**Books are to be returned on or before
the last date below**

DANIEL DEFOE
A Critical Study

DANIEL DEFOE

A Critical Study

James Sutherland

HARVARD UNIVERSITY PRESS
Cambridge, Massachusetts
1971

Distributed in Great Britain
by Oxford University Press, London

*This book was first published
by Houghton Mifflin Company in
Riverside Studies in Literature
(Gordon N. Ray, General Editor)*

Library of Congress Catalog Card Number 70-159532
SBN 674-19080-7

Printed in the United States of America

.

Preface

The aim of this book is to give a critical account of Defoe's varied achievement as a writer. The longest section is naturally concerned with his fiction, which differs considerably in theme, if not much in form, from one story to another, and which reflects many of the interests to be found in his other writings. Here I have taken note of the often conflicting views in modern criticism about his aims and methods, and about his significance in the history of the novel.

While it is mainly on account of his fiction—from *Robinson Crusoe* in 1719 to *Roxana* in 1724—that Defoe is still remembered and read today, I have availed myself of the opportunity to draw special attention to his work as a journalist. If I am not quite entitled to say, "I first adventure: follow me who list," there can be little question that a serious study of Defoe's journalism is long overdue. The *Review* has been for some time available in a facsimile edition, and has attracted some critical comment; but only a few of Defoe's numerous pamphlets have been reprinted in modern times, and in consequence this important part of his total achievement has been relatively neglected by critics. It is surely time that the best eighteenth-century pamphlets were rescued from the oblivion into which all but a few have fallen; and if that day ever comes, the best work of Defoe in this once popular genre must be given a high place. I am well aware of the objections that are usually offered: Defoe's pamphlets, it will be said, are so dependent on a reader's knowledge of long-forgotten controversies and circumstances that the effort to understand what he is talking about outweighs any pleasure we are likely to get from reading them. Yet aside from the fact that this objection would also apply to Swift's *Argument against Abolishing Christianity* and *A Modest Proposal*, the amount of knowledge needed

v

to appreciate, say, *The Shortest Way with the Dissenters* can easily be exaggerated. And if the modern reader will take the trouble to acquire the necessary minimum of information, he will often be surprised to find how similar are the circumstances with which Defoe is dealing to those of the present day. At all events, in strategy and technique, and in the employment of the various devices of rhetoric, many of Defoe's pamphlets repay the same close study as is now given to those of Swift. The advantage, no doubt, is still with Swift, but at his best Defoe is not far behind him.

Anyone who writes on Defoe is faced with the problem of selection. For this reason I have said little about his biographical and historical writings, which are on the whole a comparatively minor part of his total output, and I have dealt only incidentally with his economic writings, preferring to concentrate on other works that are more likely to interest the general reader. Even so, I have had to omit detailed consideration of several works that I should have liked to discuss more fully. The canon of what Defoe is believed to have written has been growing steadily throughout the present century: it is to be hoped that the canon of what we still read will show the same happy tendency to increase.

J. S.

Contents

DANIEL DEFOE
A Critical Study

I

A Biographical Prologue

FEW ENGLISH AUTHORS of comparable quality have written so
much as Defoe. But he was a good deal more than just a writer:
he played a considerable part in some of the most important
events of his own day, and what he wrote was so often related to
what he was doing at the time, and to the controversies in which
he was engaged, that a brief account of his career is a necessary
preliminary to any discussion of his writings.

Up to the year 1702, when he was already forty-two years
old, he was actively engaged in trade. The son of a tallow-chan-
dler, he was sent as a boy to a boarding school at Dorking, Surrey,
and then to an academy for dissenters at Newington Green, on
the outskirts of London, where he came under the influence of
an excellent teacher, the Rev. Charles Morton. Here he certainly
learned some Latin; but he also acquired a knowledge of various
scientific subjects which he would have found it hard to get in
most schools at that time. The reason why his father sent him
to a dissenting academy was that he was a dissenter himself, a
Presbyterian, and he was hoping that his son would enter the
ministry. Had Defoe belonged to the Church of England, the
next step would have been to enter him at some Oxford or Cambridge college, but the two universities were barred to nonconformists. His formal education therefore ended with his last
year at Newington Green.

There still exists a manuscript notebook in Defoe's handwrit-
ing, dated 1681, into which he had copied six sermons (presum-

ably taken down in shorthand) and a number of religious poems
of his own composition. At what precise point he decided that
he had no calling for the ministry we do not know, but it must
have been soon before, or not long after, 1681; for when, on
1 January 1684, he was married to Mary Tuffley, the daughter
of a prosperous cooper, he was described in the register as "merchant." "I acknowledge," he wrote in later life, "the pulpit is
none of my office. It was my disaster first to be set apart for, and
then to be set apart from the honour of that sacred employ."[1]
How we should interpret the word "disaster" it is difficult to
tell; but there can be no question that Defoe retained a keen
interest in church affairs for many years. The rapid succession
of pamphlets which he published from 1698 onwards on occasional conformity and on the general relationship between
the Anglican and dissenting communities is the best possible evidence of that interest. And if he was unable to preach from a
pulpit, he preached none the less to his contemporaries in the
pages of his *Review* and elsewhere.

He did not enter his father's business, but became a partner
of two brothers, Samuel and James Stancliffe, in the stocking
trade. From the evidence of various lawsuits it appears that he
also launched out into other dealings in such commodities as
wine and tobacco. One of the remarkable things about Defoe
is his extensive and apparently first-hand knowledge of so many
different branches of English commerce; and when in his early
forties he started to write about trade, this knowledge gave to
what he had to say an air of authority. Trade never ceased to
fascinate him. In the final number of his *Review*, after remarking
how the English, like the Jews, have a habit of "going a whoring
after other gods," he admits that for himself "Writing upon trade
was the whore I really doated upon."[2] There are plentiful signs
of this adulterous liaison in the pages of the *Review*, from 1704
to 1713, and in many of his books and pamphlets down to the
two volumes of *The Complete English Tradesman*, written when
he was about sixty-five, and *A Plan of the English Commerce*,
published three years later.

No doubt he had many of the qualities required to make a
successful man of business, but he had also some serious defects.
For one thing he had too many interests, and some of those

were intellectual and speculative rather than practical. He was also speculative in another sense: he took too many risks; he was guilty of the fault of "over-trading," about which he was afterwards to warn young tradesmen; he plunged into imprudent investments. "Nothing is more common," he was to write with the wisdom bought by experience,

than for the tradesman when he once finds him self grown rich, to have his head full of great designs, and new undertakings. He finds his cash flow in upon him, and perhaps he is fuller of money than his trade calls for; and as he scarce knows how to employ more stock in it than he does, his ears are the sooner open to any project or proposal that offers it self.[3]

Defoe was involved in several unprofitable ventures, including one with a diving engine and another with civet cats, and these and other speculative enterprises further embarrassed him with expensive lawsuits. Worse still, he deserted his business in the summer of 1685 to take part in Monmouth's rebellion, and was apparently made prisoner: a warrant to the Justices of Assize and Gaol Delivery of the Western Circuit, dated 31 May 1686, directs that his name "be inserted in the next General Pardon without any condition of transportation."[4] He was lucky; for three of his contemporaries at the Newington Green academy died on the scaffold. In what way he obtained his pardon is not known; but if it was by the payment of a considerable sum of money, there would be nothing unusual in that. To all these troubles must be added another for which Defoe was in no way responsible: after war had broken out with France, he sustained financial losses when ships in which he had an interest were captured by the French. The cumulative results of those various disasters was that in 1692 he became bankrupt to the extent of £17,000. If this was less than half of what Roxana made from a life of successful whoredom, it was still in 1692 a very large sum of money. But although Defoe was something of a gambler, he was never a rogue. He set about paying his creditors, and started a profitable brick and tile factory at Tilbury, on the Thames below London. By 1705 he had reduced his liabilities to £5,000, and but for further unexpected troubles in 1702–3 would almost certainly have paid off his creditors completely.

The twenty-odd years during which he was actively engaged in trade not only helped to form his character as a man, but went a long way towards determining his interests in later life. Not only was he to write constantly on trade, but he was to take an intense interest in domestic and foreign politics on which the conditions for successful trading depended. It was trade again that stimulated his unusual interest in distant countries and prompted his various schemes for colonization. As he rode about Great Britain on his numerous journeys he never failed to take note of local manufactures and markets. Buying and selling were never far from his thoughts; and when in later life he began to write fiction, he still moved imaginatively in a world of merchants and tradesmen, stocks and bank bills, shops and merchandise. He has sometimes been sneered at by critics of his fiction for his commercial mentality and morality; but perhaps we should rather wonder that a man who spent his youth and middle age in business affairs was able to translate himself so easily and confidently in his later years into a world of imaginative literature. Such a transition is rare at any time. So, too, is the sort of knowledge and experience that he brought to the writing of novels, and that gave to all his stories a firm setting in the world of his own day.

At some time in the 1690s Defoe became known to the Whig leaders of King William's government, and eventually to the King himself. For some years he was to give valuable support to the King and his ministers by writing a number of political pamphlets, culminating in *Legion's Memorial*, which are discussed in the next chapter. His most successful piece of propaganda for the King was his long bantering poem, *The True-Born Englishman*, in which he ridiculed the anti-Dutch feeling that was to be found in some sections of the English public, and more especially among the Tories. All his life Defoe was to write about William of Orange with the utmost respect and even reverence. Among his several heroes the Dutch Stadtholder who had become King of England on the abdication of James II was easily his favorite. According to his own statement he did not become personally known to the King until the publication of *The True-Born Englishman* early in 1701;[5] and if this is so, he can have known him for little more than a year.

Apart from those early political writings, one other work of this period must be mentioned. This is *An Essay upon Projects*, published in 1698. Nothing he ever wrote shows more clearly the fertility and modernity of Defoe's mind, his practical bias towards schemes for modernizing and improving the life of his own day, and for keeping his own country in the forefront of contemporary developments. In this way he outlines plans for improving the national road system; for pensions and insurance; for amending the bankruptcy laws; for an academy of military studies, and another for the education of women; and for various other feasible projects. Defoe was always ahead of his time, but rarely so far ahead that he took leave of the possible and practicable.

Among several questions that divided the nation at this time was that of the relationship between the Church of England and the nonconformists, or dissenters. As a member of the dissenting community himself, Defoe was naturally concerned about the unequal status of the dissenters as well as the enmity they often met with; and he wrote a number of controversial pamphlets on this subject, some of which are discussed in the next chapter. Here it is necessary to mention only the most famous of them, ironical in intention, *The Shortest Way with the Dissenters* (1702), which led to his arrest in May 1703. Charged with writing and publishing a seditious libel, Defoe was sentenced in July to stand three times in the pillory, to pay a fine of 200 marks, and to remain in Newgate Prison during the Queen's pleasure, this last provision being tantamount to an indefinite term of imprisonment. One inevitable consequence was the failure of his brick and tile factory, and Defoe found himself bankrupt for the second time. For the rest of his life he was never to be wholly free from the claims of creditors.

At the age of forty-three he had now to begin his life all over again. After serving his sentence in the pillory he lay in prison for several months, but in November he was set free. He owed his release to Robert Harley, the Speaker of the House of Commons, who had recently become one of the two Secretaries of State, and who had had his eye on Defoe for some time as a man who might be useful to the government. It is true that Harley was a Tory and Defoe was a Whig; but there was little real difference in their political outlook, for Harley was a moderate, middle-of-the-road man, and however immoderate Defoe may sometimes have been in his earlier years, he was from now on to cultivate and preach moderation.

One of his first assignments was to act as a secret-service agent for the government, riding all over the country and reporting back to Harley on the political temper of the various counties and boroughs. In carrying out these duties (which he undoubtedly did very well) Defoe was also laying the foundations for his unrivaled knowledge of England and of English industry, which he was to give to the world many years later in his *Tour thro' the Whole Island of Great Britain.* Later, when the negotiations for the union of the English and Scottish parliaments were opened, Harley sent him to Edinburgh to report on the political situation in Scotland, and to further the progress of the negotiations as opportunity offered. Defoe's long letters to Harley have survived, and they show him working with ant-like activity behind the scenes, dropping a word here and a word there, sitting through long debates in the Scottish parliament, and publishing a number of anonymous pamphlets designed to win over reluctant Scots to accept the terms of settlement. When the negotiations at last reached a triumphant conclusion in 1707, Defoe could look back with satisfaction on the part he had played in bringing about that Union in which he had always believed. Later he was to write a lengthy *History of the Union*, not one of his most readable works, but one in which he documented and set forth the complicated proceedings in full.

On 19 February 1704 he had published the first number of his famous periodical, the *Review*, which continued to appear (for most of its existence three times a week) until June 1713. Shortly before Harley intervened to procure Defoe's release from prison, he had written to a fellow minister, Lord Godolphin, to say it would be very useful to have an able writer on the side of the government "if it were only to state the facts right" and to answer those who played upon the people's ignorance.[6] Almost certainly he had Defoe in mind as the able writer, and although he may have been thinking of him as a pamphleteer, it may already have occurred to him that he could be still more useful

if he started a new periodical, since the false statements of which
Harley complained appeared mainly in the newspapers. At all
events, for the first year of its life Defoe's *Review* carried in its
title the words, "Purg'd from the Errors and Partiality of News-
Writers and Petty-Statesmen, of All Sides"—words which almost
echo those of Harley to Godolphin. The phrase "of all sides" was
clearly intended to suggest that the writer of the *Review* was of
no political party himself, but independent of both Whigs and
Tories; and in the first number he claimed that he would not em-
broil himself with parties, but pursue the truth. So, to some extent, he did; but in its early years the *Review* must have given
more satisfaction to Whigs than to Tories.

Yet from 1704 onwards Defoe was undoubtedly writing in
general conformity with the political policy of that moderate
Tory, Robert Harley. The precise relationship between Defoe
and Harley, and the extent to which Defoe may have lost some
of his political independence and become a spokesman for a
moderate Tory government, have been the subject of much discussion. In his own day he was accused by his old political friends
the Whigs of having changed sides, and of writing to the dictates
of his new Tory master. This is certainly a drastic simplification
of what was actually happening up to the year 1714, when Harley
was finally dismissed from office. Defoe's motives were complicated; but one of them was his genuine gratitude to Harley, and
his consequent desire to serve him in any way that was consistent
with his own principles. (From first to last "gratitude" was a word
which was frequently on Defoe's lips and in his writings; he
seems to have set so high a value on it that his estimation of
gratitude becomes a clue to his own character.) In the early years
of their association there was probably little that Harley would
have liked Defoe to do that he could not do with a clear conscience. In these troubled years of party strife, moderation was
indeed a positive political policy, and it was one to which Defoe
adhered with a persistency and an apparent conviction that angered the extremists of both sides. Without any special pleading
it may be claimed that his mature political outlook—with due
allowance for large personal differences—was similar to that of
the great Marquis of Halifax, i.e. he was a "trimmer." Why,

Halifax once asked, should men who "have played the fool with throwing *Whig* and *Tory* at one another, as boys do snow-balls," grow so angry at the word *trimmer,*

which by its true signification might do as much to put us into our wits as the other hath done to put us out of them? . . . This innocent word *trimmer* signifieth no more than this, that if men are together in a boat, and one part of the company would weigh it down on one side, another would make it lean as much to the contrary; it happeneth there is a third opinion of those who conceive it would do as well if the boat went even, without endangering the passengers. . . .[7]

This metaphor of not rocking the boat, of keeping the ship of state on an even keel, is one that Defoe resorts to from time to time. On 2 November 1710 he defends the *Review* against attacks from both parties:

All the world will bear me witness it is not a Tory paper.—The rage with which I am daily treated by that party testify for me. . . . Yet, because I cannot run the length that some of the other would have me—*new scandal fills their mouths*, and now they report, I am gone over to the new ministry. . . . I have met with none but who run themselves up to this extreme—that they had rather sink the ship than not have their own pilots steer.[8]

A good case, then, may be made out for Defoe's having remained constant to moderate principles, and even for his having courted unpopularity in his determination to cool down the heat of party wrath. As the attacks on him mounted from all quarters he took a sort of obstinate pride in his independence and outspokenness. In the *Review* of 11 November 1712 he states his position with a characteristically homely metaphor:

I have told you where your danger lies, and from what cause it proceeds. If what I say is just, I care not how much my noise offends you, for I write to please none of you, but to awaken you; when a man cries *Fire* in the night, many a soft slumber he interrupts, wakes you out of many a pleasing dream, frights your children, stuns you with the noise, and till the danger justifies him, you could throw stones at him for disturbing you; but when you see the flame about your ears, you own it was time to allarm you; and so you will acknowledge of me hereafter, whatever you think now.[9]

A few weeks later (30 December) he re-states his determination
to speak unwelcome truths:

Nor, Gentlemen, am I writing as other authors do, to court or please
you; I thank God I can openly say, I neither speak or forbear to speak
in hope or fear to please or displease any man upon earth. My case
differs from all your other writers; they court you to read, invite you,
propose to make you smile, and contrive to do it, that you may read
and buy their papers; I must force you to read your interest, your
occasion, the use you make of the subjects I write on; all these oblige
you to read this paper, and therefore the author thinks himself not at
all oblig'd to you, but you to him.[10]

This is surely the voice of the Presbyterian minister he never
became. By 1712 Defoe was probably aware that his political independence had lost him many, perhaps most, of the readers of
the *Review*. From his logical stand on occasional conformity onwards he had been taking up minority positions, and had almost
certainly found a great deal of pleasure in doing so. When the
Review finally came to an end in the following June, he was
still as intransigent as ever about his political rightness in the face
of "party rage, personal prejudice, and universal clamour"; and
he claimed, as so often before, that he had never once "acted . . .
by party, personal influence, or pecuniary reward, nor against
the principles I always profest." He had done his best to reduce
party divisions by "cool argument and calm reasoning"; but he
must have known that they were beyond his skill to cure. "I have
been like a man," he said, "who runs between two duellists to
part them, and who to prevent the losing their lives, loses his
own."[11]

That is the situation as Defoe saw it, or liked to see it; and there
is a good deal of truth in his reiterated claims that he remained
true to his principles. On the other hand, he was receiving a
gratuity (rather irregularly paid) from secret-service money, and
was in constant touch with Harley on day-to-day questions of
policy. By 1711, when the Tory government was taking determined steps to bring the war with France to an end, Defoe
began supporting their peace policy cautiously in the *Review*,
and much more openly in some pamphlets which he published
anonymously. The surviving correspondence with Harley does
tend to suggest that occasionally Defoe wrote what was expected

of him, and that sometimes he came near to asking Harley what would be acceptable. As the growing ascendancy of Bolingbroke and the High Tories after the general election of October 1710 compelled Harley to play a double game, Defoe must now and then have had to keep silence when he would rather have spoken out, and may sometimes have written what he was not very willing to write.

One of the principles, however, on which he was never prepared to compromise was the absolute necessity of a Protestant succession. As Queen Anne's health grew more precarious, the question of the succession became of paramount importance. It had been laid down by Parliament that in the event of the Queen's death (she had survived all of her numerous children) the crown should pass to the nearest Protestant successor, King George of Hanover. In 1712–13 Defoe wrote a number of pamphlets warning the nation against the danger of Jacobitism, and he also pursued the same subject in the pages of the *Review*. His complete approval of the Hanoverian succession and his detestation of Jacobitism must have been well known. Unfortunately, however, he was indiscreet enough to follow up his outright condemnation of the Jacobites with three pamphlets setting forth ironically the advantages that would accrue if the Pretender became King of England. For a man with so many enemies, this was only asking for trouble; and some malicious Whigs succeeded in having him arrested and charged with publishing treasonable libels. (Two of these are discussed in the next chapter.) Again Harley had to intervene to save him, and in due course Defoe obtained the Queen's pardon. But soon neither Harley nor the Queen could do anything more for him. On Tuesday, 27 July 1714, Harley was dismissed from office. On the following Sunday Queen Anne was dead.

The Hanoverian succession took place without incident. The new reign was only about two weeks old, however, when Defoe was again arrested on charges relating to two different newspapers, the Tory *Post Boy* and the Whig *Flying Post*. On the second charge (that of libeling a peer, the Earl of Anglesey) his trial did not come on till July 1715; he was then found guilty, but sentence was deferred, and, so far as is known, nothing further was done about it. These anxieties may have preyed on

Defoe's normally robust constitution, for earlier in the same year he appears to have been seriously ill. He was now fifty-five, and had already done more than enough for one lifetime; but he was always making fresh starts in life, and he was on the verge of a new burst of activity. Like Moll Flanders, he could always adjust himself to unexpected circumstances and set off with unabated energy in a new direction.

With the accession of George I the Whigs had returned to power, and were to remain in power for the rest of Defoe's life. In the now distant days of King William he had been himself well known as a Whig, and as such had been abominated by the Tories; in the later years of Queen Anne's reign he had come to be looked upon as a tool of the Tory party, and as such had been execrated by the Whigs. Now, with the Whigs back in control, what sort of future could he expect?

What now took place is known to us only through the fortunate preservation among the State Papers of some letters that Defoe wrote to an under-secretary in 1718. At some time in 1715 he had made a deal with the Whig ministers, and this explains why his deferred sentence was allowed to lapse. "In considering, after this, which way I might be rendered most useful to the government," he writes in the second of those letters,

it was proposed by my Lord Townshend that I should still appear as if I were, as before, under the displeasure of the government, and separated from the Whigs; and that I might be more serviceable in a kind of disguise than if I appeared openly; and upon this foot a weekly paper, which I was at first directed to write in opposition to a scandalous paper called the *Shift Shifted*, was laid aside, and the first thing I engaged in was a monthly book called *Mercurius Politicus*, of which presently. In the interval of this, Dyer, the *News-Letter* writer, having been dead, and Dormer his successor being unable by his troubles to carry on that work, I had an offer of a share in the property, as well as in the management of that work.

Although Defoe did not obtain full financial control of Dormer's *News-Letter*, "yet the conduct and government of the style and news was entirely in me," and he saw to it that "the sting of that mischievous paper should be entirely taken out, though it was granted that the style should continue Tory, as it was, that the party might be amused [i.e. have its attention diverted from the real design], and not set up another, which would have destroyed the design." Some time later he was able to extend this form of secret censorship to another paper, *Mist's Weekly Journal*:

My Lord Sunderland, to whose goodness I had many years ago been obliged, when I was in a secret commission sent to Scotland, was pleased to approve and continue this service and the appointment annexed; and, with his Lordship's approbation, I introduced myself, in the disguise of a translator of foreign news, to be so far concerned in this weekly paper of Mist's, as to be able to keep it within the circle of a secret management, also, prevent the mischievous part of it; and yet neither Mist, or any of those concerned with him, have the least guess or suspicion by whose direction I do it.

But here it becomes necessary to acquaint my Lord (as I hinted to you, Sir) that this paper called the *Journal* is not in myself in property, as the other, only in management; with this express difference, that if anything happens to be put in without my knowledge which may give offence, or if anything slips my observation which may be ill taken, his Lordship shall be sure always to know whether he has a servant to reprove, or a stranger to correct.

Upon the whole, however, this is the consequence, that by this management the *Weekly Journal*, and *Dormer's Letter*, as also the *Mercurius Politicus*, which is in the same nature of management as the *Journal*, will be always kept (mistakes excepted) to pass as Tory papers, and yet be disabled and enervated, so as to do no mischief or give any offence to the government.[12]

By his own standards Defoe would have had no difficulty in justifying what he was doing. Although the Whigs were securely in control of Parliament, there was much disaffection in the country, and the new king from Germany (who spoke no English) was far from being a popular figure with any section of the community. Satirical pamphlets and ballads attacking the new regime were circulating in large numbers; and there was some ostentatious drinking of toasts to "the King across the water," and other ritual tokens of a still smouldering Jacobitism. In September 1715 the Earl of Mar raised the standard of rebellion in Scotland. On 13 November he fought an ill-conducted and indecisive battle at Sherrifmuir, and on the same day the English Jacobites were defeated in a skirmish at Preston (in which Defoe's Colonel Jack took a fictitious part). In December the Pretender put in a tardy appearance in Scotland, but the rebellion was to all intents and purposes over. The English Jacobites had never shown any real enthusiasm for the Pretender, and even in Scotland there was considerable opposition to his cause. None the less, the rebellion of 1715 had shown how divided the country still was about its new Hanoverian king; and in undertaking to "disable" and "enervate" the more outspoken Tory newspapers Defoe was once more doing his utmost—in a characteristically indirect way—to safeguard the Protestant succession.

What is quite certain is that there was no other man in England who could have performed this ambiguous service for the government so successfully. Defoe had always had a love of mystification and an unusual talent for deception; and he seems to have had no doubt that the end justifies the means, provided the end was one of which he approved. When Harley sent him to Edinburgh in 1706, he delighted in deceiving the simple Scots about the purpose of his visit. "I am perfectly unsuspected as corresponding with anybody in England," he wrote to Harley; ". . . I talk to everybody in their own way. To the merchants I am about to settle here in trade, building ships, etc. With the lawyers I want to purchase a house and land to bring my family and live upon it (God knows where the money is to pay for it). Today I am going into partnership with a member of parliament in a glass house, tomorrow with another in a salt work. With the Glasgow mutineers I am to be a fish merchant, with the Aberdeen men a woollen and with the Perth and western men a linen manufacturer, and still at the end of all discourse the Union is the essential, and I am all to everyone that I may gain some." Later he thought up some more white lies: he was writing a History of the Union, he was engaged in a new version of the Psalms.[13] His *History of the Union* actually appeared in 1709, and a new version of the Psalms was just the sort of thing he *might* have done: Defoe's lies were nearly always plausible, although one may question the wisdom of his telling quite so many to the Scots, since there was always the danger of some skeptical listener collating one version with another.

The extension of Defoe's habit of playing a part in real life to playing one in such ironical pamphlets as *The Shortest Way with the Dissenters* is sufficiently obvious. But deception and make-believe are also prominent features in the stuff of his fiction.

Crusoe helps the ship-captain to get the better of his mutineers by pretending to be the Governor of the Island and to have the power to "hang them all if he pleased"; Moll's first husband, posing as a lord, carries her to Oxford in a hired coach and six, and they bamboozle "two or three fellows of colleges about putting a nephew that was left to his lordship's care to the University"; Roxana's life, after the murder of the jeweler with whom she has been cohabiting, is one long succession of successful deceits; and in *A New Voyage round the World* Defoe gives us a variation of the *Robinson Crusoe* episode when a mutinous Dutch pilot is similarly reduced to submission by an elaborately acted pretence that the captain is resolved to hang him. What is perhaps the most elaborate example of this play-acting occurs in *Colonel Jack*, when the offending slave Mouchat is told by Jack that he is going to be "whipped and pickled in a dreadful manner." After he has received two lashes, however, Jack intervenes and asks Mouchat what he will do if the great master can be prevailed upon to be merciful and pardon him. When Mouchat has satisfied him that he will be eternally grateful and obedient, Jack pretends to ride away to plead with the great master, and returning four or five hours later tells Mouchat that he has succeeded in persuading him "to try whether kindness would prevail as much as cruelty," and the now sobbing Mouchat is given a dram of rum out of Jack's bottle and some victuals. Getting the better of people by some form of deception—often, but not necessarily, in a good cause— was obviously something that appealed to Defoe; and his new assignment to emasculate some of the Tory journals while passing himself off as a Tory was therefore one that he was peculiarly fitted to carry out. It needed courage and skill and confidence, and Defoe had all three.[14]

Of the various periodicals he was now controlling or tampering with, Nathaniel Mist's *Weekly Journal* was much the most important, with what was then the large circulation of about 10,000 copies. Not for the first time in his life Defoe found himself forced, as he put it, to "bow in the house of Rimmon," and faced with the problem of pleasing two masters: he had to satisfy the Whig ministers by seeing to it that nothing was published in *Mist's* that would offend the government, and at the same time he had to allay the suspicions of Mist and his Tory readers by taking some risks, either by allowing things to appear that he would have preferred to suppress, or by himself writing anti-Whig paragraphs to gratify the expectations of Mist's readers. "It is a hard matter," he told the under-secretary,

to please the Tory party, as their present temper operates, without abusing, not only the government, but the persons of our governors, in every thing they write; but to the best of my skill I cause all letters and paragraphs which look that way to be intercepted, and stopped at the press.

His only hold over Mist was presumably a threat to walk out if Mist printed anything dangerous; and Defoe appears to have remonstrated with him on several occasions. On 4 June 1718 he writes of having entered into a new treaty with Mist, who has admitted going too far, and has solemnly promised not to give any further offence. Mist has agreed that he must be content

to rally the *Flying Post* [a leading Whig paper], the Whig writers, and even the word "Whig," etc., and to admit foolish and trifling things in favour of the Tories. This, as I represented it to him, he agrees is liberty enough, and resolves his paper shall for the future amuse the Tories, but not affront the government. . . . I said, Sir, all that could be said on that head, only reserving the secret of who I spoke from; and concluded, that unless he would keep measures with me, and be punctual in these things, I could not serve him any farther, or be concerned any more.[15]

On 25 October 1718, however, Mist published a letter signed "Sir Andrew Politick" that gave great offence to the government. Brought before the two secretaries of state, he asserted that the offending letter was written by Defoe, and when the publisher of the paper was also examined he confirmed Mist's statement. Defoe had made a serious slip, but on this occasion he was apparently forgiven. Shortly afterwards—presumably because he was annoyed with Mist for letting him down—he broke off his connection with the *Weekly Journal;* but he resumed it again a few months later, and he continued to write for Mist until 1724.

The early 1720s were Defoe's most active period in newspaper journalism. For Mist he was not merely translating from the foreign journals and supplying news paragraphs of his own, but he was also providing most of the essays and short discussions on a wide variety of topics that appeared on the front page. For a number of years he contributed another series of essays to *Apple-bee's Original Weekly Journal*, and he also wrote for the *Daily Post*, *The Whitehall Evening Post*, and other papers. He even found time to start in 1720 an essay paper of his own, *The Commentator*, which he wrote twice a week for about nine months. Although his connection with Mist still involved him in contemporary politics, the years from 1720 onwards show him becoming progressively interested in non-political subjects.

He was now in his sixties, and again it might have been thought that he had written himself out, and would be tempted to call it a day. But while still heavily engaged in daily and weekly journalism, and while still writing pamphlets on current affairs, he opened a new chapter in his literary career and began writing fiction. He had already made a significant step in that direction in 1715 when he published *The Family Instructor* (to be followed by a second volume in 1718), a series of cautionary tales of middle-class family life that proved to be astonishingly popular. But his works of fiction which are still widely read today began with *Robinson Crusoe* in 1719 and came to an end in 1724 with *Roxana* and *A New Voyage round the World*. He continued to write up to the year of his death in 1731, and to the last decade of his life belong a number of major works on miscellaneous subjects which will be noticed briefly in the final chapter.

Defoe is not one of the great impersonal forces of literature. It cannot be said of him, as Matthew Arnold said of Shakespeare, "We ask and ask—Thou smilest and art still." He is only too ready to talk about himself; he tells us about some personal experience, he recalls hearing or seeing something, he laments his hard fortune, he strikes attitudes. He writes constantly in the first person, and when he took to writing fiction this ingrained habit had probably a good deal to do with determining the autobiographical form of his novels. Quite apart from what he tells us about himself, some parts of his life are well documented—in public records, in his surviving correspondence, and in the observations of his contemporaries. We know what sort of things interested him most. Like Swift, however much he differed from him in outlook and temperament, he was absorbed by the topics that appealed most strongly to the masculine mind of his day. He wrote constantly, as we have seen, on politics and religion, on the war with France, on questions of morality and social behavior, and on trade and manufacture.

The nearest he came to writing his autobiography was in *An Appeal to Honour and Justice,* and this is not so much auto-biography as an *apologia pro vita sua,* obviously designed, since it appeared in 1715, to put him right with the Whigs. In this sus-tained defence of his public life he sometimes protests too much, and makes some rather obvious bids for the sympathy of his readers, who, he suggests, may not have the chance to read much more from his pen, since "the infirmities of a life of sorrow and fatigue" have brought him "very near to the great ocean of eternity." At times, too, he slips into a strain of pious self-pity:

> But such is my present fate, and I am to submit to it, which I do with meekness and calmness, as to a judgment from Heaven, and am practising that duty which I have studied long ago, of *forgiving my enemies,* and *praying for them that despitefully use me.*[16]

Defoe laying his hand on his heart and making strong claims for his consistent rectitude is at his least convincing; and his pose of injured innocence is all the more dubious and unattractive because it seems to have convinced himself. We meet with the same sort of protestations in some of his correspondence; for, whatever he may be writing, Defoe is almost always aware of someone who has to be persuaded. In his discussion of Pope as a letter-writer Johnson remarked:

> There is, indeed, no transaction which offers stronger temptations to fallacy and sophistication than epistolary intercourse. . . . Friendship has no tendency to secure veracity, for by whom can a man so much wish to be thought better than he is as by him whose kindness he desires to gain or keep?[17]

Johnson's words are certainly applicable to some of Defoe's letters to Robert Harley and to other statesmen whom he wished, in one way or another, to impress. Like Pope, too, he was some-times disingenuous in his use of language, and was given to making statements that were true only in a literal or restricted

sense, and of phrasing denials that were capable of being interpreted in different ways.

Yet to anyone who is inclined to take a harsh view of Defoe's
conduct and character it should be enough to quote some words
that he once wrote in the *Review* when discussing the unsympa-
thetic treatment of bankrupts: "You are an honest man, you say!
Pray, sir, was you ever try'd?"[18] In the course of a long life
crowded with activity Defoe was often tried severely; not merely
in the court of bankruptcy, but in many other crises which called
for resolution and endurance, and in which most other men, lack-
ing his courage or rashness, would never have landed themselves.
He lived at high pressure; and although he was essentially a
rational man, he was also subject to waves of intense feeling. In
his fiction, no less than in his private correspondence, there are
outbursts of emotionalism which will surprise only those who are
determined to think of him as nothing more than a typically hard-
headed business man who also happened to write. The national
image of John Bull or of the strong silent Englishman just won't
do for Defoe. But come to that, it won't do for Shakespeare either.

2

The Journalist

Pamphlets

A LARGE PART of Defoe's vast literary output dealt with the passing events and circumstances of the day—political, economic, religious, and social. If he had died before he wrote *Robinson Crusoe,* it is as a journalist that he would be now chiefly remembered. All through his long career as a writer the form of prose literature that was most abundantly cultivated by himself and his contemporaries was the pamphlet, a species of literary life that is now almost extinct. Of the enormous pamphlet literature of the seventeenth and eighteenth centuries very little is known to the modern reader, partly because it was almost always the product of contemporary problems and cannot be fully appreciated without some knowledge of English history and of long-forgotten controversies, and partly because (and this second reason is a consequence of the first) almost none of this literature has been reprinted in modern times. One notable exception is Swift, whose work as a pamphleteer is well known and frequently discussed; but even so the pamphlets of Swift that are generally read today are those that require least awareness on the part of the modern reader of the contemporary context and background. For one reader of *The Conduct of the Allies* or *The Public Spirit of the Whigs* there are a hundred for the Bickerstaff pamphlets or *A Modest Proposal.*

In the present climate of literary opinion there is little that one can do about this, and perhaps not much that one should try to do. Anyone who is disposed to put in a plea for what is no longer generally read is in danger of qualifying for Pope's gibe about John Dennis, and of being considered "a gentleman who can instruct the Town to dislike what has pleased them, and to be pleased with what they disliked."[1] But here the situation is rather different. It is not so much a case of trying to persuade the modern reader to be pleased with what he dislikes, as to suggest that in the pamphlet literature of the late seventeenth and early eighteenth centuries he might occasionally be pleased with something with which he has had little or no opportunity of becoming acquainted. It is true that he will have to know something about the contemporary setting if he is to appreciate the skill of the pamphleteer; but this is a small price to pay for enjoying the best work of such outstanding journalists as Sir Roger L'Estrange or Defoe.

So far as Defoe is concerned, I hope to show that he is worth the trouble; and since he almost invariably sets forth clearly and boldly what the argument is all about, the reader is usually presented with most of the information he needs. If the questions at issue no longer have the burning importance for us that they had for Defoe's contemporaries, and cannot therefore evoke the excitement they once aroused, we can still become intellectually engaged, and enjoy the logical and rhetorical effectiveness—and even at times the beauty—of the argument.

The full measure of Defoe's skill as a journalist can only be appreciated when we compare his work with that of the mob of mainly anonymous writers who were moved to express their opinions on such occasions of controversy as the Popish Plot, a standing army in time of peace, the Bill to Prevent Occasional Conformity, the negotiations leading to the Peace of Utrecht, and so on. Irate citizens passionately involved in such issues, boring citizens believing they had something of importance to communicate to the public, sat down and wrote a pamphlet, usually running to 24 or 32 pages, quarto or octavo. In this way hundreds of pamphlets were published with such titles as *A Letter from a Gentleman in the Country to His Friend in the City,* or *vice versa.* As Oldfox tells the Widow in Wycherley's *Plain Dealer,* " 'A Letter to a Friend in the Country' . . . is now the way of all such sober solid persons as myself when they have a mind to publish their disgust to the times; though, perhaps, between you

he arguments that have been advanced *pro* and *con*, he states his
ntention "calmly to consider both those extreams, and if it be
ossible, to find out the safe *medium* that may please us all."
Here we have the reasonable voice, the disarming air of im-
artiality and moderation that were partly natural to Defoe and
artly assumed for the occasion, and of course the implication
at the truth is likely to lie, as it usually does, somewhere between
e two extremes. He now addresses himself to "the honest well-
eaning English freeholder," who, he admits, has most reason to
ar a standing army since he has something to lose, in the same
ay as "he is most concerned for the safety of a ship who has a
rgo on her bottom." Defoe is being tactful, he is prepared to
ke concessions to the point of view of those he is seeking to
nvince; he can well understand their anxieties, but he hopes
show that they are groundless. He suggests that it is necessary
distinguish between England as it once was and as it is today.
 back far enough to the days when England had no standing
 my, and you will find that it was constantly invaded success-
ly—last of all by William the Conqueror. There followed a
iod when we were frequently invading the territory of our
ghbors, and "quite out of fear of invasions at home." But in the
gn of Queen Elizabeth we came very near to being invaded by
 Spaniards, and although they failed, it was chiefly because
od set the elements in battle array" against the Spanish Armada.
ce those days there has always been some sort of standing army,
 "no evil consequence followed." But be that as it may, cir-
stances have now completely changed: if we are to continue
urvive as a nation we must have continental allies, and that
ns we must be ready to play our part in a general league or
ederacy against the constant threat of French domination.

e is one neighbour grown too great for all the rest, *as they are
e states or kingdoms;* and therefore to mate him, several must join
mutual assistance, according to the Scotch law of duelling, *that if
can't beat you ten shall.*

e is addressing himself here to the isolationists who are living
e past, and is teaching them the facts of international life;
t is characteristic of him that he should make his lesson more
able by the joke about Scotch duelling. He now tries an

and I, they have no friend in the country."[2] If the custom of writing letters to newspapers had become established, most of the
pamphlets of the period would never have been written. Many of
them are shapeless, desultory, bad-tempered and intolerant, and
at their worst driveling and abusive. Most tedious of all are the
innumerable *Answers, Replies, Observations,* and *Animadversions*
which quote passage after passage from some previous pamphlet
and answer them *seriatim* with the dreariest kind of rebuttal. Let
the dead bury their dead. No twentieth-century reader, if not in
search of special information, would willingly penetrate into this
literary undergrowth. This is surely "all such reading as was never
read," and most of it may safely be left to historians, who are by
necessity coarse feeders. Yet it is worth remembering what Alexander Pope once told Bishop Atterbury:

Your Lordship has formerly advis'd me to read the best controversies
between the churches. Shall I tell you a secret? I did so at fourteen
years old (for I loved reading, and my father had no other books),
there was a collection of all that had been written on both sides in the
reign of King James the second: I warm'd my head with them, and
the consequence was, that I found my self a Papist and a Protestant by
turns, according to the last book I read.[3]

As a member of the persecuted Catholic minority, however, Pope
was an interested party: he read those controversial writers, not
as he read Homer or Shakespeare, but purely for their matter,
because the matter meant a great deal to him. But here we may
see why so much of the literature of past political and religious
controversy is almost wholly unreadable today; it was written by
and for those whose minds were made up (as an inquiring boy
Pope was an exception) and whose feelings ran high. In such
circumstances a pamphleteer had only to touch a nerve or stimu-
late a prejudice, and the committed reader would do all the rest
by the overwhelming force of his response. For such a reader
sarcasm was more effective than irony, and vituperation better
than rational argument: for the Tory any stick was good enough
to beat a Whig dog.

In almost every respect Defoe stands apart from the common
run of pamphleteers. What Matthew Arnold claimed for Burke—
that "almost alone in England he brings thought to bear upon
politics, he saturates politics with thought"[4]—is not perhaps true

of Defoe in the sense that Arnold meant it for Burke: Defoe's thinking is nearly always practical, addressed to the particular occasion and usually to a particular group of readers. Yet his political and other pamphlets are certainly saturated with thought; he is eminently reasonable, and he has always an argument which he develops clearly and persuasively. While taking sides, he yet manages to give an impression of detachment, of examining a question fairly and without prejudice, and of seeking to produce light rather than heat. He keeps his temper, he pleads for moderation and good sense. No doubt Defoe's controlled reasonableness was maddening to the fanatic and the out-and-out party man, but it must have been effective with that considerable minority that appears in modern opinion polls under the heading "Undecided" or "Don't know," and it may even have convinced those who were not too firmly committed. His strategy varies from one pamphlet to another, and as exercises in effective persuasion those short prose pieces deserve more serious study than they usually get today. I propose, therefore, to examine in some detail a few of his most interesting pamphlets, supplying where necessary the minimum of information needed to understand the point at issue.

As a political writer Defoe first caught the ear of the public in the last years of the seventeenth century, when he gave valuable support to the policies of William III. The English king was at this time at loggerheads with the majority of his subjects over the need to contain the ambitions of Louis XIV. The war with France, which had been going on for the greater part of his reign, had come to an end in October 1697 with the Treaty of Ryswick—to the relief of most Englishmen, who saw no good reason why they should be perpetually involved in foreign entanglements. England was an island and was not under attack: if the French were foolish enough to think they could launch an invasion, the Navy could take care of that. This insular attitude of the English made no sense to their more European-minded king, who believed (and who ultimately proved to be right) that the only way to secure a lasting peace was to build up an effective alliance against France, so as to achieve what was already being referred to as "a balance of power." So far from the King getting his way, however, he found himself faced with a Parliament determined not merely to reduce the size of his army, but in peacetime to

disband it altogether. In 1697 two Whig writers, Wa[...] and John Trenchard, started a lively controversy by p[...] pamphlet with the provocative title *An Argument Sho[...] Standing Army Is Inconsistent with a Free Gover[...] Absolutely Destructive to the Constitution of the E[...] archy.* To this Defoe replied with two pamphlets, th[...] which, *An Argument Shewing that a Standing Arm[...] sent of Parliament, Is Not Inconsistent with a Free [...]* was published in 1698. For what it was worth (and [...] 1698 it was worth something), he found room on [...] for a quotation from 2 Chronicles, ix.25: "And King [...] four thousand stalls for horses and chariots, and tw[...] horsemen, whom he bestowed in the chariot cities, [...] King at Jerusalem." In the event, Parliament rated [...] siderably lower than Solomon, and voted to reduce [...] to 7,000. Among the regiments that were axed w[...] own Dutch Guards, and he was with some diffic[...] from retiring to Holland and leaving the Engli[...] consequences.

It is natural to suppose that Defoe had come [...] standing with the Whig ministers who were [...] policy of the King, and that *An Argument Shewi[...] ing Army . . .* was written with their approval. T[...] that he wrote against his own convictions. In later [...] were given to dismissing him as a hireling who [...] but this is rather a tribute to the effectivenes[...] journalism than a charge that can be substantiat[...] said is that Defoe took so much pleasure in putt[...] matters on which he was indifferent, or on [...] himself (as he often did) in a middle position be[...] extremes, he would produce an equally good ar[...] side. If circumstances had been different (as [...] would have been for Defoe in the reign of Jame[...] put together an equally convincing argumer[...] armies in time of peace.

When Defoe intervened in the debate, p[...] running high. He opens, accordingly, with a[...] for moderation, and suggests that both parties [...] equally guilty of running into extremes. Aft[...]

appeal to the self-interest of his fellow countrymen. Presumably they will agree with the maxim: "Carry the war into your enemies' country, and always keep it out of your own." Well, then, if they don't want to have to fight the French on English soil there must be a regular army to fight them abroad.[5]

Opponents of a standing army in time of peace liked to argue that England could be defended quite well by its militia (lightly trained "territorial" forces), and that, if necessary, these could be sent to fight abroad. To this Defoe objects that the King has no power to send the militia abroad, and in any case, "if he could, *no body would accept them;* and if they would go, and would be accepted of, *they would be good for nothing.*" When has England been most respected in Europe? Undoubtedly when it had strong armed forces, as it had under Queen Elizabeth and Oliver Cromwell. And why is our present King William looked upon by European nations as a great leader? Undoubtedly because of his own reputation as a soldier, but also because of the valor of the regular English army under his command. No harm (Defoe feels) in making an appeal to English pride. But now he makes another of his tactful concessions. So far he has been arguing for the continuing existence of some kind of army; he has never suggested a *great* army, for that would be as dangerous as no army at all, and of course the existence of any standing army must depend upon the consent of Parliament. On the motion of Robert Harley, Parliament had recently voted to disband all those troops that had been raised since 1680, and Defoe is willing to settle for that. He reckons that the country would be left with an army of about 6,000 men—not a force likely to do much damage to English liberties. But if anyone still thinks that an army of 6,000 may be dangerous, Defoe has his answer ready: if it is, "our *militia must be very despicable.*" You can't have it both ways, he is saying: either the militia is all that you say it is, or else it is a broken reed, and in that case we certainly do need a professional army to defend us.

If a small army may enslave us, our militia are good for nothing; if good for nothing they cannot defend us, and then the Army is necessary. If they are good, and are able to defend us, then a small army can never hurt us, for what may defend us abroad may defend us at home, and I wonder this is not consider'd.[6]

Nothing infuriates an Englishman more than to have a logical
argument thrown at his head when he wishes to be left alone with
his prejudices; and it may be thought that Defoe, whose aim was
to bring over the doubtful and persuade the opponents of a standing army to think again, was being rather less than tactful here.
It is true that he was sometimes carried away by the delight of
successful disputation, but on this occasion he was not seriously
damaging his case: the militia, and more especially the London
trainbands, were something of a joke, not merely to professional
soldiers, but to the great body of peace-loving Englishmen who
had no desire themselves to strut about in a gaudy uniform and
were prepared to laugh at those who did. Nor had Defoe any
illusions that the trainbands were glorious patriots who could
always be counted upon to defend English liberties. In 1682, as he
pointed out near the end of his pamphlet, a body of them had
forcibly taken over the London Guildhall and prevented the citizens from electing two Whig sheriffs of their own choice, while
the Lord Mayor swore in two of his Tory nominees. "*This was
done by the militia to their everlasting glory,* and I do not remember the like done by a standing army of mercenaries, in this
age at least." Defoe was to recur to those illegal proceedings in the
Review (22 December 1705) when discussing the Popish Plot.
In the City of London, where the papists were "hardly one to a
thousand," the Plot was used as an excuse for all kinds of military
parading and violence, and made

our City blunderbusses be all new burnish'd, hatt and feather, shoul-
der-belt, and all our military gewgaws come in mode again; till the
City trained bands began to be rampant, that like other standing
armies they began to ride upon their masters, and trampled under foot
the liberty of that very City they were rais'd to defend. . . .

This passage shows clearly enough Defoe's contempt for the vain-
glorious and half-disciplined trainbands; but it may also be
observed that the man who spoke up for a standing army in 1698
was quite ready in 1705 ("like other standing armies they began to
ride upon their masters") to assert that regular soldiers *were*
capable of destroying the liberty they were raised to defend.
Those who look for complete consistency in Defoe are chasing a

will-o'-the-wisp. He was far from being the mercenary hack that his enemies called him, but—in political matters at least—he believed that circumstances alter cases. It is fair to suppose that in 1698 circumstances made the case for a standing army appear to Defoe to be not only reasonable but right. Yet he was careful to insist that any such army should remain in being only so long as Parliament should appoint. Defoe was arguing for a short-term policy: the King needed those troops *now*, and Defoe addressed himself to the immediate situation. Let us leave it to Parliament, he added in another tactful appeal, "the best composed House that perhaps ever entered within those walls." When he had to deal three years later with a Parliament much less to his liking, he would use very different language. *An Argument* is one of the earliest of Defoe's political tracts, and it is astonishing how quickly he had mastered the art of putting a case, seriously, persuasively, and with an unfailing intellectual agility.[7]

At what stage he became personally acquainted with the King is not precisely known; but he certainly enjoyed his friendship, and in the last two years of his reign he wrote some further highly effective pamphlets in favor of his foreign policy. The great problem that absorbed William III's attention during the last years of his life turned upon what would happen to the vast Spanish possessions when the ailing King of Spain died. William had succeeded in persuading Louis XIV to sign a Treaty of Partition (1698) naming the young Electoral Prince of Bavaria heir to the Spanish throne, but this was nullified in the following year by the death of this little boy at the age of seven. The patient William began all over again, and in March 1700 Louis agreed to the substitution of the Archduke Charles, second son of the Emperor, for the dead Bavarian prince. But once again the plans of the English king were to be frustrated. In September the King of Spain made a will bequeathing the entire Spanish empire to the Duke of Anjou, grandson of Louis XIV, and then, in the beginning of November, he died. A few days later Louis decided to ignore the second Treaty of Partition to which he had put his signature, and publicly accepted the will. The balance of power for which the English king had labored so assiduously was once more upset.

While events were working towards this crisis Defoe had been writing a pamphlet with the self-explanatory title: *The Two Great Questions Consider'd. I. What the French King Will Do, with Respect to the Spanish Monarchy. II. What Measures the English Ought to Take.* This appeared on 15 November, and in a brief preface Defoe advised his reader that since his pamphlet had gone to press the news had arrived that Louis XIV had acknowledged his grandson as King of Spain. But if Defoe for once had been overtaken by events, his pamphlet (as he claimed himself) was as relevant as ever. The greater part of his fellow countrymen were inclined to sit back and let matters take their course; and it was against this attitude of *laissez-faire* and ignorant isolationism that Defoe wished to protest. It is when he comes to what measures England should take that he really warms to his work, and he cannot resist a kind of "I told you so": the question would be easier to answer, he admits, if so many of our troops had not been disbanded, and if the nation were not so divided in policy. As a result, England "makes but a very mean figure abroad," and as a European power would be completely negligible but for the prestige of her glorious king. Defoe no doubt meant every word he said; but the first part of this statement is a deliberate appeal to English pride (who wants his country to make a "mean figure" in the eyes of other nations?), and the second part is a reminder to the English that however little love they may have for their "foreign" king, he commands the respect of Europe, and a good thing for them that he does. What sort of condition, he continues, would England now be in if James II, "a papist and confederate with France," were still on the throne? It is true we have a great fleet, and that ought to secure us from being invaded by the French. But what will happen to us if we are shut up in our own island and lose our trade?

If the French get the Spanish crown, we are beaten out of the field as to trade, and are besieged in our own island, and never let us flatter our selves with our safety consisting so much in our fleet; for this I presume to lay down as a fundamental axiom, at least as the wars go of late, 'tis not the longest sword, but the longest purse that conquers. If the French get Spain, they get the greatest trade in the world in their hands; they that have the most trade will have the most money, will have the most ships, the best fleet, and the best armies; and if once the French master us at sea, where are we then?[8]

Defoe is of course putting the Whig case for England as a nation that must depend for its prosperity on the export of its manufactures, but how incisively he puts it! There have been few like him for stating facts simply and forcibly, and for compelling the reader to accept an inescapable, if unwelcome, conclusion. There is little metaphor and no great artifice in the passage just quoted, but it rises in a crescendo movement to the unanswerable dilemma posed by the final question. To his "Where are we then?" the Tory squire might reply, "Where we were before—free from foreign entanglements, an expensive war, and crippling taxation. Free to hunt foxes and shoot pheasants, free to grow our own crops, eat our own beef and mutton, and drink our own strong ale." The division which those diverse interests represented was to continue for many years to come; but in the end it was the Whig view of England's national destiny that was to prevail. On almost every issue in which he was involved Defoe was looking forward to the future, and was often far ahead of most of his contemporaries. He was, indeed, what Professor John Robert Moore has aptly called him, a citizen of the modern world.

In a second pamphlet, *The Two Great Questions Further Considered*, Defoe repeated and developed his original argument. In advocating a defensive alliance against Louis XIV he was fighting not only the naturally isolationist Tories, but also a substantial section of the Whigs led by such men as John Trenchard, and he therefore devoted a good deal of his attention to the Whig opponents of the King's policy. But he was also replying to an anonymous critic who had published *Remarks* on his first pamphlet, and this second pamphlet suffers from his determination to answer "our wise remarker" point by point, and from a failure (quite unusual with Defoe) to keep his temper. Yet there are some able strokes in *The Two Great Questions Further Considered*, and none better than that with which he concludes his argument. In this sort of political controversy where the writer aims at clarifying an issue for the common man, one of the pamphleteer's chief weapons, as already suggested, is an ability to state the facts starkly, so as to bring them home to the man in the street in a way that he cannot possibly fail to understand. At this moment of time the one great task for a friend of the King was to make

Englishmen realize the danger of Spain falling under French domination, or, at least, becoming the ally of France:

> The debate here is not a standing army in England, but the kingdom of Spain falling into the French interests; let the King and the parliament alone to the methods, if it may be done by paying foreign forces, or by no forces, *in the name of God, Amen.* But to say 'tis nothing to us who is King of Spain is as ridiculous as to say 'tis no matter to us who has the kingdom of Ireland.

To the Englishman of 1700 a French force landing in Ireland was missiles in Cuba.[9]

Early in 1701 Defoe published two more political pamphlets within a few days of each other. Parliament had been dissolved in December 1700, and for the coming general election in January he wrote *The Six Distinguishing Characters of a Parliament Man.* This pamphlet has some general resemblance to a finer one which the great Marquis of Halifax wrote for the election of 1695, and one or two passages suggest that Defoe may have had it in mind. More interesting is *The Danger of the Protestant Religion Consider'd.* The theme of this pamphlet is still that of the need for England to wake up to the immediate danger from France, but Defoe chooses on this occasion to arouse his fellow countrymen by dwelling on the threat to the Protestant religion. For Defoe this was no doubt a real threat, and it would be unfair to suggest that he was merely making use of it to further his campaign in favor of the King's policy of containing the French drive to dominate Europe. He gives a serious historical sketch of the fluctuating fortunes of Protestantism during the past century of European warfare, and seeks to show how often the real *casus belli* has been religion. Yet it is impossible not to detect a note of exaggeration. When he says that "no war can be rais'd in Europe but what will, of course, run into a war of religion," or that "Europe has really nothing else to quarrel about," he is ignoring some of the very different arguments he had used in earlier pamphlets. In dedicating this one to the King, he tells him that "Religion is, or ought to be, the great concern of kings and nations; 'tis for this kings reign and parliaments assemble; laws are enacted; trade is carried on; manufactures are improv'd; men born, and the world made." What the King thought of all this we cannot tell, but both he and his pamphleteer were accustomed to interpreting the ambitions of Louis XIV in more mundane terms. As on so many other occasions, Defoe is putting a case, and in this concealed recruiting tract, although he is not simply writing with his tongue in his cheek, he is quite consciously playing upon the fears of religious people to further a cause that is not primarily religious at all:

Let all those who would stand neuter in this cause of religion remember that God Almighty has declar'd against such as are lukewarm Christians: there is no neuter gender in religion. . . . The defence of the Protestant religion calls upon all men who have any value for it to appear in the time of its danger. Defend religion, and politick interests will be easily secur'd; *a Jove principium;* but first God, and then your country.

For the rest, Defoe returns to some of his old topics such as standing armies and "keeping danger at a distance." One begins to feel that even this fertile writer has used up his arguments and is being driven to repeat himself.[10]

Of two other pamphlets published a few weeks later, *The Free-Holder's Plea against Stock-Jobbing Elections* and *The Villainy of Stock-Jobbers Detected,* he thought well enough to reprint them in the first collection of his writings published in 1703. In the first of these he exposes the practice of buying and selling parliamentary seats (a practice made possible by the very small number of electors qualified to vote in many constituencies), and characteristically makes a number of suggestions for a general reform of parliamentary representation. As he was later to tell Robert Harley, he was never one "for searching an evil to be amazed at it, but to apply the remedies."[11] In the second pamphlet he attacks the wealthy speculators who have been deliberately creating a run on the Bank of England, and so endangering the public credit. His hatred of stock-jobbers was such that he appears to have put them considerably lower in his moral scale than pirates like Captain Singleton or thieves like Moll Flanders.

Defoe's services for King William culminated in May 1701 in one of the climactic moments of his career. The new Parliament was showing no sense of urgency in dealing with the threat from France, and on 21 April a petition was drawn up in the name of the Gentlemen, Grand Jury, Justices, and Freeholders of Kent,

calling attention to the dangerous state of Europe and begging
Parliament to take immediate steps to safeguard the country:

We most humbly implore this honourable House to have regard to
the voice of the people! that our religion and safety may be effectually
provided for, that your loyal addresses may be turned into bills of
supply, and that His most Sacred Majesty (whose propitious and
unblemished reign over us we pray God may long continue!) may be
enabled powerfully to assist his allies, before it is too late.

When this petition was presented in person by five gentlemen of
Kent a few days later, a predominantly Tory House of Commons
ordered the Sergeant-at-Arms to arrest them, and they were
removed to the Gatehouse Prison. The five gentlemen had acted
entirely within their rights as English freeholders in petitioning
Parliament on a matter of national urgency; but the angry Tory
majority interpreted their action as a piece of Whig propaganda
(as indeed it was), designed to bring extra-parliamentary pressure
to bear on the elected representatives of the people. If they
thought they had settled the matter by their high-handed action,
they were much mistaken. On 14 May, guarded, it was said, "with
about sixteen men of quality," Defoe entered the House and presented to the Speaker, Robert Harley, a paper of his own composition, usually known as "Legion's Memorial," which the Speaker
was "commanded by two hundred thousand Englishmen" to deliver to the House of Commons. In this astonishingly outspoken
and forthright document all pretence of merely petitioning the
House was abandoned. Members of Parliament were reminded
more than once that they were the servants of the people of
England, and must act in accordance with the laws of the country.

You are not above the people's resentments, they that made you
members may reduce you to the same rank from whence they chose
you; and may give you a taste of their abused kindness in terms you
may not be pleased with.

Accordingly, they are called upon to release the five gentlemen
of Kent they have illegally imprisoned, to address the King with
a view to an immediate declaration of war against France, and to
vote suitable supplies to enable him to carry on the war. These and
other things, the Commons were told, "we do require and demand."

Thus, Gentlemen, you have your duty laid before you, which it is hoped you will think of; but if you continue to neglect it, you may expect to be treated according to the resentments of an *injur'd nation;* for Englishmen are no more to be slaves to *parliaments* than to a king. *Our name is Legion, and we are many.*[12]

As Sir George Clark has pointed out, the claim that the people have a right to control the proceedings of Parliament marks a return to the position taken by the Earl of Shaftesbury near the end of the reign of Charles II. Defoe is willing to revive this claim now because there seems to be no other way of resolving a dangerous crisis threatening the whole future of England as a nation. Yet *Legion's Memorial* shows how easily he could shift his position. Early in 1701, before the new Parliament had been elected, and when a tactful approach seemed desirable, he could write in *The Danger of the Protestant Religion Consider'd*: "I know better than to reflect on parliaments." But now, with a Parliament opposed to the King, he was prepared to take a very different line: to threaten, to speak out boldly on behalf of "two hundred thousand Englishmen," to "command" and "demand." *Legion's Memorial* is a mixture of bluff and genuine indignation. As a journalist Defoe could sense the feeling of the English people; he must have known that the tide was turning against isolationism, the comfortable pretence that if England kept quiet Louis XIV would leave England alone. In taking his bold stand he must have been counting on the same sort of surge of popular feeling as had swept the country a generation earlier at the trial of the Seven Bishops, when the Cornish supporters of Bishop Jonathan Trelawny chanted their defiant ballad,

> And shall Trelawny die?
> Then thirty thousand Cornish boys
> Will know the reason why.

Such heady moments are not uncommon in English history, and Chesterton's lines about the English people—

> Smile at us, pay us, pass us; but do not quite forget.
> For we are the people of England that never have spoken yet.—

hardly represent the truth about them. But although Defoe may have been riding the crest of a popular wave, it took real courage to do what he did on that May morning; nor would he be the

interesting man he is if he had not been ready on several other
occasions to live dangerously and chance the consequences.[13]

Legion's Memorial is not a great piece of literature, but it had
all the virtues that were proper to the occasion. Defoe's style
varies very considerably from one work to another, and what was
needed here was the plainest of plain speaking.

We do hereby claim and declare,
1. That it is the undoubted right of the people of England, in case
their representatives in parliament do not proceed according to their
duty, and the people's interest, to inform them of their dislike, disown
their actions, and to direct them to such things as they think fit, either
by petition, address, proposal, memorial, or any other peaceable
way. . . .

The language is almost legal in its considered precision; the tone
is authoritative, final, and deadly serious. For emotional overtones
Defoe invokes "the great law of Reason," "the undoubted Right
of the People of England," posterity, liberty and slavery, legality,
justice, and other equally vague and powerful concepts, and he
makes effective play with the idea that "the good people of England" are the masters, and Parliament their inferiors who may be
called to account for their misdemeanors. Dangerous stuff; but
Defoe was obviously enjoying himself, and thousands of ordinary
citizens accustomed to being pushed around by their betters must
have welcomed his blunt and irreverent treatment of a Parliament
that had shown itself intolerant and inflated by its own importance.[14]

When the House rose in July the five gentlemen of Kent were
released, and were given a magnificent Whig banquet in the City,
at which Defoe was an honored guest. Events now moved so fast
that no further intervention was needed from Defoe or from
anyone else. Early in September the exiled James II died, and
Louis at once proclaimed his thirteen-year-old son King James III
of England. This was too much even for the Tories, and the
country was at last united in opposition to the French. William
seized the chance to dissolve an uncooperative Parliament, and
when the new House met in December the Tory majority was
much reduced. At last the King could proceed with his prepara-

tions for a war that he had long known to be inevitable; but he was not to live to see it. In March 1702 his horse stumbled while he was riding at Hampton Court, and he was thrown heavily. He died on 19 March. Two months later, in the reign of Queen Anne, England and France were once again at war. As a journalist Defoe was soon to be deeply involved, with new friends and old enemies.

ii

The political pamphlets which he wrote from 1697 to 1701 had by no means absorbed all his attention. There were other issues on which he felt called upon to pronounce. One of the most effective pamphlets he ever wrote, *The Poor Man's Plea* (1698), was concerned with a moral and social, rather than a political, problem. As the full title makes clear, this had reference to "all the Proclamations, Declarations, Acts of Parliament, etc. which have been, or shall be made, for a Reformation of Manners, and suppressing Immorality in the Nation." Ever since the new King and Queen had come to the throne in 1688 they had shown concern about the state of public morality, and in the early 1690s a number of Societies for the Reformation of Manners had come into being with the expressed purpose of implementing several royal proclamations and acts of Parliament directed against various forms of immorality and irreligion. The best-known expression of this new social conscience is Jeremy Collier's famous counterblast to the lax drama of the day, *A Short View of the Immorality and Profaneness of the English Stage* (1698); but by the time Collier entered the lists there was already a considerable pamphlet literature on the subject of reformation.

The problem facing a writer who wishes to reform his fellow citizens is, first, how to make them listen at all, and then how to avoid alienating those who are unwilling to give up their pleasant vices and have no desire to be preached at. Collier obtained the ear of the public by the exercise of some wit and a good deal of sarcasm, and by having a case with which many of his readers were inclined to agree. It is true that he quoted so liberally from the bawdier passages of Restoration comedy that some of his readers may have enjoyed his book for the wrong reason; but if

so, he could have said, as Defoe said in the preface to *Roxana*, that
if any reader makes a wrong use of a book "the wickedness is his
own." In *The Poor Man's Plea* Defoe's approach to the problem
of public morality is both original and provocative. Whether they
would have been willing to admit it or not, what the members of
the reformation societies were chiefly concerned about was immorality and profanity in the working class. In so far as the laws
were put into effect at all, they were usually invoked against the
poor, who were frequently arrested on blank warrants, filled in by
members of the societies, when found drunk and blaspheming in
the streets. Defoe, who was in full sympathy with the movement
towards reform, held no special brief for the poor, and was ready
enough on many occasions to complain about their shiftlessness
and improvidence; but he was convinced that there was little hope
of a general reformation unless the upper classes were prepared to
show a better example than they had hitherto done, and unless
the laws were enforced against them as rigorously as they were
against the poor:

These are all cobweb laws, in which the small flies are catch'd, and
the great ones break through. My Lord Mayor has whipt about the
poor beggars, and a few scandalous whores have been sent to the
House of Correction; some alehousekeepers and vintners have been
fin'd for drawing drink on the Sabbath day; but all this falls upon us
of the mob, the poor *plebeii*, as if all the vice lay among us, for we do
not find the rich drunkard carri'd before my Lord Mayor, nor a
swearing lewd merchant. *The man with a gold ring and gay cloaths*
may swear before the Justice, or at the Justice; may reel home through
the open streets, and no man take any notice of it; but if a poor man
get drunk, or swears an oath, he must to the stocks without remedy.[15]

Defoe has cleverly shifted the basis of the argument from straight-
forward denunciation to an appeal for fair play, and in so doing
has greatly reinforced the popular appeal of his reforming crusade.
One law for the rich and another for the poor just isn't good
enough; it is not being fair to "us of the mob." In so writing Defoe
is availing himself of all the natural antagonism of the underdog
to his superiors, of the poor to the well-to-do, of the proletariat
to the "establishment." Like so many of the positions he adopted,
this one is potentially dangerous to the established order of
"gentlemen and others"; but when Defoe gets caught up in an

argument that is logically irrefutable, nothing is going to stop him pursuing it to its conclusion.

This pamphlet is also notable for being the first in which he made effective use of a *persona*. All that is said here is said by "the poor man," a decent, unpretentious citizen who knows his place and writes more in sorrow than in anger, but who is not afraid to criticize his betters. The style is therefore adapted to its supposed writer. Since Defoe is more concerned with his argument and its effect on middle- and upper-class readers than with a close imitation of a poor man's way of writing,* he does not risk offending them by introducing too many vulgarisms or illiterate expressions. But the style is noticeably colloquial and simple, and its colloquialism is certainly not that of the upper class:

The parson preaches a thundering sermon against drunkenness, and the Justice of Peace sets my poor neighbour in the stocks, and I am like to be much the better for either when I know perhaps that this same parson and this same Justice were both drunk together but the night before.

We should not find Addison and Steele writing about "a thundering sermon"; nor should we meet in Swift (unless he was finding words for an equally humble *persona*) with such an expression as "I am like to be much the better for either." So, too, with the homely illustrations:

If my own watch goes false, it deceives me and none else; but if the town clock goes false, it deceives the whole parish.

A vicious parson that preaches well, but lives ill, may be like an unskilful horseman who opens a gate on the wrong side, and lets other folks through, but shuts himself out.[16]

In *The Poor Man's Plea* Defoe has already come close to the method that he invariably used when writing his works of fiction more than twenty years later: he has identified himself with an invented person, and (except when he occasionally forgets) is writing *as* that person.

---

* References to "my Lord Rochester" and "Lycurgus" may be thought to be rather beyond the reading of the Poor Man.

The modern reader may find it difficult to realize what a large
part religious differences played in the life of Defoe's England,
and the extent to which religion was involved with politics. The
historic national church was the Church of England, but in a
population of about six million people there was a large minority
of dissenters, estimated by Defoe to amount to two million. In the
minds of many Anglicans (and more especially of the Tories) the
dissenters were associated with the Puritans who had taken arms
against Charles I and ended by cutting off his head in 1649, and
who, during the ensuing Commonwealth, had come near to
destroying the Church of England altogether. After the Restoration the uncompromising attitude of Anglicans to dissenters was
expressed in the Test Acts of 1673 and 1678, which made it
obligatory for anyone holding public office to take the sacrament
at least once a year according to Anglican ritual. As a consequence, the practice known as occasional conformity had grown
up: if a citizen chosen to be, say, Lord Mayor of London happened to be a dissenter, he could qualify for office by taking a
token communion in the Church of England, and continue to
worship for the rest of the year among his fellow dissenters. By
the close of the seventeenth century most dissenters had no desire
for martyrdom and were only too glad to be left in peace, even if
they were to some extent looked upon as second-class citizens.
Occasional conformity, therefore, seemed to many to be a reasonable compromise, and a price they could well afford to pay for the
privilege of being otherwise unmolested and free to worship as
they thought best.

But not to Defoe. To Defoe occasional conformity was logically indefensible, and ultimately destructive of the basis on
which dissent rested. As a dissenter himself, he made this abundantly plain early in 1698, when he published *An Enquiry into the
Occasional Conformity of Dissenters, in Cases of Preferment*, and
firmly emphasized his convictions on the title-page with a provocative text from 1 Kings, xviii.21: "If the Lord be God, follow
him: but if Baal, then follow him." Defoe's argument is simple, but
inescapable: the only possible reason for anyone being a dissenter
from the established church is that he is convinced "he can really

serve God more agreeable to His will, and that accordingly 'tis his duty to do it so, *and no otherwise.*" The whole issue turns upon what a man's conscience tells him to do, and if it does not tell him he must dissent, then he is actually doing wrong in *not* conforming to the established church. What is intolerable is the pretence that occasional conformity is only a civil act, and not a religious one; for *all* sacraments are religious. Occasional conformity, therefore, is merely *"playing Bo-peep* with God Almighty," and is "such a bantering with religion as no modest Christian can think of without horror." Defoe is determined to leave the occasional conformist without a shred of justification for his practice:

> But if I shall thus dissent, and yet at the same time conform; by conforming I deny my dissent being lawful, or by my dissenting I damn my conforming as sinful.[17]

There is no reason to suspect Defoe of insincerity in his condemnation of what was a typically English compromise; he clearly believed that occasional conformers would be no loss to the dissenting community. Yet, as on other occasions, we may also suspect that he was taking an intellectual pleasure in carrying an argument to its logical conclusion. Among his fellow countrymen Defoe was something of a maverick, a sort of George Orwell who continually ignored the party line, and who was therefore unpredictable and often exasperating to those who had expected him to be on their side. As a dissenter he might have trodden a little less hard on the toes of his co-religionists; but instead he went out of his way to twit those prominent dissenters who accepted the easy compromise of occasional conformity. No man was compelled to be a mayor or a magistrate; but if he was a dissenter and refused office because his conscience would not let him take the sacrament according to the rites of the Church of England, he was liable to a substantial fine. Defoe rubs his point home:

> If the service of their country be so dear to them, pray why should they not chuse to expose their bodies and estates for that service, rather than their souls?
>
> The penalty of the law in accepting the publick employments is wholly pecuniary; the difference lies here, *they chuse the trespassing on their consciences before the hazard of their estates,* as the least evil.

To a second edition of his pamphlet Defoe addressed a preface to the aged and respected Presbyterian minister John Howe, more or less challenging him to answer the arguments set forth in his *Enquiry*, or else "the world must believe that dissenters do allow themselves to practise what they cannot defend." Howe, who happened to have in his congregation a prominent nonconformist, the current Lord Mayor of London, was understandably nettled, and issued a rather bad-tempered reply, which Defoe answered in *A Letter to Mr. How*. What probably annoyed Howe more than anything else was the intrusion of this layman and amateur into a field which should be left to the professionals: Defoe, in fact, was offering to teach the dissenting ministers their own business. When, two years later, he was to need their Christian charity, he found that he had alienated the greater part of the dissenting community.[18]

With the accession of Queen Anne the High Church party felt that their hour had come at last. A number of sermons, notably one preached at Oxford in June 1702 by Dr. Henry Sacheverell, were clearly intended to inflame public opinion against the dissenters, and to suggest that the days of toleration were numbered. In November the new confidence of the Tories was expressed in a bill introduced into the House of Commons to prevent occasional conformity. For some Tories this bill may have seemed a measure to protect the Church of England from schism, and to win back some of the dissenters to the Anglican community; for most, perhaps, it was no more than an adroit political move directed against the Whigs, in whose ranks the great majority of the dissenters was to be found. It is significant that one of the most enthusiastic supporters of the bill was the brilliant young Henry St. John (afterwards Lord Bolingbroke), who was already known as a freethinker, a libertine in his morals, and a clever politician. Meanwhile the pamphleteers got to work. In *An Enquiry into Occasional Conformity. Shewing that the Dissenters Are No Way Concern'd in It*, Defoe re-stated his belief that the dissenters had nothing to lose by getting rid of the practice of occasional conformity. While recognizing that the bill was a malicious one promoted by the High Church faction, and while emphasizing that dissenters had every reason to dislike that part of the bill "which excludes us from the native honours and preferments of our country, which are our due, our birthright, equally with our neighbours," he still refused to lament the proposed ending of occasional conformity as a recognized practice, and even suggested that its termination would strengthen the dissenters by making them close their ranks. "We would humbly propose to have the title of the Act alter'd, and to have it entitl'd, An Act for the Better Uniting the Protestant Dissenters." Once again Defoe had taken a stand that isolated him from the great majority of his fellow dissenters; and what is interesting here is that he positively gloried in his independence, and was confidently prepared to justify it. " 'Tis hard," he observed, "for a man to say, all the world is mistaken but himself; but if it be so, who can help it?" And again: "It is a wonderful thing to find no body of my mind, and yet be positively assur'd that I am in the right." Defoe never lacked confidence in his convictions; the intense approval and disapproval he aroused among his contemporaries were largely due to the firmness with which he held and stated his beliefs. As he was soon to find out, such utter confidence is hubristic, and invites nemesis. Apart from this, his pamphlet is notable for some plain speaking about the economic power of the dissenters, and even some threats about how they might have to exercise it if they were driven too far:

Let us fraight our ships apart, keep our money out of your bank, accept none of our bills, and separate your selves as absolutely from us in civil matters as we do from you in religious, and see how you can go on without us.

Legion's Memorial, and now this: Defoe was getting a little above himself.[19]

The bill to prevent occasional conformity never became law. It passed through the House of Commons with large majorities, but was thrown out by the House of Lords. While the controversy was still at its height, Defoe—the self-styled advocate of moderation—published a famous pamphlet that had the effect of enormously increasing the tension on both sides, and that was to lead to his own arrest, bankruptcy, and imprisonment. *The Shortest Way with the Dissenters* appeared anonymously early in December 1702, apparently the work of an extreme High Church fanatic whose patience was exhausted, but in fact a brilliant hoax by Defoe. In writing this pamphlet Defoe was hardly concerned at all with occasional conformity; he had passed beyond that particular issue to an exposure of the rabidly intolerant attitude of the Anglican diehards. By impersonating one of those High Church zealots and making him use the extravagant language of men like Sacheverell, he aimed at condemning them out of their own mouths.

'Tis vain to trifle in this matter; the light foolish handling of them by mulcts, fines, etc.—'tis their glory and their advantage. If the gallows instead of the Counter, and the gallies instead of the fines, were the reward of going to a conventicle, to preach or hear, there wou'd not be so many sufferers. The spirit of martyrdom is over; they that will go to the church to be chosen sheriffs and mayors would go to forty churches rather than be hang'd.

If one severe law were made, and punctually executed, that whoever was found at a conventicle shou'd be banish'd the nation and the preacher be hang'd, we shou'd soon see an end of the tale; they wou'd all come to church, and one age wou'd make us all one again.

Not even Sacheverell would have written this, but he might easily have *said* it after his second glass of college port. In later years, when seeking to justify what he had written in *The Shortest Way*, Defoe was given to asserting that there was nothing said in that pamphlet that had not been said time and again by some of the High Church writers. In the *Review*, 9 October 1705, he asked his readers whether all that was ironically said in his pamphlet "was not seriously, as well as with a malicious earnest, published with impunity in print a hundred times both before and since." It was "those warm gentlemen of the Church of England," he claimed in *The Shortest Way to Peace and Union*, who were "the proper authors of *The Shortest Way*." His fullest statement of what he had intended to do in 1702 occurs in a lengthy work of 1712, *The Present State of the Parties in Great Britain*:

Some people have blam'd the author of the aforesaid pamphlet called *The Shortest Way*, etc. for that he did not quote either in the margin, or otherwise, the sermon of Sacheverell aforesaid, or such other authors from whom his notions were drawn, which would have justify'd him in what he had suggested; but these men do not see the design of the book at all, or the effect it had at the same time taken off the edge of the book, and that which now cut the throat of a whole party would not then have given the least wound. The case the book pointed at was to speak in the first person of the party, and then thereby not only speak their language, but make them acknowledge it to be theirs, which they did so openly that confounded all their attempts afterwards to deny it, and to call it a scandal thrown upon them by another.[20]

Defoe's claim that in *The Shortest Way* he had done nothing but "speak their language" has been questioned; he comes nearer the truth in his *Brief Explanation of a Late Pamphlet* (1703), when he asserts that he had put "the persecution and destruction of the Dissenters, *the very thing they drive at*, . . . into plain English." His technique here bears a general resemblance to that used by a greater satirist to attack a freethinker. In *Mr. Collins's Discourse of Free-Thinking, Put into Plain English, by Way of an Abstract for the Use of the Poor*, Swift spelled out in full what Collins had sometimes only implied discreetly. But neither Swift nor Defoe was satisfied with merely making explicit what was only implicit: into both pamphlets there entered an element of exaggeration, and even travesty. In *The Shortest Way*, however, both exaggeration and travesty were necessarily limited by the author's intention. Defoe had set himself a nice problem. He wanted to pass off *The Shortest Way* as a genuine High Church diatribe against the dissenters, so that High Church zealots would read it and publicly approve of it, and then, when the true authorship became known, be self-exposed for the intolerant fanatics they were. Too much exaggeration would therefore defeat his purpose. At the same time he wanted to make sure that *The Shortest Way* would attract the maximum amount of attention by going further than Sacheverell or any other High Church fanatic had yet gone; and this involved him in making statements so outrageous that there was a danger the hoax would destroy itself. At this distance of time it is hardly possible to say how effectively Defoe's pamphlet worked as pure hoax, and how many of his contemporaries were, at least temporarily, taken in by it. Most of our evidence comes from Defoe himself, and may therefore be a little suspect. In *More Short-Ways with the Dissenters* (1703) he cites one "Esquire M——" who "has given it under his hand that he heartily prays God wou'd give her Majesty the grace to put all that was wrote there in the book call'd *The Shortest*

Way in execution"; and elsewhere he suggests that many of his
fellow dissenters were alarmed at what they took to be only
another, if severer, attack by a High Church spokesman. Defoe
had certainly shown great skill in catching the triumphant tone of
the High Church party, who, under a new queen entirely sym-
pathetic to the Church of England, were now cock-a-hoop:

No, Gentlemen, the time of mercy is past, your *day of grace is over;*
you should have practised peace, and moderation, and charity, if you
expected any your selves. . . . What account can you give of the
multitudes you have forc'd to comply, against their consciences, with
your new *sophistical politicks,* who, like new converts in France, sin
because they can't starve? And now the tables are turn'd upon you,
you must not be persecuted; 'tis not a Christian spirit.

You have *butcher'd* one king, *depos'd* another king, and made a
mock king of a third; and yet you cou'd have the face to expect to be
employ'd and trusted by the fourth.

He also reproduced with remarkable accuracy the inflammatory
preaching style of Sacheverell, with its conventional biblical
metaphor and its uncompromising and derisory vocabulary. On 5
November 1705, when he preached his notorious sermon on "The
Perils of False Brethren" before the Lord Mayor of London,
Sacheverell was still beating the same old drum:

That the old leaven of their forefathers is still working in their present
generation, and that this traditional poyson still remains in this brood
of vipers, to sting us to death, is sufficiently visible from the dangerous
encroachments they now make upon our government, and the treasonable reflections they have publish'd on her Majesty, God bless her! . . .
A man must be very weak, or something worse, that thinks or pretends that Dissenters are to be gain'd or won over by any other grants
and indulgences than giving up our whole constitution. And he that
recedes the least tittle from it, to satisfy or ingratiate with these
clamorous, insatiable, church-devouring malignants, knows not what
spirit they are of. . . .
And yet if our Dissenters had lived in those times [of St. Paul], they
would have branded him as an intemperate, hot, furious zealot, that
wanted to be sweeten'd by the gentle spirit of charity and moderation,
forsooth! Schism and faction are things of impudent and incroaching
natures; they thrive upon concessions, take permission for power, and
advance a toleration immediately into an establishment; and are therefore to be treated like growing mischiefs, or infectious plagues, kept

at a distance lest their deadly contagion spread. Let us therefore have
no fellowship with these works of darkness, but rather reprove them.
Let our superior pastors do their duty in thundering out their ecclesiastical anathemas. . . .

Sacheverell preaching about his fellow Christians: such passages
could be slipped into Defoe's parody without any reader detecting
a difference. Indeed, if one wished to question Defoe's right to be
called a satirist in *The Shortest Way*, it would be on the grounds
that he merely reproduced the extravagance he wished to satirize.
This is not quite true; he does exaggerate a little, he carries High
Church fanaticism to a stage of absurdity that not even Sacheverell
had reached. But on this occasion he was dealing with a set of
men who went to such extremes that only a few additional strokes
were required to achieve the *reductio ad absurdum*. Defoe only
paid out enough additional rope to enable the High Church party
to hang itself.[21]

Unfortunately he had also laid himself open to the retaliation
of his enemies, and was now to find how dangerous wit could be
in a literal world, and how easily it could be one of those
"mistaken things":

> 'Tis what the *vicious fear*, the *virtuous shun*;
> By *fools* 'tis *hated*, and by *knaves undone!*

It is clear from the savage sentence which he now incurred (jail,
pillory, and a large fine) that his enemies had only been waiting
for the opportunity to settle old scores with the propagandist of
the late King. But Professor Moore is undoubtedly right in his
suggestion that Defoe's outspoken satire in *Reformation of Manners*, in which he had attacked various city magnates and magistrates, helps to account for the treatment he received when on
7 July he stood trial at the Old Bailey for writing and publishing
a seditious libel. For the sort of situation in which he had now
landed himself he needed the best legal advice available, but his
counsel, William Colepeper, one of the Kentish petitioners, was
not much better than well-meaning. At all events, Colepeper
advised Defoe to plead guilty and to throw himself upon the
Queen's mercy. It is easy to be wise after the event; but if Defoe
had pleaded not guilty, he would at least have forced the prose-
cution to explain why *The Shortest Way* was a seditious publica-

tion if the sermons of Sacheverell and others which said practically the same thing were apparently harmless and inoffensive. No doubt the Solicitor-General would have explained this to his own satisfaction and have brushed aside the ineffective Colepeper; but he would have been compelled to find reasons which he was never in fact called upon to give.[22]

As part of his sentence Defoe was ordered to find securities for his good behavior during the next seven years. This meant, in effect, that if he wrote and published anything that could be construed as inflammatory or unwelcome to the government of the day he could expect little mercy. In fact he paid little attention to this warning, and published, even while still in prison, some astonishingly outspoken comments on those who had just passed sentence on him. What sustained him was partly a streak of recklessness and an unshakeable confidence in his own rightness (a legacy, perhaps, from his puritan ancestry), but partly too some concept of a natural justice that must ultimately triumph over every manipulation and malpractice. He did manage, however, to avoid serious trouble for the next ten years or so.

iv

Although he was still very much involved in contemporary politics, another interest was now to absorb more and more of his attention. From 1704 onwards he wrote constantly about trade, a subject on which even Defoe would have found it difficult to be seditious, but on which he could be, and often was, highly provocative. He began to write seriously on trade when his second bankruptcy made it impossible for him to carry on trading any longer. "He who can, does," said Shaw. "He who cannot, teaches." But if the jibe is not altogether inapplicable to Defoe, he gave far more to the world by his writings on trade and commerce than he would ever have done by running a successful brick and tile factory.[23]

To 1704 belongs the earliest and one of the liveliest of his purely economic pamphlets, *Giving Alms No Charity*. This had its origin in a bill for the relief of the poor introduced into Parliament by Sir Humphry Mackworth, who proposed setting up parochial factories, supported by public funds, to give work in spinning, weaving, and so on to the unemployed. To Defoe this suggestion was utterly wrong-headed; it could only result in "giving to one what you take away from another; enriching one poor man to starve another." What was the point of throwing an honest man out of work in order to subsidize beggars and vagabonds in one of Sir Humphry's factories? Defoe had two main objections to Mackworth's bill; one based on an abstract economic principle, and the other on a realistic assessment of the English working man.

The abstract principle was that the prosperity of a country depends upon the natural circulation of trade through as many hands as possible:

> The manufactures of England are happily settled in different corners of the kingdom, from whence they are mutually convey'd by a circulation of trade to London by wholesale, like the blood to the heart, and from thence disperse in lesser quantities to the other parts of the kingdom by retail. . . . By this exchange of manufactures abundance of trading families are maintain'd by the carriage and re-carriage of goods, vast numbers of men and cattle [i.e. horses] are employed, and numbers of innholders, victuallers, and their dependencies subsisted.

So why ruin this happy state of affairs by setting up factories in every village and making each little community self-supporting, since "this breach of the circulation of trade must necessarily distemper the body"? It will be noticed that Defoe's conception of trade as a natural process is reinforced by his biological metaphors ("like the blood to the heart," "distemper the body"). One of the factors that made Defoe so effective a journalist was the impression he invariably gave of really knowing what he was talking about, of being a writer with expert knowledge of his subject, of having been on the spot and seen for himself what was happening. Already, he points out, the stocking trade of Norwich is in decay because most of this traditionally East Anglian manufacture is now concentrated on the knitting frames of London, and the same is true of the Norwich weavers.

> If it be so at Norwich, Canterbury is yet more a melancholy instance of it, where the houses stand empty, and the people go off, and the

trade dye because the weavers are following the manufacture to London; and whereas there was within few years 200 broad looms at work, I am well assur'd there are not 50 now employ'd in that city.

By giving such specific examples and not confirming himself to generalities Defoe drives home his point that any interference with the natural and traditional order of things can only lead to economic dislocation and distress. For him trade had its inexorable laws as the physical universe had for Newton, and the literary universe for Pope.[24]

As for the English working man, Defoe speaks again from personal knowledge as an employer of labor. He is ready to recognize that poverty may sometimes be due to the sickness of the breadwinner, or to some incapacitating accident. Such "meerly providential" infirmities can be left out of the reckoning, for they "ever were, will, and ought to be the charge and care of the respective parishes where such unhappy people chance to live." But those unfortunates represent only a small fraction of the poor in England. The two main causes of poverty are luxury and sloth. By luxury Defoe means the English working man's high standard of eating and drinking, on which he is prepared to spend every penny he earns. He just cannot, or will not, save money. "Good husbandry is no English virtue"; and indeed the average Englishman despises anyone who is provident, and tends to look upon him as "a covetous old miserable dog." Here again Defoe was able to cite an example from his own experience as an employer:

I am ready to produce to this honourable House the man who for several years has gain'd of me by his handy labour at the mean scoundrel employment of tile-making from 16s. to 20s. *per* week wages, and all that time would hardly have a pair of shoes to his feet, or cloaths to cover his nakedness, and had his wife and children kept by the parish.

Since twenty shillings a week was a handsome wage at the beginning of the eighteenth century, the assumption must be that Defoe's employee drank it all away in the alehouse. As for sloth, he is unwilling to give the whole working class a bad name. The English have "the title of an industrious people, and so in general we are"; but he prefers to characterize them as "the most lazy diligent nation in the world." Too many Englishmen will work till they have got a pocketful of money, and then just stay away from their job, or go on drinking, until it is all spent. What it all amounts to, in Defoe's opinion, is that there are far too many work-shy people in England who could easily find employment, but who make such a good thing of begging that begging has become a form of employment. Once again Defoe confirms his argument with an example from his own experience:

I affirm of my own knowledge, when I have wanted a man for labouring work, and offer'd 9s. *per* week to strouling fellows at my door, they have frequently told me to my face, they could get more a begging, and I once set a lusty fellow in the stocks for making the experiment.

More of this sort of treatment, he believes, is what is needed with men who won't work when there is plenty of work to be had. He had clearly no belief in a "welfare state." If there were genuine unemployment (and not just casual unemployment due to work-men taking the week off to booze away their earnings), there would not be the difficulty there is in finding recruits for the army:

'tis poverty makes men soldiers, and drives crowds into the armies; and the difficulties to get English men to list is because they live in plenty and ease, and he that can earn 20s. *per* week at an easie, steady employment must be drunk or mad when he lists for a soldier, to be knock'd o' th' head for 3s. 6d. *per* week; but if there was no work to be had, if the poor wanted employment, if they had not bread to eat, nor knew not how to earn it, thousands of young lusty fellows would fly to the pike and the musquet, and choose to die like men in the face of the enemy, rather than lie at home, starve, perish in poverty and distress.

All in all, then, Sir Humphry Mackworth's bill is directed at helping people who could quite easily help themselves. He would have been better employed in devising legal methods to compel those idlers "to seek that work which it is plain is to be had."[25]

That, then, is the main drift of Defoe's argument. But into this vigorous tract he also introduces some of his other favorite topics, notably the great gain to England of giving a home to the refugees from various European countries. The early pages of his pamphlet are devoted to a historical account of the immigrants who arrived from the Low Countries in the reign of Queen Elizabeth to escape the persecution of the Spanish governor, the Duke of Alva, and who brought with them their skill in spinning and weaving, to the lasting benefit of the English manufacture. So far is England from being now overpopulated that it could with advantage absorb more such foreigners. Echoing Sir William Petty, whose works on "political arithmetic" were appearing when Defoe was a young man, he insists that "number of inhabitants are the wealth and strength of a nation." On the other hand, Defoe is against this sort of human migration when it goes in the opposite direction: it was all right for the Flemings to come to England, but it is all wrong for Englishmen to go to Russia "to teach that unpolish'd nation the improvements they are capable of," and instruct them "in such manufactures as may in time tend to the destruction of our trade." On economic matters Defoe's views are strictly practical and national. He is not incapable of taking a philosophical view of economic processes and of seeing them as subject to their own laws (as he does, for example, at the beginning of *A Plan of the English Commerce*, 1728); but when he writes on trade, he is usually concerned with the inland and foreign trade of his own country—not with the Wealth of Nations, but with the growth of English commerce.[26]

In style and tone *Giving Alms No Charity* differs from the general run of Defoe's controversial pamphlets. For one thing, it was addressed to "the Knights, Citizens and Burgesses in Parliament Assembled," and he was at some pains to express himself with due deference to that august assembly. The tone is not obsequious, but it is certainly deferential and uniformly polite: Defoe is behaving with his party manners. He may possibly have been remembering that he had given sureties for his good behavior for seven years; but it is more likely that the mixture of flattery and deference in this pamphlet was intended to placate those members of Parliament who were still smarting from his escapades of 1701 and 1702. The author of *Legion's Memorial*, who had no hesitation in telling Parliament in 1701 that the English people *demanded* a certain line of action, was now in 1704 prepared to be more respectful in order to gain a hearing for his arguments. It is true that he wrote anonymously, as an English freeholder with the good of his country at heart, but he knew that the secret of authorship was hard to keep, and that he would almost certainly be identified as the writer. (His mention of his tile factory would be a sufficient clue for most readers.) He therefore resolved to be tactful. "GENTLEMEN," he begins,

He that has truth and justice, and the interest of England in his design, can have nothing to fear from an English parliament.

He continues with references to "this honourable House" and "so honourable and august an Assembly"; he "humbly" appeals and suggests, and "craves the liberty" to offer his opinion, trusting that "no freedom of expression which the arguments may oblige him to may be constru'd as a want of respect, and a breach of the due deference every English man owes to the representing power of the nation." It is obviously something of a strain for Defoe to keep this sort of thing up; and at one point he suggests that all will be well if the deliberations of Parliament are "blest from Heaven, *as now we trust they are*, with principles of unanimity and concord"—as they were *not*, presumably, in the Parliament to which he had presented *Legion's Memorial*. But this is almost the only lapse into intransigence, and the pamphlet ends with another polite tribute to " a body so august, so wise, and so capable as this honourable assembly." Since he is addressing members of Parliament, most of whom had some education and some of whom were perhaps better educated than himself, he writes a more "correct" and less colloquial English than he normally used, and at one point slips in a Latin quotation to heighten the tone of polite discourse.[27]

None the less, Defoe succeeds in saying what he has to say with all his customary forthrightness; and if he professes respect for Sir Humphry Mackworth, whose efforts on behalf of the poor "merit the thanks and acknowledgment of the whole nation," he leaves us in no doubt that he thinks his bill ill-considered and potentially disastrous, and that all such schemes are "public nuisances." (His politeness to Mackworth is the more significant because he had recently had a fairly sharp exchange with him over the occasional conformity bill in a pamphlet called *Peace without Union*.) What sets *Giving Alms No Charity* apart from pamphlets of the same kind is Defoe's obvious familiarity with the whole range of English manufacture and commerce, his ability to drive home his arguments with a realistic appeal to the facts of life, and his characteristic assurance. Always positive and self-confident, Defoe is nowhere more so than when he writes on trade.[28]

v

The question of Defoe's political integrity is one that his biographers must try to settle. But it is relevant to his work as a political journalist in so far as it may affect his method of presenting a case, and the arguments he is prepared to use. Between 1705 and 1713, in addition to writing the *Review*, he published over seventy political pamphlets of varying quality, and he was especially active from 1711 to 1713 when the Tory government was engaged in negotiations for peace with France. Early in 1709 Marlborough's victories over the French in a succession of hard-fought campaigns had looked like bringing the war to a triumphant conclusion, and peace negotiations were opened at the Hague. The Allies, believing that they had got the French beaten, presented Louis XIV with forty preliminary articles, to all of which he assented except one, concerning the future of Spain, and the negotiations were broken off. The onus of prolonging the war undoubtedly lay with the Allies, who had been overconfident, and who refused to make peace while the grandson of Louis remained King of Spain. War weariness had been growing in England, and the prospect of peace had raised hopes which were now cheated. In September 1709 came the Pyrrhic victory of Malplaquet, in which the French, who had been considered dispirited and demoralized, fought with great resolution, inflicted on the Allies heavier losses than their own, and retired in good order. From this point on, the demands for peace became more insistent in England; and when the general election of October 1710 sent up to London a predominantly Tory House of Commons, and the Queen began replacing her Whig ministers with Tories (Harley becoming the effective head of the government), the movement to end the war was well under way. The Tories were committed to making peace, the Whigs to the unconditional surrender of the French, and the country at large was more and more inclined to support the Tories.

In this changing situation Defoe had to effect an unobtrusive transition from outright support of the war to advocacy of the peace policy of Harley and the Tories. Whatever his own views may now have been, it can't have been easy, but he managed to do it. While still writing in the *Review* for Whig readers as the moderate Whig he had always been, he had to try to put forward arguments for ending the war that could conceivably come from a Whig. But when writing anonymous pamphlets in support of Harley's peace policy he was not under the same restriction. In one of the most interesting of these pamphlets, *Reasons Why This Nation Ought to Put a Speedy End to This Expensive War*, published in October 1711, he takes more trouble than usual to conceal his identity; for his argument bears a general resemblance to that of the Tory pamphleteers, notably to that of Swift in his celebrated piece, *The Conduct of the Allies*, which was published rather less than two months later, and which ran through six editions in about eight weeks. (Defoe's pamphlet had a less spectacular success, but it reached three editions in the month of publication.) Swift, the convinced Tory, with his hatred of the moneyed interest and his dislike of "red-coats" and military power, did not hesitate to capitalize on Tory prejudices and to appeal to the selfish interests of his readers. But Defoe, faced with saying something effective which would not violate his principles, but which might bring over some wavering Whigs, made out his own skilful case for bringing the war to a "speedy end."

He opens with an emotional appeal to the feelings of all decent Englishmen:

A mind possest with any tenderness for the miseries, sufferings, and distresses of its native land, that has the happiness of any generous principles and shares something of that sublime quality called by the Ancients *Love of our country*, cannot look upon the present condition of this nation without being in the highest degree affected. . . .

One is reminded of the mock-humanitarian opening of Swift's projector in *A Modest Proposal*, when he says what a melancholy sight it is to see the streets crowded with beggars of the female sex, followed by their ragged children "importuning every passenger for an alms." Characteristically, Defoe mixes his sobs and groans with a more practical appeal: the long and bloody war which has been going on for more than twenty years has become so "chargeable" that the slightest talk of peace has the effect of sending up the price of stocks immediately. At this point he probably considers that he may be in danger of alienating some patriotic readers who are conscious of the sacrifices they have made, either vicariously through their sons and brothers who have fought in Marlborough's campaigns, or through the heavy taxes they have themselves had to pay to support the war. He therefore pauses for a moment to praise the patience and resolution which have been shown by the nation, whose fortitude cannot be reproached. Yes, he continues, but our strength is not inexhaustible; and now, after all those years of attrition, we are in danger of bleeding to death:

Now we see our treasures lost, our funds exhausted, all our publick revenues sold, mortgaged, and anticipated; vast and endless interests entail'd upon our posterity, the whole kingdom sold to usury . . .

—and of course an immense debt. These are the very arguments that Swift and Arbuthnot were to use; and they were directed mainly against the Whig magnates and money-lenders whose loans to the government were helping to finance the war.[29]

So far, so good; but if Defoe is to turn the minds of his readers completely against the war, he must go further. He must show that beating the French in a series of bloody battles has not really paid off. Since the war has now reached a stalemate, what is the point of persevering with it any longer?

In our land armies we expend mighty sums to perform trifling exploits, and please our selves with a few inches of the enemy's ground, bought too dear, and paid for with a double price of money and blood.

Defoe had little of Swift's abhorrence of war; and in the past he had gladly celebrated British successes in the field with panegyrics and hymns to victory. When, therefore, we find him going on to attack the carnage at Malplaquet, and Marlborough by implication, it is impossible to absolve him completely from the charge of "writing to order." After the battle of Malplaquet in 1709 he had not, it is true, burst into verse, but he had given up several numbers of the *Review* to celebrating and justifying that costly victory. Describing how the enemy had been beaten out of "all the woods and fastnesses," and successfully engaged "through all the barricadoes of trees cut down and earth cast up at the head of every avenue," he had continued:

To say it is a dear-bought victory *is to say nothing;* we must pursue victory, and we must have it, how dear soever we buy it; and 'tis our happiness that we have troops who dare pay for such a victory every campaign, and will give the price, as long as France can take the purchase.

Loss of men, he tells his readers a week later, must not dispirit us; we *must* lose men. "Our soldiers are the *enfans perdues* of Europe, and must be sacrific'd to the compleating of the war; if we could spare the honest brave fellows, we would; *but it cannot be. . . .*" One *could* say that by October 1711 Defoe had changed his mind about the imperative need to sacrifice those "honest brave fellows"; or one could say that when he was writing in 1709, the predominantly Whig administration of Godolphin was in power, and that by 1711 it had been replaced by the Tory administration of Harley and St. John. At all events, he put a very different construction on the battle of Malplaquet in his pamphlet of 1711. This victory, he told his readers, had cost 22,000 lives,

sacrificed meerly to the pique of glory between the haughty generals, and to decide the mighty contest between us and the French, who should possess the hedges of Taniers, or be masters of the little coppice of Blareignes.

He was not, he insisted, seeking to lessen the esteem we ought to have for our generals (he had just done so), but rather to make it clear that all their victories were not bringing peace any nearer. How many more towns must we capture? At the rate of one town a summer the war could go on forever.[30]

The real obstacle to peace, Defoe now argues, was the demand of the Allies for unconditional surrender; the last negotiations failed because we were too imperious and unyielding in our terms. Now he touches on the delicate subject of England's need for peace. "It is an unpleasant work for any writer," he admits, "to expose the weakness of his country." But be that as it may, English trade is now almost at a standstill, as may be seen from the number of shops closed between Cheapside and Charing Cross,

and the names of bankrupts in every *Gazette*. Here Defoe was
on one of his favorite topics, and it might have been expected he
would dwell on it. On this occasion, however, he was much more
concerned not to give his identity away, and even to suggest to
the reader that whoever the author was he couldn't be Daniel Defoe. Hastily observing, therefore, that "Discourses of trade are
not the particular talent of the author of this," he passes on to
consider the crippling burden of taxation, and draws a grim picture of what is in store for the country if the war is allowed to
drag on—taxes on food and clothes, and (this mainly for the
Whigs) the stopping of interest on government funds. He has
another thrust at the Whigs when he refers to attempts to destroy
public credit, and here again he deliberately misleads the reader
as to his identity when he refers to "one of their own writers"
(i.e. Defoe himself) who had issued warnings against the danger
of this. But the most remarkable instance of his carefully laying
a false scent in this pamphlet is still to come. The chief reason for
the Whig opposition to peace negotiations was their belief that the
Tories intended to make peace with France by "giving up Spain,"
i.e. by allowing Louis XIV's grandson to remain king. Some gentlemen, Defoe says, have written about this eventuality

as a thing so fatal that it was all at one with giving up Britain, and the
Review has the modesty to say that no minister of state dares sign a
treaty of peace for the delivery of Spain. However, upon this supposition let us expostulate a little with the *Review*, or his party, upon the
point. . . .

"The *Review*, or his party": Defoe is again seeking to convince
his readers that he cannot be the author of *Reasons Why This Nation;* he is also, perhaps, hoping to persuade them that the author
of the *Review* is still to be reckoned a good Whig, and has never
been anything else. As recently as the *Review* of 1 September
1711 he had scoffed at the notion of giving up Spain to the House
of Bourbon as something "not to be nam'd or thought of among
us":

To give up Spain to the House of Bourbon is a thing so absurd, so
ridiculous, you ought as soon to think of giving up Ireland to
them. . . .[31]

No wonder he had to take steps to conceal his authorship of a pamphlet in which he was making such a complete *volte-face*. Yet even in this extremity he was able to find an argument that would go some way to clearing him of having betrayed his principles. The young Emperor Joseph had died unexpectedly of smallpox in April, and his successor had still to be named. But, as Defoe told the readers of his pamphlet, the Emperor's death had made a world of difference, since his successor would almost certainly be the Archduke Charles,* whom the Allies (but not the French) had already recognized as King of Spain, and who, as ruler of the Empire *and also of Spain*, would upset the balance of power quite as much as it was upset by having the grandson of Louis XIV as King of Spain. If, as he had always maintained, the war was being fought to maintain the balance of power in Europe, one kind of imbalance was as bad as another. Yet why had Defoe not seen this a month before when he was telling the readers of the *Review* that there was no question of the ministry making a peace that left Louis XIV's grandson on the throne of Spain? The argument he was now using in his anti-war pamphlet had already become common property among the Tory writers, and he must have been perfectly familiar with it. If he now used it himself, it must have been because Harley had made it clear to him that the government meant to resume peace negotiations, and that it was his business to write against the war.[32]

It is scarcely surprising that the next time Defoe found himself in serious trouble it was caused, not by his old enemies the Tories, but by his old political friends the Whigs. In 1713, when the question of who would succeed Queen Anne was becoming a very real issue, his old fondness for irony landed him briefly in prison for the second time. In 1712 he had published two anti-Jacobite pamphlets, *A Seasonable Warning and Caution against the Insinuations of Papists and Jacobites in Favour of the Pretender* and *Hannibal at the Gates. Or, The Progress of Jacobitism*, in which the danger to the Protestant succession was clearly and directly stated. Now in 1713 he published in quick succession three further pamphlets on the same theme, but with highly ambiguous and provocative titles: (1) *Reasons against the Succession*

---

* He became Emperor in October 1711.

of the House of Hanover; (2) *And What If the Pretender Should Come? Or, Some Considerations of the Advantages and Real Consequences of the Pretender's Possessing the Crown of Great Britain;* (3) *An Answer to a Question that No Body Thinks of, viz. But What If the Queen Should Die?*

Of these three pamphlets the first two were intended to be ironical throughout. The titles, as Defoe aferwards claimed, "were amusements, in order to put the books into the hands of those people who the Jacobites had deluded, and to bring the books to be read by them." He had always had the journalist's flair for an arresting title, and he was counting on securing immediate attention for a pamphlet that appeared to set forth the reasons *against* a Protestant succession, or to dwell on the advantages of the Pretender becoming king. Back in 1701, some months after *Legion's Memorial,* he had published what on the face of it must have looked like an anti-war pamphlet, *Reasons against a War with France,* but which in fact developed an argument for going to war for the right reasons. His reason for the misleading title was no doubt the same as that which he gave in 1713, but the anti-French bias of the 1701 pamphlet was quite unmistakable. The same cannot be said of the first two unlucky pamphlets of 1713, and Defoe had only himself to blame for the trouble they brought him.[33]

Reasons against the Succession of the House of Hanover falls between several stools; and it is never made clear whether the author is supposed to be a Jacobite, or a detached and cynical observer of the contemporary scene, or a satirist writing with heavy irony. The pamphlet begins in Defoe's lively and colloquial manner with a description of the public excitement now raging over the succession:

Why, hark ye, you folk that call your selves rational, and talk of having souls, is this a token of your having such things about you, or of thinking rationally; if you have, pray what is it likely will become of you all? Why, the strife is gotten into your kitchens, your parlours, your shops, your counting-houses, nay, into your very beds. You gentlefolks, if you please to listen to your cookmaids and footmen in your kitchens, you shall hear them scolding, and swearing, and scratching, and fighting among themselves; and when you think that the noise is about the beef and the pudding, the dish-water, or the kitchen-stuff, alas, you are mistaken; the feud is about the more mighty affairs of the government, and who is for the Protestant succession, and who for the Pretender. Here the poor despicable scullions learn to cry, High Church, No Dutch kings, No Hanover, that they may do it dexterously when they come into the next mob. Here their antagonists of the dripping-pan practise the other side clamour, No French peace, No Pretender, No popery.

Well and good; but what does the author deduce from those divisions in the kitchens and "up one pair of stairs"? That this is not a fit time for the Hanoverian succession:

if Hanover should come while we are in such a condition, we shall ruin him, or he us, that is most certain.

Not only that, but King George of Hanover can hardly be expected to risk coming to England at all if the nation is so divided:

What prince, think you, will venture his person with a party or a faction [i.e. the Whig party], and that a party crush'd, and under the power of their enemy . . .? And if they cannot be in a posture to defend and maintain him when they have him, how shall he be encouraged to venture him self among them?[34]

One must assume that by making such statements Defoe intended to call for unity, and to frighten people (the Whigs more especially) into uniting behind the Protestant succession by drawing attention to the dangerous effects of the present discord. But the discord was there; and all that he had succeeded in doing was to magnify it, and to make the timorous feel that the cause of the Pretender was more widely supported than in fact it probably was. He can hardly be said to have made things any better by proceeding to a historical parallel between the present situation and that on the death of Edward VI, when "your bloody papist persecuting Queen Mary" succeeded to the throne:

The late King Edward VI had settled the Protestant succession upon the Lady Jane; it was received universally as the Protestant succession is now. The reasons which moved the people to receive it were the same, i.e. the safety of the Protestant religion, and the liberties and properties of the people; all the great men of King Edward's court

and council came readily into this succession, and gave their oaths . . .
for the standing by the successor in her taking possession of her said
just right. Mary, daughter of Catherine of Spain, was the pretender. . . .

But what happened? If the English people had stuck to their
Protestant principles, they would have had a Protestant queen;
but instead of that they divided into parties, and "fell out with
one another; high Protestants against low Protestants." Such was
their zeal for the hereditary principle that they were quite ready
to put themselves under Spanish tyranny, and let the Protestant
religion "go to the devil," with the result that the Catholic Mary
came to the throne, and Lady Jane Gray was beheaded. And the
moral of all this?

What! would you bring over the family of Hanover to have them
murder'd? No, no; those that have a true value for the House of
Hanover would by no means desire them to come hither, or desire
you to bring them on such terms. . . .

To Defoe any betrayal of the Protestant succession was so un-
thinkable, and any clinging at this late date to the principle of
hereditary right so foolish, that he obviously felt he had only to
remind his readers of what happened in the reign of "Bloody
Mary" to make them repudiate the Pretender and really start
working for the Hanoverian succession. But if all this seemed
obvious to Defoe, it was a good deal less than obvious to many
Tories who had no enthusiasm for the future George I, and
to the much smaller body of active Jacobites who would not have
him at any price. Merely to point out what had happened before
was only to make many Englishmen feel that it could well happen
again, and that there was nothing they could do about it. The
desire "not to become involved" is not peculiar to the twentieth
century.[35]
  But Defoe, proceeding from one ineptitude to another, goes on
to play upon the Englishman's unwillingness to have another civil
war on his hands:

No question but every honest Briton is for a peaceable succession;
now, if the Pretender comes, and is quietly established on the throne,
why then you know there is an end of all our fears of the great and

formidable power of France; we have no more need to fear an invasion, or the effects of leaving France in a condition by the peace to act against us, and put the Pretender upon us; and therefore, peace being of so much consequence to this nation, after so long and so cruel a war, none can think of entering upon a new war for the succession without great regret and horror.

Defoe is tying himself in knots. Once again he must have been counting on every right-minded Englishman repudiating such cowardly considerations and recognizing the speciousness of the arguments put forward. But by this time many of his simpler readers could have been only in a state of hopeless confusion, and to some of them the argument that any attempt to secure the Protestant succession could only lead to bloodshed must have made sense. "I do not contend," they read a little further on,

that it is not a lawful succession, a reasonable succession, an established succession, a sworn succession; but if it be not a practicable succession, and cannot be a peaceable succession—if peace will not bring him in, and war cannot—what must we do? It were much better not to have it at all than to have it and ruin the kingdom, and ruin those that claim it at the same time.[36]

At this point Defoe may have felt that his ironies were becoming a little too involved and subtle, for his next reason against the succession of the House of Hanover breaks entirely new ground. Some diseases, he now contends, can only be cured by antipathies, and perhaps the coming of the Pretender is the only way left to cure the nation's present distemper. It may well be that

there is no way for us to learn the true value of a Protestant successor so well as by tasting a little what a popish pretender is, and feeling something of the great advantages that may accrue to us by the superiority of a Jacobite party. . . . Even let him come that we may see what slavery means, and may inquire how the chains of French galleys hang about us, and how easy wooden shoes are to walk in; for no experience teaches so well as that we buy dearest, and pay for with the most smart.

This argument is reinforced with some robust imagery of taking a Tory vomit to "spew out . . . your Tory filth, your idolatrous filth, your tyrannic filth." Here at last the irony is obvious enough, and from this point to the end of the pamphlet the case against the Pretender is not in doubt. But the total effect of the pamphlet is one of blur and muddle. Defoe shifts ground too often; he is not consistently ironical, and he offers arguments, meant to be ironical, which could too often be taken at their face value, and which, if the reader is meant to reject them as ridiculous, ought to have been shown quite unambiguously to be so. That they were obviously ridiculous to Defoe himself is not enough. What he was struggling to say in this unlucky pamphlet was that all the scandalous divisions in the country, the quarreling and the name-calling, were not merely weakening the nation, but were the surest way to bring in the Pretender and popery:

Why then, while you are obliquely and by consequences joining your hands to bring in popery, why, O distracted folk! should you think it amiss to have me talk of doing it openly and avowedly. Better is open enmity than secret guile; better is it to talk openly, and profess openly, for popery, that you may see the shape and real picture of it, than pretend strong opposition to it, and be all at the same time putting your hands to the work, and pulling it down upon your selves with all your might.[37]

But it would have been better for Defoe if he had spoken more openly for Protestantism, and not chosen the method of irony and indirection which he handled so uncertainly. One can imagine his beloved daughter Sophy pleading with him: "No more irony, dear papa! You *know* you aren't good at it."

And What If the Pretender Should Come covers some of the same ground as the pamphlet just examined—a circumstance that may perhaps suggest that Defoe was not satisfied that he had made himself clear. This later pamphlet, however, is more consistently ironical: the supposed author is clearly intended for a Jacobite, and what he has to say makes sense from his point of view, with enough extravagance to make his views seem ridiculous to everyone else. Take no notice, he tells us, of "that scandalous scribbler, the *Review*," who keeps harping away about the terrible things that would happen if the Pretender ever became king—popery, slavery, subservience to France, the destruction of credit, etc. There are perfectly good answers to all his charges. All this talk about the danger from France would be pointless if the Pretender came to the throne, for in that case Louis XIV, who is his friend, would be the friend of England. "How strange is it that none of our people have yet thought of this way of securing their native country from the insults of France!" Defoe is counting, fairly enough, on an immediate reaction of national pride to provide the necessary answer to this argument. Yet when his Jacobite *persona* goes on to argue that trade with France, which has always shown a balance in favor of England, would be increased, to the encouragement of English manufactures, the irony once again becomes so thin as to be almost non-existent. It is true that when he mentions in passing "the constant flux of money in specie which we drew from them every year upon court occasions," Defoe is counting on his readers recalling the days when Charles II received a secret subsidy from Louis that enabled him to rule without Parliament; but the remark is made so incidentally that the point might well be overlooked.[38]

Various objections are now considered, and answered one by one. It is said that the coming of the Pretender might introduce the French mode of absolute government among us, and make us miserable. Well, aren't we miserable enough already—miserably divided, with a miserably weak government, and miserably subjected to rabbles and the mob? How unlike the French! They are united in willing obedience to the absolute will of their king; they don't miss what they never had, and "entertain no notions of that foolish thing LIBERTY which we make so much noise about; nor have they any occasion of it, or any use for it if they had it." They are just as happy with their wooden shoes "as our people are with their luxury and drunkenness." Defoe's method here is to mention in succession the things that every normal Englishman likes and takes for granted—the liberty of the subject, freedom of speech, the Protestant religion, representative government, beef and beer —and then admit that all these would have to go if the Pretender became King of England. And then, having admitted what would be lost, he goes on to re-state that loss indirectly by dwelling upon the corresponding gains, which are either footling or plainly undesirable. This method of meeting objections by feeble or silly answers which answer nothing is that used by Swift in *An Argument against Abolishing Christianity,* which had appeared two years before, and which Defoe would certainly have known. Indeed, he comes closest to Swift when he is answering the objection that the Pretender would probably stamp out the Protestant religion:

There seems to be but one thing more which those people who make such a clamour at the fears of the Pretender take hold of, and this is Religion: and they tell us that not only French government, and French influence, but French religion, that is to say, POPERY, will come among us; but these people know not what they talk of, for it is evident that they shall be so far from being loaden with religion, that they will rather obtain that so long desired happiness of having no religion at all. . . . This is an advantage so fruitful of several other manifest improvements, that though we have not room in this place to enlarge upon the particulars, we cannot doubt but it must be a most grateful piece of news to a great part of the nation, who have long groan'd under the oppressions and cruel severities of the clergy, occa- sion'd by their own strict lives and rigorous virtue, and their imposing such austerities and restraints upon the people; and in this particular the clamour of slavery will appear very scandalous in the nation, for the slavery of religion being taken off, and an universal freedom of vice being introduced, what greater liberty can we enjoy?[39]

Defoe is now well into his stride, and he proceeds to consider still further benefits that the Pretender would bring. He would certainly repudiate the national debt, the interest on which now amounts to almost six million pounds to be paid to "the common people." It may be objected that it is unjust to ruin thousands of families; but the Pretender will have to consider the interests of the nation as a whole. In any case, "is it not remarkable that most part of the money is paid by the cursed party of Whigs, who from the beginning officiously appear'd to keep him from his right?" Still, if it is thought that justice is not being done, the Pretender can also continue to tax the landed men, who are mostly Tories.

Thus both sides having no reason to envy or reproach one another with hardships, or with suffering unequally, they may every one lose their proportion, and the money may be laid up in the hands of the new sovereign for the good of the nation.

With all this money at the disposal of the Pretender, the nation will be free from "the burthen, the expence, the formality, and the tyranny of parliaments"; and those members of Parliament who have spent vast sums bribing the electors to vote for them will be spared that expense. Better still, the new king will be able "to set up, and effectually maintain, that glorious and so often-desir'd method of government, . . . a standing army." Finally, under his reign, any pamphleteer daring to criticize the government will not just be whipped and pilloried: he will be hanged. Ministers of state will no longer have to proceed against anti-government writers in the courts of law, and prove their case against them:

But when these happy days arrive, juries and judges shall find and determine in these, and all other cases, bring verdicts and give sentence, as the Prince in his royal justice shall direct.

Had Defoe's satire often been as good as this, "it had been vain to blame, and useless to praise him." Compared with *Reasons against the Succession,* this second pamphlet may be regarded as a highly successful exercise in sustained irony, although even here he once or twice fails to make it clear that he is not to be taken literally.[40]

What followed the publication of his three pamphlets must have seemed to Defoe incredible. For weeks on end he had been writing vigorously in the *Review* against the Pretender and the Jacobites. As he was to say himself in *An Appeal to Honour and Justice,* "Had the Pretender ever come to the throne, I could have expected nothing but death." At all events, he was the last man to be reasonably suspected of writing against the Protestant succession; but his own consciousness that he had stated his position unmistakably so many times before may have made him too confident that his ironical approach in the pamphlets of 1713 could not possibly be taken at its face value. He had failed to reckon, however, with the more embittered Whigs, who were exasperated with him for writing in the *Review* in favor of the Peace of Utrecht, or at any rate not writing against it, and who regarded him as a turncoat in the pay of the Tory party. They now saw their chance of revenge, and took it. Three prominent Whigs lodged a complaint with Lord Chief Justice Parker that Defoe's three pamphlets were treasonable; a warrant was issued for his arrest, and on 11 April 1713 he was taken into custody and obliged to give bail for £800. The subsequent proceedings (which Defoe exacerbated by commenting on his case in the *Review* while it was still *sub judice*) and his eventual pardon from the Queen are related by Defoe himself in the *Review* and in *An Appeal to Honour and Justice.*[41]

vi

Defoe never lost his skill as a writer of pamphlets. The 24 or 32 pages to which they normally ran gave him room to state a case clearly and persuasively without fatiguing the ordinary reader, and enabled him to introduce enough examples, anecdotes, reminiscences, and so on to hold that reader's attention. In his later years his mind turned more frequently to various social abuses. Like other elderly men, he found that the world wasn't getting any better, and that indeed it had in many ways deteriorated since the days of his youth. Always prepared to speak his mind, Defoe was never more emphatic and never more sure of himself than in some of the pamphlets he wrote in his late sixties. Intellectually he may have grown a little rigid, but his writing was as fluent and lively as ever. As a final example of his pamphleteering I take *Everybody's Business Is Nobody's Business* (1725), in which he addressed himself to the problem of "the pride, insolence, and exorbitant wages of our women-servants, footmen, etc." That he had not lost his touch may be seen from the fact that this topical pamphlet ran through five editions in less than two months.

He had already dealt with this subject at length the year before in *The Great Law of Subordination Considered,* a work running to over 300 pages, and written in the form of a series of letters from a Frenchman resident in England to his brother in France. This failed to reach a second edition, and the unsold sheets were re-issued about 1726 with a new title-page. The length of this book may have put readers off, but one may reasonably blame the portentous title, which suggests an abstract and general discussion instead of the highly concrete and particular account of the servant problem that Defoe in fact gave his readers. Indeed, *The Great Law of Subordination* deserves to be better known than it is; for it contains a succession of stories illustrating the insolent and at times outrageous behavior of servants, told with great liveliness and suitable indignation. Into his far smaller sixpenny pamphlet, however, Defoe manages to compress most of the points he had made in the larger work, and he has the advantage of not using a sledgehammer to crack a nut.

As always, he is completely master of his facts, writing with first-hand knowledge of the tricks of servants, their habit of getting together to push up wages, their demand for perquisites, their way of getting a rake-off from tradesmen, their petty thefts, and so on. In developing this theme he treats the reader to the kind of entertainment he had learnt so well how to provide. Writing under one of his pseudonyms, Andrew Moreton, he gives a spirited account of how he answered the door to a well-dressed young female who asked for his sister, and how he entertained her downstairs while his sister dressed herself to receive her unknown guest. "At last she came down dress'd as clean as her visitor; but how great was my surprize when I found my fine lady was a common servant-wench." In the ensuing dialogue the girl announces that she can clean the house and dress a common family-dinner, but that she will have nothing to do with washing and ironing or needlework, and she expects the family to hire a charwoman for scouring the floors. "Then get you gone for a lazy impudent baggage," said I, "you want to be a boarder, not a servant. Have you a fortune, or estate, that you dress at that rate?" Defoe has here made all the points he wanted to make, and made them dramatically: maidservants nowadays dress like "a fine London-madam," they expect far too high wages for the little they are prepared to do, they are pert and don't know their place.[42]

Perhaps the practice of writing fiction for the last few years had given Defoe the habit of making his points in the form of story; perhaps he was just growing more anecdotal in his old age. At all events, anecdote and reminiscence come thick and fast. A little further on he takes exception to those gentlemen who make it a custom "to kiss and slop the maid," so putting ideas into a girl's head, and spoiling many a good maid. (One thinks of Lady Charlotte's nephew Jackey in *Pamela*: " 'A charming girl though,' said her rakish nephew, and swore a great oath; 'dear aunt, forgive me, but I must kiss her.' ") Worst of all are the girls serving in coffee-houses and taverns, who often have their heads turned by idle compliments, and "put on all the flirting airs imaginable." Those creatures, Defoe says,

being puff'd up with the fulsome flattery of a set of flesh-flies that are continually buzzing about 'em, carry themselves with the utmost insolence imaginable; insomuch, that you must speak to them with a great deal of deference, or you are sure to be affronted. Being at a coffee-house t'other day where one of these ladies kept the bar, I had bespoke a dish of rice-tea; but madam was so taken up with her sparks that she had quite forgot it. I spoke for it again, and with some temper, but was answer'd after a most taunting manner, not without a toss of the head, a contraction of the nostrils, and other impertinencies, too many to enumerate. Seeing myself thus publickly insulted by such an animal, I could not chuse but shew my resentment. "Woman," said I sternly, "I want a dish of rice-tea, and not what your vanity and impudence may imagine; therefore treat me as a gentleman and a customer, and serve me with what I call for. Keep your impertinent repartees and impudent behaviour for the coxcombs that swarm round your bar, and make you so vain of your blown carcass."[43]

Defoe's reaction is so excessive that one must believe he was still smarting from some recent encounter like the one he describes: the elderly gentleman kept waiting while the girl rattled away with her younger and more attractive customers. The insolence of the wench, chattering there with her sparks! She could not know that the man she was treating in this pert and off-hand manner had enjoyed the friendship of King William (and if she had known, would she have cared?), had been admitted to the confidence of Robert Harley, Earl of Oxford (had she ever heard of him?), had written a story called *Moll Flanders* which she had almost certainly read, and was in fact Daniel Defoe, of Stoke Newington, Gent. What were things coming to? Where was the respect due to old age and one's social superiors?

But Defoe's emotional involvement (if he was involved) did not interfere with his writing: the whole episode is admirably told. There is a certain formality in the expression, for a serious complaint is being made, but any danger of stiffness is removed by such colloquial turns as "buzzing about 'em" and "t'other day." Contempt for the barmaid and her sparks is well conveyed by the imagery of the flesh-flies buzzing about the counter (an image only too appropriate in an eighteenth-century, or even twentieth-century, English coffee-house), and Defoe returns to it again at the end with "the coxcombs that swarm round your bar" and "your blown carcass" (blown = 1. swollen, fat; 2. inflated with pride; 3. fly-blown). The barmaid is referred to separately as "an animal" and (ironically) as "madam," and is addressed peremptorily as "Woman." Professor James T. Boulton has observed that "the recording of relatively brief dramatic moments is Defoe's forte," and "with the kind of detail that adds authenticity":[44] such sharp detail is to be found in the description of the barmaid, "not without a toss of the head, a contraction of the nostrils, and other impertinencies." And in conclusion it will be noted how the anecdote proceeds in a steady crescendo movement to the shattering rebuke of its climax.

It would be foolish to regret such explosions of wrath and indignation (and they are fairly frequent) in Defoe's later writings. It may be saddening to find the once robust Fielding, in *The Journal of a Voyage to Lisbon*, irritated and exasperated by little matters that he would once have taken in his stride, and driven by sickness to complain of what he would have laughed at in the days of his health. But Defoe's asperities were of a different kind. At every stage of his career he had written naturally, and with an immediate response to the situation in which he found himself. Now in his old age it was natural for him to be occasionally peevish and a *laudator temporis acti*; but he was still setting down his thoughts as they came to him, still finding apt and forcible words to express his feelings, still being inevitably and indelibly himself.

Periodicals

MUCH of Defoe's finest work as a journalist was done for the periodicals which he owned or with which he was connected. The first and most famous of these was the *Review*. Starting as a weekly on 19 February 1704, with the title of *A Weekly Review of the Affairs of France*, and therefore concentrating on the war, it began to come out twice a week from 1 April, and from 22 March 1705 three times a week (Tuesday, Thursday, Saturday). On 1 January 1706 Defoe changed the title to *A Review of the*

State of the English Nation (from 8 March 1707, *the British Nation*), until on 2 August 1712 it became simply *Review*. On that date he announced that owing to the recently imposed tax on newspapers it would in future be published only on Tuesdays and Saturdays, but that "if there appear room for it, and that it may be worth the expence, it shall come out oftener hereafter." From 8 January 1713 he reverted (with some irregularity) to thrice-weekly publication until the last issue on 11 June 1713, when he finally laid down his pen with the words *"Exit REVIEW."*

The *Review* was not just a periodical that Defoe edited. Apart from the advertisements, and some poems and letters sent in by readers, he wrote almost every word of it himself. Except incidentally, when he happened to have some special information, it was not a newspaper, but a paper of comment on current affairs and contemporary topics. Sometimes he would stay with the same subject for many consecutive numbers; e.g. the war with France (and later the peace negotiations), the High Church party, Scottish affairs (and more especially the Union), parliamentary elections, trade, and so on. But from time to time he would leave the larger issues of the day to write on such questions as immigration, imprisonment for debt, public mourning and its effect on trade, the existence of spirits and apparitions, the plundering of wrecked ships and the inhuman treatment of distressed sailors, and immediate problems of the day such as that of the young bullies known as "Mohocks" who roamed through the streets of London at night terrorizing the citizens, or the French religious fanatics called the "Modern Prophets," or the transformation of a Presbyterian meetinghouse into a theatre, and much else. To give some light relief to his more serious discussions he experimented with various supplements, beginning with a section which he called "Mercure Scandale: Or, Advice from the Scandalous Club," in which he twitted his fellow journalists on their mistakes, and dealt (as the *Tatler* and *Spectator* were to do after him) with manners and morals and various social and other problems, by the method of answering questions. Although the questions sent in by his readers (if they were not just invented) were settled by a supposed club, Defoe never gave to the Scandalous Club the human interest that Addison and Steele gave to the *Spectator* club with its little group of typical characters. This section proved so popular, however, that for five numbers Defoe published a 28-page supplement of "Advice from the Scandal Club," and he followed this with twenty-three numbers of a separate publication, *The Little Review*, in which he again borrowed from *The Athenian Gazette* John Dunton's idea of answering questions sent in by correspondents. Defoe always said that he provided this sort of light entertainment reluctantly, and only to please those readers who needed relief from the more serious parts of the *Review*. Although he treated such readers to both humor and facetiousness, it is significant that he often answered questions (e.g. on marriage problems) in a serious manner. After dropping *The Little Review* he occasionally included a short section headed "Miscellanea" in which he might discuss some topic in a lighter vein; but for the most part he stuck to a discussion of the main political, religious, and economic problems of the day.

This serious discussion, however, was carried on with unabated liveliness, and in such a way as to make the issues clear to the least erudite of readers. Most of the stylistic features of the *Review* are also to be found in his pamphlets, but Defoe was perhaps in closer contact with his readers in the *Review* than in any of his other writings. The public to which he was consciously addressing himself (and one is tempted to substitute the word "audience" for "public") was predominantly middle-class, consisting perhaps mainly of tradesmen, but including readers from a wider range of the population, both Anglican and nonconformist. In the *Review* of 24 May 1705 Defoe explains that "this paper is writ to enlighten the stupid understandings of the meaner and more thoughtless of the freeholders and electors," and he suggests that it would be a useful service if some gentlemen would "help the country people to a sight of this paper" by distributing copies gratis. "This paper" clearly refers to this particular number of the *Review*, but it is stylistically indistinguishable from Defoe's normal way of writing his periodical. Some months later (13 October 1705) he remarks:

I have hitherto preach'd to my inferiors and equals, men of the same class with my self; I hope I have slip'd into no indecencies, and have studied nothing more than to suit my language to the case, and to the persons.

Again, on 11 March 1712, "I am writing," he says, "to the common understanding." The plain-spoken, down-to-earth, unpedantic and colloquial style of the *Review* is not his only manner of writing, even in the *Review* itself; but it may be called the staple of his style, not differing noticeably from that in which he wrote *Robinson Crusoe* and *Moll Flanders*. In the preface to his first volume of collected *Reviews* he offers a justification of his way of writing:

Let not those gentlemen who are cricks in stile, in method or manner, be angry that I have never pull'd off my cap to them in humble excuse for my loose way of treating the world as to language, expression, and politeness of phrase; matters of this nature differ from most things a man can write. When I am busied writing essays and matters of science, I shall address them for their aid, and take as much care to avoid their displeasure as becomes me; but when I am upon the subject of trade, and the variety of casual story, I think my self a little loose from the bonds of cadence and perfections of stile, and satisfy my self in my study to be explicit, easie, free, and very plain; and for all the rest, *nec careo, nec curo*.[45]

By claiming the liberty to be "a little loose from the bonds of cadence" and to be "easie" and "free," Defoe is telling his readers that he has not troubled to write shapely sentences, regularly and formally constructed. But of course he has a delightful cadence of his own, the natural cadence of colloquial speech. No writer ever established a more immediate and friendly familiarity with his readers. He continually addresses them in phrases like "Well, gentlemen," "Pray, gentlemen, let us go hand in hand back a little," "Now, good people . . ."; he exhorts, advises, reminds, warns, interrogates them. All through the *Review* Defoe is "I" and his readers are "you"; the personal relationship of speaker and listener is never broken. While, much of the time, he writes as he might speak to a group of acquaintances in a coffee-house, at other times he mounts the pulpit and preaches or harangues. He has the egotism of the talker accustomed to engrossing attention. "I am still upon trade," he will write in his opening sentence; or, "I have always said, and say it still. . . ." He has, too, the talker's way of breaking off to say, "I'll tell you a story"; and his first readers must often have been pleased with his ability to refer to some recent or well-known event (or, in newspaper language, "story") to illustrate the point he was making. In the spring of 1712, for example, new developments in the international scene led Defoe to a fresh discussion of the balance of power, and to a reiteration of his old argument that while it would completely upset that balance if the King of France had the crown of Spain as well, it would be no better if the Emperor had it. If a choice *must* be made, he was for giving it to the Emperor; but it was "a dreadful choice," for the Emperor was a Roman Catholic, and one whom God seemed to have prepared "for a scourge to the Protestant churches of Europe." At this point Defoe clearly felt that these matters of high policy would be all the better of a simple illustration to bring the dilemma home to his readers:

But I must own, the choice to me appears to be the same that Sir William Windham's two maid-servants were put to last week, when his house was on fire, *viz., to be burnt, or to leap out of the window,* by which they both perish'd.—If you give Spain to France, you run into the fire; if to Austria, you leap out at window. It is true, the last must be chosen, as it is the best of the woful circumstances to choose from, because, *here we are sure to be burnt,* there, *we may escape,* tho' it be a thousand to one, and next to an impossibility.[46]

Another of Defoe's habits that may be associated with his colloquial way of writing is that of sliding suddenly into a passage of dialogue, either between himself and his readers, or between himself and someone of his own invention, or simply between two or more imagined characters. One of the most striking examples occurs in his satirical paper (8 June 1708) on a country election, where his colloquial ease is at its most effective. After a Hogarthian description of the rough, hiccuping, vomiting, farting, belching electors, Defoe concentrates more especially on one who has not yet sold his vote:

Well, M—— comes and makes his leg, and Sir William speaks to him for his vote.—"Ha, ha, an't like your worship, I han't promised anybody yet; I am as like as another not to be against your worship, ha, ha."—"And what hast got there, Goodman M——," says Sir William, "what hast brought to market?"—"A sow and piggs; an't please your worship to buy them, it will do me a kindness." The butcher whispers Sir William, "Buy them, buy them; your worship shall be sure of him then." "Well," says Sir William, "buy them for me. If you give him a little more than they are worth, you understand the thing." Up gets the butcher. "Let's see them, M——. What shall Sir William give you for them?"—"Why, I'll have three mark for them."—"No, no, look you, M——, that is too much; but you know Sir William stands for our shire, you shall vote for him, and he shall take the sow and piggs, and leave the price to us."—"Well, well, I an't against him, I'll give you my word for that." *So they make the bargain;* the butcher comes back.—"Sir William, I have bought the sow and piggs, and he promises; your worship must give him three mark for them." Sir William orders the steward to pay the money; the sow and piggs are worth about half the money, the fellow promises he won't be against Sir William, but never promises to vote for him; goes away after that to Sir Thomas, gets *ditto* of him, and keeps his word with both by voting for no body.

Among Defoe's more effective passages of dialogue are those between two simple characters commenting upon the contemporary situation (a trick he may have learned from L'Estrange's *Observator*), as in the short dialogue between two honest countrymen who discuss in their west-country dialect the negotiations for peace at Utrecht ("*You-trik* or *We-trik*, or zomething like that, but shure I doon't remember, vor I doon't use those outlandish words much").[47]

Defoe has the popular writer's gift for simplification, for bringing an abstract issue down to concrete terms that appeal to the ordinary reader. We can see him doing this in his discussions of the negotiations that led to the Peace of Utrecht. As those negotiations dragged on, one of the clamors of the Tory party was that the Dutch had not been pulling their weight in the war, and had not supplied the full quota of men and materials that they had promised. Arguing the case in the *Review* (21 February 1712), Defoe is in favor of England supporting the claims of the Dutch in any peace treaty, but if it is suggested that England should carry on the war against France single-handed, that is quite another matter. The Dutch are our allies, but friends must act like friends:

I love my friend, and will do any thing for him I can, but if he, forgetful of the civility of a true friendship, puts forth his hands and endeavours to pick my pocket, he destroys all the notion of friendship which he pretended to before.

This may indeed be thought an oversimplification, and with the metaphor of picking a pocket, a falsification of the true state of affairs: Defoe was now committed to writing in favor of peace, and at this time he was allowing himself to be critical of the Dutch in a way that his old Whig friends could not have approved. In general, however, his gift of reducing a complex situation to simple, homely terms (as Dr. Arbuthnot did in *The History of John Bull*) was used fairly enough, and must have increased his popularity with unlearned readers.[48]

In his constant endeavor to be easily intelligible he was greatly helped by his ready command of simile and metaphor. His imagery, as we should expect, is drawn from a wide range of common human experience, and is therefore familiar and easily assimilated. He has his favorite images, such as that of a house on fire or a sinking ship. (On one occasion a government tax on newspapers and pamphlets which was designed in part to suppress libelous publications is dismissed by Defoe as "sinking the ship to drown the rats.") He draws freely, too, for his imagery on agriculture (ploughing, sowing, etc.), on medicine (purges, the physician "breathing a vein," etc.), and of course on trade and shopkeeping. He is fond of proverbial, or near-proverbial, images: a man is "drunk as a drum" or he "works like a horse"; unjustified railing and abuse are like "a man spitting against the wind, which blows it all back in his own face."[49]

What is especially characteristic of Defoe is the expanded metaphor; and here again one sees the popular writer making things easy for his readers. On 8 December 1709 he lays down the right treatment for the hot-brained and intolerant Dr. Sacheverell:

You should use him as we do a hot horse.—When he first frets and pulls, keep a stiff rein, and hold him in if you can; but if he grows mad and furious, slack your hand, clap your heels to him and let him go, give him his belly full of it.—Away goes the beast, like a fury, over hedge and ditch, till he runs himself off of his mettle, perhaps bogs himself, and then he grows quiet of course.—And after you have us'd him thus a-while, he pays for his experience, and grows wiser for himself.

So with this wild, hot, furious man who "flies, champs, foams, and stinks," let him have his head and he may "bog himself in a gaol, and then he'll be as tame as a lamb." Widening the discussion to the High Church party in general, Defoe now gives his readers an anecdote ("I'll tell you a story") about an old lady who was barked at by a huge mastiff dog which was luckily chained to its kennel. "*Ah*, says the lady, *thou art a terrible beast, but thank God, thou art like Satan, thou art chain'd.*" Having told his story, Defoe feels that there is plenty of metaphorical life in the old dog yet, and proceeds to develop the canine parallel:

Besides, good people, do you not know the nature of the barking creatures?—If you pass but by, and take no notice, they will yelp and make a noise, and perhaps run a little after you; but go but on, and mind them not, and they give over again, but offer to strike them, or throw stones at them, and you'll never have done, nay, you'll raise all the dogs in the parish upon you.—The only way is to ride on, take no notice of the cur that follows you—and he goes back quietly, with his tail between his legs, or for anger bites a post, or the ground, or any thing that's next him, as if he was mad you would not turn again upon him.—Indeed, if he follows you close, and offers to bite your horse's heels; if he comes within reach of your whip or cudgel, and you can come at him fairly, you may lend him a lash or two; but it is not worth your while—unless you strike home.—For you'll only raise a dust and noise, which, tho' there is nothing of damage, is nevertheless unpleasant.

It is hardly necessary to point out that by comparing Sacheverell to a horse that foams and stinks, and the High Church fanatics to yelping curs, Defoe is successfully denigrating and belittling the objects of his derision. For all his professions of moderation, he frequently lashes his opponents with a rough scorn. When the Whigs, who were outnumbered in the House of Lords, made a deal with the Tory Earl of Nottingham and obtained his support at the cost of voting for his bill to prevent occasional conformity, Defoe fell on "this piece of party treachery" which had sacrificed "no less than the civil and religious liberties of 2 millions of the good people of England, I mean the Dissenters, who, *as the negroes in Afric sell their fathers, mothers, brothers, and children, into perpetual bondage, for bells, glass beads, and gewgaws,* were all sold and given up for the unperforming insignificant vote of a *High-Flyer.*"[50]

One of Defoe's most elaborate metaphors was that used by him, on 1 March 1712, to satirize the peace negotiations at Utrecht, which he compared to a horse-fair. The French jockeys (i.e. horse-dealers) had been the first on the scene, and now the time was at hand "when our beast must come to the market." Defoe then proceeded to draw out his metaphor so as to suggest the disagreement among the Allies about the terms to be offered to the French:

It seems there has been some strife among us how he shall come dress'd up into the market, and what he shall be call'd when he comes there; some moved that he should have a fine horse-cloth thrown over him, painted and embroider'd with all the several dominions and titles of the partners [i.e. the Allies], and that in the middle, in one large schedule or column, should, in fine capital golden letters, be set down the price they should agree to ask for him; to which also was to be affix'd the names of all the partners and owners of the horse, with this particular, as the consequence, that this was the price of the horse, and that we would not abate a farthing.

Well, but says an old jockey among the horse-owners, this is never the way to sell the horse, for if we do not leave ourselves room to abate some small trifles, we may injure ourselves; for if the French jockies should bid us so near our price that we may think it better at last to part with him than keep him any longer at so great a charge, if our hands should be ty'd up we may out-stand our market.

Rough John, an old horse-scourer and a bold chapman, answer'd readily to this, It is not our business only to sell our horse, but to sell him at our own price, and since the French chapman has jocky'd us so often, if you will be rul'd by me, I would have us put a general price upon him, and tell him plainly, thus: *Look ye, monsieur, there is our horse, and that is our price, and we expect you will make no words about it, but take him and go about your business.* Well, jockey John, says another, but then it may be he will answer in an old phrase, *Two words to a bargain,* and so we may break off all. . . .

Defoe stays with his metaphor of a horse-fair right on to the end, concluding this number of the *Review* with the reflection that what is now needed is "to bring the horse-trade to a ballance, and preserve the market, that both buyers and sellers may go on quietly with their business." In such concrete terms Defoe habitually discusses with his readers the political issues of the day, setting his scene, bringing on his characters, and making them talk in homely and idiomatic dialogue.[51]

All this makes for popular writing and easy reading. But Defoe was a popular writer for an even better reason. He had the thoughts and feelings of the common man, for he was himself an uncommon example of the common man—more articulate, more clear-headed, better informed, but still one of the ordinary people. In the dichotomy between "them" and "us" he was almost always on the side of "us," or at least succeeded in giving that impression. A good example of his power of appeal to the man in the street will be found in the *Review* of 1 April 1712, where he expressed with great skill the growing desire among all sections of the nation for an honorable peace. It is true that this particular *Review* also reflects the Tory policy of bringing the war to a speedy end; but Defoe manages to transcend or by-pass party politics by making his appeal to one of the permanent feelings of ordinary humanity —the plain man's dislike of pomp and ceremony and fussy in-essentials, a dislike that is frequently expressed in the homely admonition to "cut the cackle, and come to business." The pre-liminary peace talks at Utrecht (so similar to those at Paris to end the war in Vietnam) were being protracted from day to day, and week to week, over what appeared to the man in the street to be mere trifles of procedure—not, perhaps, over the right shape of the conference table and where the various delegates should sit, but on matters of equal moment. When nations go to war, Defoe told his readers, they don't tie themselves to any rules or stand upon ceremony, but simply fall on each other without more ado. But when it comes to making peace and repairing the damage—

What ceremony! what punctilios! what niceties! what adjusting of precedencies! what conferences! whether the coaches of this or that prince's ambassadors shall give way! how the footmen must behave! *and the like;* what mighty debates about receiving and conducting! and whether the bottom of the stairs or the top shall confine their civilities! How many nauseating impertinencies attend the elbow chair, and the giving of the hand at visits, *and the like!* And how often are the conferences which they come about delay'd for several days, and sometimes broke up, till these more weighty things are adjusted!

When they come together, innumerable difficulties arise about who shall keep the *protocol!* the granting passports! the form of these passports, the stile of their respective princes! the exchanging powers! the form of treating, whether by writing or conference! *and the like.* —Are these men met to put an end to a bloody war, to prevent the ruin of nations, the burning of cities, and the destruction of people? Do these men act as if they design'd to stop the bleeding of Europe, or to check the crimson deluge? Merciful God! If thy gracious providence had not more compassion on mankind than these wretched politicians and courtiers, to what ruin and destruction would the world be expos'd!

Do these men know that the sun has pass'd the equator, and is advancing towards the tropick? Do they see the days lengthening, the season coming forward to action? Do they hear the drums beat a march? Do they think of the armies coming into the field, the campaign beginning, and that every day's delay may bring blood and devastation upon the world? *Do they consider* that in one day an action may happen in which the lives of 20 or 30 thousand may be lost? That *on one hour of the time* which they throw away in foolish forms, and dancing in the circle of their ridiculous niceties, the fate of Europe may depend?

On a subject on which the nation was still divided—whether to make peace now without obtaining all the concession from the French that were desired, or to carry on the war until the French agreed to unconditional surrender—Defoe has succeeded in uniting almost all his readers on what was essentially a side issue, but one which made war seem foolish, and peace all the more desirable because so idiotically delayed. As on other occasions, Defoe is against "them," these wretched politicians and courtiers, and *for* "us," the suffering people of England. His scorn and contempt are expressed in the rhetorical effectiveness of the peace delegates "dancing in the circle of their ridiculous niceties"—a phrase which the English reader would perhaps apply more especially to the French, that "dancing nation" which Defoe had satirized in *The True-Born Englishman.* It will be noticed, too, how Defoe's homely style can on occasion give way to one more eloquent. In the passage just quoted there is a cumulative effect in all three paragraphs, brought about by balance and by the repetition of the same general idea with varied examples, and driven relentlessly home by exclamation or interrogation. The language, too, rises to the level of the occasion, with such emotional abstractions as "the ruin of nations," such metaphorical expressions as "the bleeding of Europe" and "the crimson deluge," such circumlocutions as "the sun has pass'd the equator, and is advancing towards the tropick," followed by the ominous immediacy of "Do they hear the drums beat a march?"[52]

In his various pronouncements on writing, Defoe laid emphasis most frequently on the virtues of a plain and homely style. "Easy, plain, and familiar language," he wrote in *The Complete English Tradesman*, "is the beauty of speech in general, and is the excellency of all writing, on whatever subject, or to whatever persons they are we write or speak. The end of speech is that men might understand one another's meaning. . . ." In the *Serious Reflections . . . of Robinson Crusoe* he practically equates stylistic plainness with moral integrity:

The plainness I profess, both in style and method, seems to have some suitable analogy to the subject, honesty, and therefore is absolutely necessary to be strictly followed; and I must own, I am the better reconciled, on this very account, to a natural infirmity of homely plain writing, in that I think the plainness of expression which I am condemned to will give no disadvantage to my subject, since honesty shows the more beautiful, and the more like honesty, when artifice is dismissed, and she is honestly seen by her own light only. . . .[53]

This seems to be the style in which the greater part of the *Review* was written. With a personality so complex as Defoe's we must be careful not to take everything at its face value; but certainly the impression we get from reading the *Review* is that of a man who set down his thoughts as they came to him, more concerned to be explicit and forcible and plain-dealing than to be correct, or to worry about "cadence and perfections of style." He may have worried more than we are apt to suppose; but no man could have written so much and so rapidly as Defoe unless, by natural ability and as a result of constant practice, the thought and the expression of it had become almost simultaneous. As with Shakespeare, so with Defoe, "his mind and hand went together." At the same time, in the *Review* and in many other of his writings, there are passages in which we may detect a more deliberate use of the resources of rhetoric, and in which he is concerned to move and persuade, and not merely to be understood.

When Defoe began writing for *Mist's Weekly Journal* in 1717, he was approaching sixty years of age; and although the real reason for his connection with Nathaniel Mist was the job of censorship which he had secretly undertaken for the government, the greater part of what he wrote for the journal was non-political. This is even truer of his contributions to *Applebee's Weekly Journal*, for which he began to write in 1720. The Defoe of those later years was no longer commenting on every political move and development as he had done in the days of his *Review*, but was drawing upon the stores of his past experience (including his reading) to write short essays and comments on topics of general interest.

The weekly papers normally ran to six pages. An Act of 1712 imposing a tax on newspapers had levied one penny on papers of a whole sheet and a halfpenny on those of a half sheet; but the drafters of the Act had overlooked the possibility of someone publishing a newspaper of a sheet and a half. It was not long before advantage was taken of this loophole in the law, and *Mist's* was one of a considerable number of weekly journals that appeared regularly as a sheet and a half, i.e. six pages, and so evaded the stamp duty, until a new Stamp Act in 1725 imposed a halfpenny tax on every half sheet. To fill six pages with news, however, was an almost impossible task in the early eighteenth century, for news-gathering was still at a relatively primitive stage; when the wind blew hard from the west for several days on end (and this is the prevailing wind in England), none of the packet-boats from the continent could reach Harwich or Deal or Dover, and there was a dearth of foreign news. The difficulty of filling six pages was therefore met by publishing literary matter of various kinds; and the Stamp Act of 1712, designed in part to discourage and even suppress periodical publications, may be said to have accidentally stimulated the growth of English journalism.

Nothing was certainly known about Defoe's connection with Nathaniel Mist until in 1864 his nineteenth-century biographer, William Lee, discovered in the Public Record Office the six letters which Defoe had written to Under-Secretary Charles Delafaye. Lee printed those letters in his Life of Defoe, published in 1869; and in two further volumes of the same date he printed a selection from Defoe's contributions to various periodicals between the years 1716 and 1729. Much the greater part of this material was drawn from the essays that Lee believed Defoe wrote for Mist and Applebee; but he also included excerpts from *Mercurius Politicus, The Whitehall Evening Post, The Daily Post, The Universal Spectator*, and *Fog's Journal* (a successor to *Mist's*). Since 1869 those two volumes of extracts have been silently and trustfully accepted into the Defoe canon, and no doubt most of what Lee printed *is* by Defoe. The custom of ascribing anonymous publications to him began in his own lifetime, and evoked several sarcastic comments from him, and some outright, and some equivocal, denials. In the *Review* of 26 February 1712 he jeers at "these wise judges of stile" who are sure they can identify him by the way he writes:

I know it by its stile, say they, *it is his way of writing;* . . . and thus twenty Tory books are call'd mine which I have no manner of knowledge of, or hand in.

And these same judges of style, he adds, often applaud as an excellent piece something that he *has* written, but because they happen to approve of it, never guess that it is his. We have been warned; but the ascription of new pieces to Defoe goes on, and many of the attributions are certainly correct. "Long and critical study of a great author," said Lee, "may result in so full an acquaintance, that his writings will be recognised by the student in a moment, as the voice of a familiar friend." Lee certainly had that full acquaintance with Defoe's writings (as Professor Moore has in our own day), and he lists a number of Defoe's most characteristic expressions to support his attributions based on style. He does not, however, rely upon style alone to identify Defoe's contributions to the various journals for which he wrote; many of the ideas he expressed were either peculiar to Defoe, or they appear frequently in his other writings, or they contain allusions to matters that particularly interested him. When, for instance, we find two letters on 21 and 28 November 1724, written to "Mr. App" (John Applebee) by someone who says she was born in Newgate "and the famous Moll Flanders was my aunt," and when we take into account the style in which the letters are written, we need have little hesitation in ascribing them to Defoe.

Lee may have been too confident in reprinting short news items as being certainly by Defoe, and some of his longer pieces may also be questioned; but there seems little reason to doubt that most of his ascriptions are sound.[54]

In writing essays for Mist and Applebee, Defoe was still addressing readers of the same social class as those who had read his *Review*. It is of course impossible to be quite precise about this; but there are enough contemporary sneers at the readers of *Mist's Weekly Journal* to make it seem likely that it circulated mainly among the working class, and had not the largely middle- and upper-class public of that other Tory journal, *The Craftsman*. If you enter into a dispute with Mist, a correspondent told the author of *The St. James's Journal* (2 August 1722), "you will very much lessen your importance in several families of distinction where you are received, and be perhaps obliged to write only for porters and coblers, and such dirty customers as are his greatest patrons." But if Mist's readers were mainly of humble origin, and were therefore unlikely to have had much education, Defoe's chief concession to them was to be endlessly interesting. It cost him no pains to write unpedantically, without abstract arguments and learned allusions, for he had been doing that all his life. As he grew older, his anecdotal manner, his dry humor, and his ability to make lively and apposite allusions to past events and circumstances tended, if anything, to become more pronounced. When Jack Sheppard was making his remarkable escapes from Newgate in 1724, Defoe covered his escapades from week to week in *Mist's* and *Applebee's*, and his contribution to *Mist's* on 24 October is a good example of his anecdotal style:

The great talk which the strange escape of John Sheppard has occasioned, has reviv'd an old story which happen'd in the reign of Queen Elizabeth, when Walsingham was Secretary of State. This minister, suspecting that Spain was carrying on some designs against the Queen's government, suppos'd that he could discover the bottom of the whole affair if he could have a sight of the Spanish ambassador's papers. He might have seized him, but that was look'd upon as a violation of the laws of nations; he therefore compass'd his end by a stratagem. He sent for the then Keeper of Newgate, and ask'd him if he had a thief in his custody who was very expert at opening of locks? The Keeper told him of one who was wonderful that way, a fellow that lay in for several robberies, and who would certainly be convicted. The Secretary order'd the fellow to be brought to him, and gave him instructions to convey himself into the ambassador's house, and open such a cabinet; but to take nothing but papers from thence, promising him not only a pardon, but also a reward. The fellow executed his orders without being discovered, only that he could not forbear the temptation of taking a parcel of gold which lay in the cabinet with the papers. Upon his delivering the papers, the Secretary ask'd him if he had taken nothing else? He frankly own'd he had; at which the Secretary seeming very angry, the thief gave him to understand that he was out in his politicks; for if he had left the gold, the ambassador would have known it could be no common thief who had broken open his cabinet, but now he would never suspect from what quarter the robbery came. . . .[55]

Defoe still wrote on some of his old subjects: politics, religion, marriage problems, bankruptcy, the evils of stock-jobbing, bribery at elections, journalists and journalism, and so on. But the old subjects were adapted to the times: when he wrote on religion now, it was less likely to be on High Church and dissenters, and more likely to be on free-thinking and atheism; when he wrote on stock-jobbing, it was about William Law in France and the South Sea Bubble in England. Other new topics were the riots of the weavers against the importation and wearing of printed calicoes, the plague in France and the danger of its spreading to England, education (with particular reference to the charity schools), fraudulent lotteries, and the indecent literature being published by Edmund Curll. It must have been more especially for the "porters and coblers" that he wrote so frequently on thieves and pickpockets and highwaymen, on dreams, omens, and apparitions, and on comets as portents, although on all those matters he shared the interest of his humbler readers. He wrote against astrology and exposed quack doctors; but (unless someone else was responsible for the insertion) he published accounts of a sea monster, and of a floating island near Gibraltar from which came "the roaring of wild and ravenous beasts." He was much ridiculed by his fellow journalists for a long circumstantial story in *Mist's*, 5 July 1718, based on accounts from "many several hands," of the blowing up and total destruction of the island of St. Vincent. On 2 August, by which time it was apparent that no such thing had happened, Defoe (or Mist) made the best of an embarrassing situation by a show of skepticism:

They pretend to tell us a strange story, viz., that the Island of St. Vincent is found again, and is turn'd into a volcano, or burning mountain; but we must acknowledge we do not believe one word of it.

After describing how the island exploded, Defoe had gone on to offer scientific explanations of this imaginary event; an element of popular science in his accounts of natural phenomena was another reason for his appeal to his less educated readers. On the other hand, writing in *Applebee's*, 16 May 1724, of an eclipse of the sun which was "eclipsed on Monday last . . . by the dulness of the day," he used the general disappointment which this occasioned to write a delightful essay on "the temper and disposition of our people in England . . . on all occasions in which anything of novelty appears." Unless the worst happens, he suggested, people are never satisfied:

"D—— these *clipse-mongers* and *stronomer men*," says a learned cit that gave a guinea to come into Mr. Whiston's Great Room; "they picked my pocket," says he, "of a guinea, and when it come to, there was nothing to be seen. Why it was not an eclipse worth a farthing! I expected it would be quite dark, that the birds would fall down dead; that it would be cold, damp, and dismal, as it was nine year ago; that the old women would fall down to their prayers, the young women be frighted into fits, that the breeding ladies would miscarry, the children would be born with the eclipse marked in their faces; that the Catholick women would run to confession, and all the maids that had been lewd would cry, and tell their mistresses of it, for fear the Day of Judgment was come. But instead of this, there was a great piece of the sun left uncovered, and light enough to harden all the pretty sinners; so that none of those little useful secrets came out which would otherwise have been told.

There is a good deal of this relaxed good humor in Defoe's later journalism; and when he writes on such topics as a dearth of news, or ballad-making, or old maids, he can be as humorous and urbane as Addison or Steele.[56]

But, like Addison meditating in Westminster Abbey, he is also capable, when the occasion calls for it, of a solemn and impressive oratory. Such an occasion in 1722 produced one of Defoe's most memorable pieces of writing. On 16 June of that year the great Duke of Marlborough died, and his death made the same kind of massive impact on his fellow countrymen as that of the Duke of Wellington over a hundred years later. As the weeks passed, elegies and panegyrics and obituaries flowed from the press; and preparations went steadily forward for giving the Duke a magnificent funeral—an art form in which the English excel. It is true that Marlborough was more especially a hero of the Whigs, and that many of the Tories saw no reason to shed tears for a man they had always disliked;* but none the less the nation as a whole was now mourning the loss of a great military hero whose place in history was secure. Marlborough had once been a hero to Defoe, who had celebrated his victories in the *Review*, and perhaps he still was. By 1722, however, Defoe may have had second thoughts about him; and in any case he was now writing for Applebee, whose Tory readers could hardly be expected to welcome a panegyric on Marlborough. At all events, Defoe published on 23 June a rather guarded tribute, weighing the dead Duke's great merits against his very considerable defects. When he returned to the same subject four weeks later (the Duke was not buried until 9 August), the elaborate and pompous preparations for the funeral may have caused something of a revulsion in Defoe's mind. Stands were going up all along the route by which the procession would pass; three regiments of the Foot Guards were being put through special funeral exercises in Hyde Park; the newspapers reported that a magnificent hearse was being built, that the Company of Upholders (undertakers) had ordered a thousand yards of black velvet, and that the funeral was going to cost £30,000. Nobody was talking about anything else than the great coming event, the burial of the Duke in Westminster Abbey. As a journalist Defoe could not ignore it; but he could, and he did, get beyond and above it:

How have we skreen'd the ashes of heroes to make our mortar, and mingl'd the remains of a Roman general to build a hog-stye! Where are the ashes of a Caesar, and the remains of a Pompey, a Scipio, or a

* See, for instance, Swift's "Satirical Elegy on the Death of a Late Famous General."

Hannibal? All are vanish'd—they and their monuments are moulder'd into earth—their dust is lost, and their place knows them no more.

We are told, he continues, that the Duke died immensely rich,

but HE IS DEAD; and, some say, the great treasure he was possess'd of here had one strange particular quality attending it—which might have been very dissatisfying to him if he had consider'd much on it— namely, that he could not carry much of it WITH HIM.

But now Defoe passes beyond the dead Duke to a contemplation of the mortal lot and the instability of human glory:

What then is the work of life? What the business of great men that pass the stage of the world in seeming triumph, as these men we call heroes have done? Is it to grow great in the mouth of fame, and take up many pages in history? Alas! that is no more than making a tale for the reading of posterity, till it turns into fable and romance. Is it to furnish subjects to the poets, and live in their immortal rhimes, as they call them? That is, in short, no more than to be hereafter turn'd into ballad and song, and be sung by old women to quiet children; or, at the corner of a street, to gather crowds in aid of the pickpocket and the whore. Or is their business rather to add virtue and piety to their glory, which alone will pass with them into eternity, and make them truly immortal? What is glory without virtue? A great man without religion is no more than a great beast without a soul. What is honour without merit? And what can be call'd true merit, but that which makes a person be a good man, as well as a great man?[57]

Even though Marlborough and his state funeral was a party issue, and Defoe was writing for a Tory paper, this cannot be just party writing. In so far as he *was* "rallying the Whigs," he was doing so here with consummate tact: he couldn't possibly get into trouble for saying that all men must turn to dust, and that true greatness is to be found in virtue and piety rather than in military glory, although by saying these things he was deflating the coming pomp and ceremony, and to that extent pleasing his Tory readers. Yet the whole passage has the genuine ring of Defoe's deepest convictions; he is drawing upon a legacy of puritanism that may have become rather worn and dinted over the years, but that he still carried with him to his own grave not many years later. In those reflections upon death and the true meaning of life, the man who was set apart from the sacred office has momentarily come back to it; and although we may be aware, as we read, of the rhetorical balance of question followed by answer, the studied repetition, the careful juxtaposition of words and phrases, and the effective contrasts between the grand or grandiose and the mean or contemptible, we cannot surely allow this conscious artistry to make us doubt the seriousness of the writer, or his sincere belief in what he is saying.

3

The Poet

IT TOOK A LONG TIME to convince Defoe that he was not a poet, if indeed he ever accepted the fact. Bernard Shaw once claimed to be able to write blank verse more easily and expeditiously than prose;[1] and without pressing the parallel too far or taking Shaw's joke too seriously, it may be said that much of Defoe's verse was obviously written at about the same speed, and with the same facility, as his prose. There is certainly plenty of it: the Collected Verse of Daniel Defoe would fill at least two large volumes. A good deal of what he wrote is best described as journalism in verse, and most of it has worn less well than his journalism in prose; but once or twice, by a combination of wit and intellectual vigor, he succeeded in writing effective satire which can still be read with pleasure.

Most of his work in verse is either in the heroic couplet, which he normally used for satire, or in the loose irregular pindaric form of the period, which he learned to handle no worse than most of his contemporaries. His earliest known verse is preserved in a notebook, dated 1681, and must therefore have been written when he was about twenty-one. Consisting of six verse meditations and an uncompleted "Psalm of Thanksgiving and a Vow," these religious poems bring us close to the young man who had intended to become a Presbyterian minister, but who had for some unknown reason abandoned the ministry for trade. They are poems of self-examination and self-abasement, expressing the genuine spiritual experience of one whose conscience is still tender, and whose heart can still be easily bruised. Although the young **Defoe** writes of "strong lusts" and a "gulph of sins," he probably comes nearer to his own case when he describes less carnal temptations:

> Chiefly I come,
>   (Ah that I were at home!)
> From all that gawdy righteousness of myne,
>   To dress in that new robe of Thyne.
>   And from my self,
>   That fatall shelf
> On which my soul would splitt and drown,
> Lord, I have nothing of my owne![2]

Self-righteousness was something that Defoe was never to find easy to shake off; but it is significant, so early as this, that he realized it was part of his nature.

So far as is known, his first verse to be published was a satirical piece, *A New Discovery of an Old Intreague* (1691), and he thought well enough of it to reprint it in the second volume of his collected writings in 1705. Any interest it once had has long since evaporated; and the modern reader may be excused if he finds himself baffled by its allusions to obscure City magnates, and repelled by its crude rhymes and its rough and sometimes imperfect couplets. Even so, there are some good lines. Defoe has his satirical laugh at some nameless major in the City trainbands whose horse was accidentally shot by a trooper, who

> Pick'd out the animal, and spar'd the beast.

He liked this thought so well that he used it again eleven years later in *Reformation of Manners*, when he was attacking one of the City sheriffs for his lewd life:

> The brute he rides on wou'd his crimes detest,
> For that's the animal, and this the beast.[3]

In 1690 John Dunton had launched a highly successful periodical, *The Athenian Mercury*, in which he undertook with the help of a few learned assistants to answer questions sent in by his readers. A number of poets, including the young Jonathan Swift, sent Dunton congratulatory poems, and among those published in 1692 was one from Defoe "To the Athenian Society." This poem attempts in seventy lines to sketch the intellectual history of man from his beginnings to modern times, and is full of biblical allusions and of personified abstractions such as Memory, Forgetfulness, King Ignorance, Sloth, and so on. Perhaps the most remarkable feature of the poem is that Defoe makes only an oblique reference to the Athenian Society. Wisdom and Learning (the two sons of Knowledge) having waged war with Ignorance, the one in Italy and the other in Greece,

> Their empire to the world's extremes extend,
> And viceroys to remoter kingdoms send,
> Their faithful agents through the world disperse,
> And these we sing in our immortal verse;
> These now we sing, and willing trophies raise,
> To their just value, and their Master's praise.[4]

It is not clear whether the "Master" is God or John Dunton; if it *is* Dunton, this is the only reference to the Athenian Society.

Defoe had a better subject, and made good use of it, when in 1697 he wrote an elegy on Dr. Samuel Annesley, the minister in whose church he had worshipped. The poem is interesting as a verse "character," and also as an indication of the qualities Defoe admired in a man. He praises Annesley for his courage, his sincerity, and for being "just the very person that he seem'd"; but he also singles out for commendation

> *His native candor, and familiar stile,*
> Which did so oft his hearers' hours beguile,

so that "We lov'd the doctrine for the teacher's sake." He remembers, too, Annesley's equable temper and his love of moderation:

> If e'er his duty forc'd him to contend,
> *Calmness was all his temper, peace his end.*[5]

When we remember that Defoe sat at Annesley's feet every Sunday during his formative years, we may perhaps see where he could have learned some of those principles which he afterwards practised or tried to practise.

When, early in 1700, he published his long poem *The Pacificator*, he emerged as a successful satirist. A poetical war had recently broken out between Sir Richard Blackmore and the wits. In the prefaces to his epic poems, *Prince Arthur* and *King Arthur*, and again in his *Satyr against Wit* (1699), Blackmore had taken his stand with Jeremy Collier against the profaneness and immorality of the dramatic literature of the day and the general licentiousness of much contemporary writing. The wits retaliated with satirical epigrams, and Sir Samuel Garth ridiculed Blackmore in his poem *The Dispensary*. Finally, about a week after the publication of Defoe's poem, there appeared a satirical collection with the ironical title, *Commendatory Verses on the Author of the Two Arthurs, and the Satyr against Wit*. In *The Pacificator* Defoe adopted what was to become his favorite stance of peace and moderation. In vain "victorious Nassaw" had defeated the French abroad,

> Since from those conquests he is hardly come
> But here's a civil war broke out at home.

Englishmen, who seem never to be happy unless they are quarreling, and who "for want of wars with one another fight," have now started a domestic conflict between the men of sense and the men of wit. The men of sense are under the command of Blackmore ("great Nokor"), and he is supported by Jeremy Collier, and by Cowley, Milton, Rochester, Waller, Roscommon, Howard (presumably the Hon. Edward Howard), and, surprisingly enough, by Alexander Radcliffe, the ribald and bacchanalian verse-writer, and, more surprisingly still, by Mrs. Aphra Behn—all these being "giants . . . of wit and sense together." Defoe's pronouncements are often those of the typical puritan (he never, for instance, showed any real willingness to tolerate the theatre), but he sometimes surprises us by an unexpected tolerance. Although he cannot have approved of some of Rochester's writings or the wild life he led, he quotes or refers to his work frequently, and obviously admired him for his wit. As for Mrs. Behn, who had contributed her fair share to "the steaming ordures of the stage," Defoe may have developed the same reluctant admiration for her as he seems to have felt for Moll Flanders: she was a woman living by her wits and making a success of it. In his notable plea for the education of women in *An Essay upon Projects* he had remarked that "what they might be capable of being bred to is plain from some instances of female-wit which this age is not without." Mrs. Behn was clearly one of the most remarkable of those instances of female ability; and if Defoe would have preferred her wit to be less libertine, he could still admire her ingenuity and mental energy.[6]

The most interesting feature of *The Pacificator* is Defoe's structural device of a battle between two contending armies. The men of sense are heavily armed with "a coat of sense"; the wits rely on their "satiric dragoons" and their "light horse call'd lampoons," but they also draw upon seven "pindarick legions" and ten thousand "lyrick foot . . . Arm'd with *soft sighs,* with *songs,* and *billet-doux,*" and they have, too,

> several little bands of dogrel wit,
> To scowre the ways and line the hedges fit.

All this, of course, reminds us of Swift's more fully developed satirical fun in *The Battle of the Books,* but there can be no question of plagiarism here: Defoe's poem was published four years before *The Battle of the Books,* and although Swift's satire had been written at least two years before *The Pacificator* appeared, it seems quite improbable that Defoe could have seen it in manuscript. Both writers presumably hit upon the same satirical plot independently, and in any case they had been anticipated by at least two other writers.[7]

Defoe's battle ends with the troops of wit "disorder'd and o'er-run," and with Blackmore left in possession of the field. But this is not the end of the poem. Defoe is concerned to prevent a renewed outbreak of literary hostilities, since it is the public that suffers from this sort of civil strife, and total victory for either side can only result in "a dearth of sense, or else a plague of wit." He therefore calls for the mediation of neutral powers, to limit the bounds of wit and to purge "sullen sense" of its pride and insolence: both sides must be prepared to concede something, and "submit to Reason's high commands." There follows a long and excellent passage on Wit and Sense:

> *Wit,* like a hasty flood, may over-run us,
> And too much *sense* has oftentimes undone us; . . .
> *Wit* is a king without a parliament,
> And *sense* a democratick government:

Wit, like the French, where'er it reigns destroys,
And *sense advanc'd* is apt to tyrannize:
Wit without sense is like the *laughing-evil*,
And *sense* unmix'd with fancy is the *d——l*.
Wit is a standing-army government,
And *sense* a sullen stubborn p——t:
Wit by its haste anticipates its fate,
And so does *sense* by being obstinate:
Wit without sense in verse is all but *farce*,
Sense without wit in verse is all *mine a——*. . .
United, *wit* and *sense* makes science thrive,
Divided, neither *wit* nor *sense* can live;
For while the parties eagerly contend,
The mortal strife must in their mutual ruin end.

This passage of over forty lines is perhaps Defoe's most successful venture into "wit writing"; his imagery is apt and varied and topical, and his antithetical couplets are more polished and pointed than is customary with him. He displays in fact that successful combination of wit and sense which he is advocating for other writers. *The Pacificator* suggests, as in a different way *The Consolidator* was to do a few years later, that at the beginning of the eighteenth century Defoe had ambitions to be classed among the "polite" writers in the neo-classical mode. In a passage advocating that there should be "Some judge infallible, some Pope in wit" to show each writer where his special talent lay, he suggests that such a judge might

> Let C—— write the comick, F—— lampoon.

"C——" is obviously Congreve, and if "F——" stands for Foe, we have an indication of how Defoe thought of himself in the little world of contemporary English literature. In that case it looks as if some of his early verse has remained unidentified, for little of his published work at this date could be described as lampoon. At all events, now in his fortieth year, he was still very much interested in *belles-lettres;* and if trade, politics, and religion were already competing for his attention, and in time were to dominate his thinking, he continued for some years more to write effective satirical verse, which would have been even more effective if he had taken a little more care with it.[8]

Now, however, he wrote *The True-Born Englishman,* a long poem which was to make him famous. The English, who are more given to xenophobia than they care to admit, had recently been concentrating their dislike of strangers on their new Dutch king and his fellow countrymen, and more especially on one or two of his Dutch favorites in high office. Those insular prejudices were given rough expression in the summer of 1700 by John Tutchin's publication of his satirical poem, *The Foreigners,* an early example of the cry of "England for the English." Any attack on his hero King William was bound to provoke Defoe, and we have his own word for it that Tutchin's poem filled him "with a kind of rage." What is surprising, in view of the journalistic rapidity with which he usually wrote, is that his reply to Tutchin did not appear until January 1701. Although it runs to more than 1,200 lines, Defoe was fully capable of dashing off a poem of that length in much less than six months, and its comparatively late appearance is something of a mystery, more especially as he excuses in an Explanatory Preface "the hasty errors of my verse" on the grounds that "the time I have been upon it has been but little." At all events it was an immediate success. At least nine authorized editions were printed in the year of its publication, and Defoe reckoned that a further 80,000 pirated copies had been sold in the streets for a penny or twopence.[9]

The poem is in two parts, and Part I is structurally much superior to Part II. Defoe opens in proverbial fashion:

> Wherever God erects a house of prayer,
> The Devil always builds a chappel there.

He begins with the Devil, partly because he may really believe in the existence of an Evil One endlessly tempting men to sin, and partly because by naming his various "vice-gerents and commanders" he sees a way to describe the darling sins of the various European peoples. The Devil knows the genius and inclination of each, and "matches proper sins for ev'ry nation." So Pride, "the first peer and President of Hell," rules in Spain; Lust in Italy; Drunkenness in Germany, and so on. The prime sin of the English is Ingratitude; and this must be linked, it is suggested (but in what way is never made clear), with the very mixed origin of the English nation. Defoe is now launched on his main theme. England has been repeatedly invaded and conquered over the centuries, and each new race of conquerors has begotten true-born English-men on the existing stock—Romans, Saxons, Danes, Normans, and the rest. If we search for the origins of the English nobility,

> 'Tis that from some French trooper they derive,
> Who with the Norman bastard did arrive: . . .
> The silent record blushes to reveal
> Their undescended dark original.

And yet, strangely enough, it is those very men of "noble mean extraction" who

> despise the Dutch,
> And rail at new-come foreigners so much.

If it is suggested that all this happened in the remote past, the answer is that the infusion of foreign blood has continued down to the present day, if not by conquest, then by peaceful immigration. Large numbers of Protestant refugees came to England in the reign of Queen Elizabeth; the Scots followed King James of Scot-land south in 1603 (and those "interloping Scots" were greeted with the same uproar as the Dutch are now); Charles II, the "royal refugee," returning from exile in 1660, restored the breed

> with foreign whores:
> And carefully repeopled us again
> Throughout his lazy, long, lascivious reign,
> With such a blest and true-born English fry,
> As much illustrates our nobility.

(Defoe loses no opportunity to explode the myth of ancient lineage; his insistence that most of the English nobility aren't noble at all, or only very recently so, must have been one of the grounds for the popularity of the poem with humble readers.) It was, too, in the reign of Charles II that thousands of "the banish'd Protestants of France" (Defoe says 200,000) came to England:

> We have been Europe's sink, the jakes where she
> Voids all her offal out-cast progeny.

Yet they all became Englishmen, and in one generation learned to dislike and despise foreigners. What, then, are we to make of this mongrel race?

> A true-born Englishman's a contradiction,
> In speech an irony, in fact a fiction.[10]

If Defoe had stopped there he would have written a more coherent poem. Part I is based on an excellent polemical argument, carried on with zest and good humor. Defoe has made his point: the English are the last nation in the world from whom one would expect xenophobia, since they are themselves a mixture of so many different races. Defoe's talent for *reductio ad absurdum*. has had full play, and his humorous exaggerations are an effective way of deflating English pride and complacency. But he had still a lot to say about his fellow countrymen, and in Part II he proceeds to widen the basis of his satire by a fuller consideration of the real nature of Englishmen. Although his aim is still to attack the complacency of the English ("An Englishman ne'er wants his own good word"), he allows them certain redeeming qualities, and so gives his satire the appearance of impartiality. The real emphasis, however, falls upon their faults. The laboring poor, for example, are saucy, mutinous, and improvident, and they are far too much given to boozing. Returning next to the main theme of *The Poor Man's Plea*, Defoe insists that a drunken clergy and a drunken and swearing gentry set a poor example to their inferiors, and that intemperance is rife among university men, poets, statesmen, and indeed in almost every class and profession. In what appears to be another reference to Charles II he tells us:

> Drunk'ness has been the darling of the realm,
> E'er since a drunken pilot had the helm.

He now turns to the quarrels and divisions in religion, where "each man goes his own by-way to heaven" and "fancies none can find the way but he," and where there is a complete lack of Christian charity and tolerance. Later he passes to a consideration of the Englishman's strong sense of liberty and property, his hatred of any restraint, his proneness to what Matthew Arnold was to call "worship of freedom in and for itself," leading him to disrespect laws and magistrates, and even to affront his kings:

> The bad with force they eagerly subdue;
> The good with constant clamours they pursue:
> And did King Jesus reign, they'd murmur too.[11]

Defoe's rambling progress now leads him to an excursus on recent English history: the resistance to the arbitrary rule of James II; the gratitude to William of Orange for preserving English liberties, soon followed by a typical English reaction into discontent and a longing for the worthless king they had deposed. At this point Defoe feels that he cannot possibly allow such folly to pass unanswered, and accordingly he gives us a defence in about a hundred lines of the Whig settlement of 1689, anticipating the arguments that he was to set forth again at inordinate length in his *Jure Divino*. And now, since

> English gratitude is always such
> To hate the hand which does oblige too much,

he is led inevitably to a panegyric of William in some sixty lines spoken by Britannia. Returning to the Dutch, who came to England to maintain our freedoms, and who "Were paid, and curs'd, and hurry'd home again" (no standing army in time of peace), he defends the King's decision to rely on Dutchmen he can trust, since he obviously can't trust the English:

> Experience tells us 'tis the English way,
> Their benefactors always to betray.

This couplet enables Defoe to introduce a long digression on the wealthy financier Sir Charles Duncombe, which has little to do with the matter in hand, except that Duncombe, who "hopes e'er long to be a lord," is typical of that fluid English society in which it is possible to move from poverty and obscurity to the ranks of the nobility in one generation. A short Conclusion now brings the poem to an end; but Part II, it will have been seen, is something of a rag-bag, with little of the steady relevance of Part I.[12]

The True-Born Englishman, however, is an original and hard-hitting satire, and only Defoe could have written it. The "rage" he felt at the attacks of Tutchin and others on his beloved hero

no doubt accounts for his sharp and at times contemptuous retaliation on his fellow countrymen. But he kept his temper. He knew
as well as Swift that "anger and fury, though they add strength
to the sinews of the body, yet are found to relax those of the
mind, and to render all its efforts feeble and impotent." One good
reason why Defoe so often exasperated those he attacked is that
he always kept cool, and even flaunted his self-control in their
faces.[13]

In one of his pronouncements on satire he made three conditions: the character should be just; the thing satirized should be a
crime; the language, though keen, should be decent. To take the
second of these requirements first, Defoe was probably quite
satisfied that the ingratitude with which he taxed the English was
in the circumstances criminal; and in any case he said more than
once that he looked on ingratitude as "the worst of crimes." He
felt almost as strongly about the intemperate habits of the nation,
to which he devoted nearly a hundred lines of invective. As to
the character being just, it should be remembered that his description of the Englishman admits a number of virtues among the
vices. But here we have to face a difficulty that Defoe, like many
other satirists, tended to overlook or play down. The satirist,
wishing to hit hard, is apt to give the impression that the vice he
is castigating is universal, or at least general; if he limits the application of his censure to a minority, or to the exceptional few, he
lowers the pressure of his satire, and gives every individual reader
the chance to count himself out. In the original preface to his
poem—realizing, perhaps, that he had made it appear as if the
King hadn't a friend in all England—Defoe sought to modify the
effect of his wholesale condemnation of ingratitude by insisting
that the men he had in mind were mainly the High Church
Tories. In the Explanatory Preface which he added to a later
edition he similarly limited his charge of drunkenness to those
individuals who were actually guilty of intemperance, and expressed the belief that all candid readers would interpret his satire
in that spirit, "without thinking the whole profession lash'd who
are innocent." This is all very well, but it is not what Defoe says
in the poem. He was sometimes oddly off-hand, or even disingenuous, when challenged about his statements. In the *Review*
of 15 February 1709 he printed a very temperate letter from a

clergyman who suggested that his habit of "falling upon" the
Anglican clergy could only result in making the Church of England "odious and contemptible." To this Defoe made his usual
reply, that he was quite ready to acknowledge there were very
many virtuous and pious clergymen in the Church, and that his
strictures were intended only for the profligate:

*No man is concern'd in a charge of vice but the vicious; no man is
touch'd in a scandal but the scandalous.* And if any clergyman complains of my saying there are drunkards, or whore-masters, or swearers
among them, is it not most natural to say, *Why are you angry, sir?*
Are you ONE of them? Does the garment fit you?—Is the picture
drawn there your likeness?—If it be not, why are you angry? Why
are you mov'd, if you are not touch'd?

But this won't do. You cannot, let us say, accuse the universities
of being nurseries of idleness and debauchery, and then, if some
indignant professor objects to such a sweeping condemnation,
retort that he must be idle and debauched himself, or else he
would not try to rebut your charge. Defoe, in fact, was often
carried away by the ardor of the pursuit, as Swift was in *A Tale
of a Tub*. The only surprising thing is that either Swift or Defoe
should have been surprised at the hostile reaction. With those
reservations, it may be admitted that the character given of the
English in *The True-Born Englishman* was a just one (and still
is), allowing for the necessary exaggeration of satire, and the
satirist's desire to shock his readers into self-examination, and, if
possible, to self-reformation.[14]

As for the language of Defoe's poem, it was certainly keen, but
by the standards of 1701 not indecent. There were, it is true, some
expressions that would have offended the nicer ear of Pope, whose
own obscenities were given a more polite and delicate turn; but
the poem was primarily addressed to the John Bull Englishmen
of the day, and spoke to them in the same vigorous and semi-
colloquial language in which Defoe was soon to address the
readers of his *Review*. We meet therefore not only with the plain
downright English of "urinals," "jakes," and excretion, but with
such colloquialisms as "the Lord knows what," "God knows
who," "the devil and all," "brimstone whores," and England
repining that foreigners are "put upon her." The poem has a

more varied range of metaphor than is common in Defoe's verse;
and while some of this is characteristically homely (e.g. "As folks
cry *Fire* to hasten in relief"), a good deal is biblical (e.g. "thick
as the locusts which in Aegypt swarm'd"; "harps of praise . . .
on the willows hung"; "burnt-offering"; the "thirty pieces" of
Judas, and so on). In his reference to the "eager rapes . . . Betwixt
a painted Britain and a Scot," and the resulting offspring who

> quickly learnt to bow,
> And yoke the heifers to the Roman plow,
> From whence a mongrel half-bred race there came,

Defoe is echoing Judges, xiv.18; but he may also be allowing himself the witty sexual *double entendre* that we should more usually
associate with Dryden or Congreve.[15]

What is perhaps most interesting in Defoe's metaphors and
allusions is the extent to which they spring out of the contemporary political and religious situation. He is the most unpedantic of
writers, and his thought and expression are saturated with the life
of his own day. We have not read far in *The True-Born Englishman* before we come upon his lively description of the Devil,
whose absolute rule over mankind Defoe expresses in highly
topical terms:

> No Nonconforming sects disturb his reign,

and

> He needs no standing army government.

So, too, when he writes of the lesser infernal powers,

> They rule so politickly and so well,
> As if they were *Lords Justices* of Hell,

he is again referring to contemporary circumstances. Most English
kings had passed the whole of their reign without ever leaving the
country; but in William's reign of thirteen years he was out of
England for periods amounting to over five years. While Queen
Mary was alive, she acted as sole sovereign during his absences,
but after her death in 1694 the nominal rule was in the hands of
Lords Justices, chosen mainly from the holders of high office. The
term was therefore immediately topical, and would arouse a quick

response in Defoe's readers. Again, when he makes Sir Charles
Duncombe say,

> Our gallants need not go abroad to Rome,
> I'll keep a whoring jubilee at home,

the reference is once more topical—to the Roman Catholic Year
of Jubilee in 1700.[16]

That Defoe could write in the pointed style of the wit as well
as in the vigorous and colloquial style of the market-place may be
seen from the many sententious lines scattered through his poem
(e.g. "Restraint from ill is freedom to the wise"; "For whores and
priests will never want excuse"; "Knaves rail at laws, as soldiers
rail at peace"; "And all men learned poverty despise"). Many of
his couplets are distinguished by an effective balance and antithesis, and by a nice turn of phrase:

> But Virtue seldom does regard the breed;
> Fools do the wise, and wise men fools succeed.
> What is't to us, what ancestors we had?
> If good, what better? Or what worse, if bad?
> Examples are for imitation set,
> Yet all men follow virtue with regret.

Pope would no doubt have eliminated the "does" and the "do"
from the first couplet, but he would certainly have approved the
chiasmus of the second and fourth lines. The fourth line especially is a good example of Defoe's ability to achieve not only
balance but a high degree of compression. ("If we spring from
good ancestors, what are we the better for it? Or, if we spring
from bad ancestors, are we any the worse for that?"). In the sixth
line we have another example of Defoe's gnomic writing. Many
of his passages move in a steady crescendo towards a climax; and
in his frequent return to the words "true-born Englishman" he
makes a good use of repetition to hammer home his central idea.
As an exercise in the ridicule of national weaknesses the poem
appears to have achieved its purpose. There is every reason to
believe the claim Defoe made for it many years afterwards:

National mistakes, vulgar errors, and even a general practice, have
been reform'd by a just satyr. None of our countrymen have been

known to boast of being *true-born Englishmen*, or so much as to use the word as a title or appellation ever since a late satyr upon that national folly was publish'd, tho almost forty years ago.[17]

In 1702 Defoe published three substantial poems. Faithful to the memory of King William, who had died on 8 March some days after being thrown from his horse, he wrote *The Mock Mourners*, a poem partly panegyrical on the late King and on the English constitution, but mainly satirical on those of his subjects who had frustrated his policies, and who now drank to "the horse's health that threw him down." Again Defoe shows little but contempt for the English nobility, who failed to take their place in the field of battle, but "sent their King abroad, and staid at home." And what shame future generations will feel when they reflect how much this glorious king "was lov'd abroad, and scorn'd at home"! Among the interesting features of this poem are an elaborately-worked-out metaphor of the state as a great machine, and one passage in which Defoe comes close to writing like a metaphysical poet. The King's death came so unexpectedly, he says, that the English people had no time given them to supplicate the Almighty for his recovery; it was almost as if "Almighty Power had been afraid" to allow time for the people's prayers, since they would have come in such multitudes that He would have had to change his mind:

> For Prayer so much the Sovereign Power commands,
> E'en God himself sometimes as conquer'd stands,
> And calls for quarter at the wrestler's hands.

This desperate vision of an Almighty God whose will is sometimes diverted from its course and whose omnipotence is negated by the prayers of his suppliants at least suggests the measure of Defoe's grief at the death of his beloved king.[18]

In *Reformation of Manners* he embarks on a wholesale denunciation of immorality and profaneness, both in London (Part I) and in the country at large (Part II); but he finds room for sideswipes at stock-jobbers, beaux, and in one abusive passage at Matthew Prior. There are flashes of wit and humor as good as any to be found in the poetry of the period; for example:

> Indulgent Heaven for decency thought fit
> That some shou'd have the money, and some the wit.
> Fools are a rent-charge left on providence,
> And have equivalents instead of sense. . . .

There is, too, a lively passage giving ironical instructions for literary success in an age in which "Vertue's the faint green-sickness of the mind" and in which "One man reads Milton, forty Rochester." Even if Apollo were to descend and write in praise of virtue, it would never do today:

> The bookseller perhaps wou'd say, *'Twas well:*
> *But 'twould not hit the times, 'twould never sell.*

Some of the satire in *Reformation of Manners* is general, but most of it is directed against named individuals, more especially magistrates who, while punishing or rebuking immorality in others, have no thought of reforming themselves. Defoe, it will be seen, has returned to a favorite theme.[19]

His views on personal satire were stated on a number of occasions. In the *Review*, 20 January 1708, he gave it as his opinion that when a satirist was attacking the enemies of the public he should back up his satire with the names of the offenders,

or at least speak so plainly that things and people might be guess'd at; . . . for either the satyr is just or it is unjust; if it be just, it ought to be pointing as well as pointed, and the crime should describe the person, or the person the crime. . . .

In his own practice, he claimed, he had concealed a thousand times more "follies, crimes, vices, and ridiculous actions" of even his worst enemies than he had exposed; and indeed, since his aim has always been reformation,

I expose none but what I think incorrigible, and who first really expose themselves, seem past shame, advice or correction; and with these I think my self not ty'd up to rules.

In another *Review* (12 June 1711) he repeated his claim that when there was any hope of a man repenting he had not exposed him by name:

If I give a character of a man, 'tis always he that has made his own character so publick that any man may see he never designs to have it conceal'd; that he proclaims war against the laws, and is too great for resentment; whose scandals are protected by his power, and grown too flagrant to be reform'd. These I think are the just subject of a satyr, nor is there any other way left to attack them.

Late in life, in *Conjugal Lewdness* (1727), he set forth his views on satire at some length, and again gave special stress to its usefulness in dealing with those who were above the law, or not easily made subject to it:

Satyr can scourge where the lash of the law cannot; the teeth and talons of the pen will bite and tear; and the satyr has a sting which is made for the correction of such offences and such offenders as bully justice, and think themselves out of the reach of prisons and punishments; as small arms are of use in battle where the cannon and mortars cannot play, and the point of the lance can wound where the balls cannot fly. If men are fenc'd against one thing, they may not be fenc'd against another, and the sense of shame may restrain where even a sense of punishment will not. There are crimes which a lash of the pen reach'd when a lash at the cart's-tail would not; and a time when men that have laugh'd at the law, and ridiculed all its powers, have yet been laugh'd out of their crimes by a just satyr, and brought to the necessity of hanging themselves for shame, or reforming to prevent it.[20]

This was also the view of Swift and Pope; and indeed it was, and is, a widely accepted way of justifying satire. Defoe's most successful exercise in satirical ridicule was undoubtedly *The True-Born Englishman*. In *Reformation of Manners*, on the other hand, he lashes rather than mocks at such flagrant offenders as Sir Salathiel Lovell, the City Recorder, and the cumulative effect of such sustained and unvaried vituperation soon becomes monotonous. In any case, long-forgotten reprobates mean nothing to us, however much they may have meant to Defoe and his contemporaries, unless the satirist can make us realize their true character and motives—as Swift succeeds so remarkably in doing in his *Short Character of His Excellency Thomas Earl of Wharton*.

In Defoe's third long poem of 1702, *The Spanish Descent*, he gives a satirical account of the bungled expedition against Cadiz under the command of the overcautious Admiral Rooke, and then celebrates the capture of the French treasure ships in Vigo Bay. It is little more than a piece of verse journalism; but there is some effective satire on the "quidnuncs" who pass on false news and lay down the law on political and military strategy.

In July 1703, while he was a prisoner in Newgate and waiting for his ordeal in the pillory, Defoe published another bitter satire, *More Reformation*. Although he was partly concerned to reproach his fellow dissenters for their stupidity in not understanding the true purpose of *The Shortest Way*, and to rebuke their uncharitableness in abandoning him in his hour of distress, he also allowed himself some reckless comments on one or two of his judges, notably Judge Powell and Sir Salathiel Lovell, and even on Sir Simon Harcourt, the Solicitor General, who had appeared against him for the Crown.

Even more outspoken, however, was *A Hymn to the Pillory*, the publication of which was so timed that the poem was selling in the streets of London while Defoe was actually suffering punishment in what he called "the state-trap of the law." If Defoe was a martyr to anything when he stood in the pillory, it was to good journalism. From some of his surviving letters we know that he had been dreading this punishment. "Jayls, pillorys and such like with which I have been so much threatn'd," he wrote to William Paterson in April 1703, "have convinct me I want passive courage, and I shall never for the future think my self injur'd if I am call'd a coward." Yet this irrepressible journalist, whose sentence had included giving sureties for his good behavior for the next seven years, had spent some of his time in Newgate writing this uncompromising hymn of defiance to those who had put him there. Once again he fearlessly attacked Lovell, Sir Robert Jeffreys and others for their immoral lives, and ran over most of his favorite satirical topics—cowardly and incompetent admirals, drunken magistrates and clergy, time-serving lawyers "who by the slight of tongue can crimes create," immoderate High Church divines—and so on to the thundering climax, in which he calls upon the Pillory to tell mankind the real reason why, "so full of fault, and yet so void of fear," he is now enduring his punishment:

> Tell them it was because he was too bold,
> And told those truths which shou'd not ha' been told,
>   Extol the justice of the land,

> Who punish what they will not understand.
>   Tell them he stands exalted there
>   For speaking what we wou'd not hear. . . .
> Tell 'em the M[en] that plac'd him here
> Are sc[anda]ls to the times,
>   Are at a loss to find his guilt,
>   And can't commit his crimes.

It seems clear that on this occasion Defoe was something more than the fearless journalist securing a scoop from his own misfortune. Some words in his preface to *More Reformation* may give us the clue to how he felt about the treatment he had received at the hands of the law:

England is particularly famous for the most generous way of fighting in the world, I mean as to the common people's private quarrels. . . . The English men fairly box it out, and in this way of fighting the rabble stand by to see fair play, as they call it. . . .

Defoe had not received fair play, and his sense of natural justice was outraged. In his preface to the second volume of his collected writings (1705) he claimed that the *Hymn to the Pillory* "was the Author's declaration, even when in the cruel hands of a merciless as well as unjust ministry, that the treatment he had from them was unjust, exorbitant, and consequently illegal." (So much for the seven years' ban on plain speaking which his judges had imposed on him.) But Defoe went further still: his poem "was taken for a defiance of their illegal proceedings," and the very fact that they had not thought fit to prosecute him for it was a clear indication they knew they were guilty.[21]

Apart from the light it throws on Defoe's character, the *Hymn to the Pillory* has considerable interest as a poem. It is one of the most successful of his pindaric effusions, his steady indignation carrying him buoyantly along on its irregular rhythms. Metaphor is profuse and varied: the pillory is in turn a "hieroglyphick state machine," a "stool of state," the "state-trap of the law," "great engine," a "spreading stage," "great monster of the law," a "pulpit" (for the "drunken priest"), a "bar" (for the lawyers), a "throne," a "pageant," a "herald of reproach," and a "bugbear of the law." With its exhortations, exclamations, apostrophes, its bold imperatives and unqualified statements, and its reiterated "Tell them . . . Tell them," the *Hymn to the Pillory* strikes with tremendous rhetorical force, and with the sustained excitement of Defoe's moral indignation. He has become fearless because he has become desperate.

   To 1704 belongs *An Elegy on the Author of The True-Born Englishman*, another long essay in the pindaric mode which again attacks most of Defoe's now-familiar victims, and which has some outspoken lines on the manipulation of the law:

> *For Law is but a heathen word for power;*
> A metaphor invented to confess
>   The methods by which men oppress;
> By which with safety they destroy mankind,
> While Justice stands before, *and Fraud behind.*

There are, too, some interesting autobiographical passages; and one especially in which he makes his point by suddenly quoting and adapting a stanza from Rochester's "Phyllis, be gentle, I advise":

> Thus like old Strephon's vertuous miss,
>   Who, foolishly too coy,
> Dy'd with the scandal of a whore,
>   And never knew the joy;
> So I, by Whigs abandon'd, bear
>   The satyr's unjust lash,
> Die with the scandal of their help,
>   But never saw their cash.

Rochester's poem is a witty invitation to Phyllis to commit what Defoe would normally refer to as fornication, and to be what he would normally call a whore. That he should so cheerfully avail himself of a well-known bawdy poem to make his own very different statement about the ingratitude of the Whig party is an indication not only of how angry he was with the Whigs, but how far he had moved from the dissenting academy at Newington Green. In the excitement of composition, however, he was often carried away into a world of fantasy and intellectual enjoyment; and in any case Rochester appears to have been a poet to whom he was nearly always ready to grant a special kind of indulgence for the sake of his wit. It was an indulgence that he was not prepared to extend to Jonathan Swift. If ever I write another satire again, he says in this same poem. I shall not hesitate to name the men whose crimes I have in mind:

> Young S——t shall not the House of God debauch,
> And meet with neither censure nor reproach.

"Young S——t" I take to be the author of *A Tale of a Tub*, which had been published a few months earlier than Defoe's poem. In 1704, it is true, Swift was thirty-seven years of age, but he was, comparatively speaking, a new author, and Defoe probably thought of him as a young man. However he might pitch into drunken parsons and High Church zealots himself, Defoe was not prepared to joke about religion, and Swift's ribald treatment of nonconformists especially could only have angered him.[22]

When the Great Storm broke over southern England late in November 1703 and winds blew with hurricane force for two days, causing unprecedented destruction, Defoe wrote another pindaric poem, *The Storm. An Essay*, which he published along with the *Elegy* in 1704. In an age when such natural disasters were looked upon as a judgment from heaven, it is not surprising to find Defoe improving the occasion by suggesting that the Great Storm was a punishment for the divisions within the country:

> Since storms are then the nation's choice,
> Be storms their portion, said the heavenly voice.

But the preacher in Defoe also seized the occasion to confute atheism, and the moralist and humanitarian in him protested against the callous men of Deal, who left shipwrecked sailors to perish on the Goodwin Sands while they plundered their cargoes —a subject to which he was to return in the *Review* of 18 December 1708. All this is expressed with Defoe's usual direct and unsparing vigor; and there are some passages of near-Miltonic grandeur as he dwells on the fury of the storm, or contemplates the great First Cause, "Ancient as Time, and elder than the Light."[23]

In August 1704, news of the great victory at Blenheim reached London. Before the end of the month Defoe had composed *A Hymn to Victory*, which must have met with considerable suc-

cess, since on 5 September he was warning readers of the *Review*
against "three sorts of counterfeits, or shams, called by the same
title . . . full of faults, the sence mangled, and several lines altered
in some near to blasphemy." It is, however, one of his less readable
poems, a period piece with much dreary apostrophe (Victory is
addressed as "Nymph"), and it suffers from the fact that detailed
accounts of the battle had not yet reached London when Defoe
was composing his paean.[24]

He did much better in *The Double Welcome. A Poem to the
Duke of Marlbro*, published early in 1705. The great Duke was
now back in London, and Defoe welcomed him not only as the
brilliant general, but as the warrior-statesman who would "calm
our wild debates" and lower the immoderate heat of party warfare at home. In developing this second reason for his "double
welcome," Defoe warns Marlborough against High Church fanatics especially:

> Pardon the poet, all your wars are jests,
> *You've fought with men*, you never fought with *priests*.

Warming to his work, he writes of "the strong banditti of the
gown," and launches an attack on Dr. Sacheverell—a "High
Church buffoon" and a "noisy, sawcy, swearing, drunken priest."
It never seems to have occurred to Defoe that immoderate language of this kind was hardly calculated to "calm our wild
debates" or bring about that peace which he kept on saying he desired. One other satirical thrust may be noted. Addison had recently been made a Commissioner of Appeal in the Excise, an
office worth £200 a year, and had undertaken to celebrate the
victory of Blenheim in the poem which he later published as
The Campaign. Reflecting, no doubt, on the ingratitude of the
Whigs and his own unrewarded state, Defoe slipped in some acid
lines about his young rival:

> Maecenas has his modern fancy strung,
> And fix'd his pension first, or he had never sung.

In his prose allegory *The Consolidator*, published some weeks
later, he referred again to Addison, who (he claimed) refused to
write *The Campaign* until the Court had settled £200 per annum
on him, "since 'tis known they have but one author in the nation

that writes for 'em for nothing." The one author was, of course, that virtuous and long-suffering patriot Defoe.[25]

It is unnecessary to pursue his poetical activity much further. In 1705 he published a long political satire, *The Dyet of Poland*, "printed at Dantzick" and with a preface signed "Anglipoloski, of Lithuania." The Polish Diet represents the English Parliament; and in a thin disguise Defoe satirizes his old enemy Daniel Finch, Earl of Nottingham ("Finski"), Admiral Rooke, Sir Edward Seymour, and other Tories, and under other similar disguises praises Lord Somers, Harley, and the moderate statesmen of whom he approves. Past experience led him to throw this thin disguise over his satire of contemporary statesmen, and any good lawyer could have defended him successfully in 1705 on the ground that Nottingham, Seymour, and the rest were nowhere actually named. The danger to Defoe was rather that one of the outraged victims of his satire might take the law into his own hands, and possibly hire ruffians to cudgel him, or worse; but this was a danger he was prepared to face. In the *Review* of 7 July 1705 he told his readers, with a kind of jaunty indifference, that he had his answer ready for those who threatened to cut his throat on account of what he had written:

I move about the world unguarded and unarm'd, a little stick not strong enough to correct a dog supplies the place of Mr. O[bserva-to]r's great oaken-towel, a sword sometimes perhaps for decency, but it is all harmless to a meer nothing; can do no hurt any where but just at the tip of it, call'd the point.—And what's that in the hand of a feeble author?

It is well to remember that for many years Defoe walked on the edge of real danger to his person, and perhaps to his life; and no doubt he had learned to "snatch a fearful joy" from his own te-merity. No doubt, too, the very risks that he knew he was taking gave an added point to his satirical thrusts.[26]

In 1706 he published *Caledonia*, a poem in heroic couplets varied with octosyllabic couplets, in which he complimented the Scots on their learning, their brave soldiers of fortune, their ancient families, and so on. But it was characteristic of him that he also seized the occasion to argue that Scotland was an under-developed country—

> What pains has Scotland taken to be poor,
> That has the Indies at her door.

(The Indies were her insufficiently exploited herring fishery.)
The whole country, he insisted, cried out for improvements in
agriculture and stock-breeding, and in lead, copper, and coal
mining:

> Wake, Scotland, from thy long lethargic dream . . .
> To land improvement and to trade apply,
> They'l *plentifully* pay thine industry.
> Thy barren muirs shall weighty sheaves bestow,
> Th'uncultivated vales rich pastures show,
> The mountains flocks and herds *instead* of snow. . . .

The boundary line between verse and prose in the eighteenth
century was often wavering and indeterminate.[27]

One last poetical labor must be noticed. As early as 26 September
1704 Defoe had announced in the *Review* a new poem called *Jure
Divino. A Satyr. In Twelve Books*, to be published by subscrip-
tion at ten shillings a copy. As the months passed, the announce-
ment was repeated from time to time. On 13 February 1705 a
subscriber who had inquired about the date of publication was
informed that the volume had been "stop'd on an extraordinary
occasion," but was now "perfecting in the press" and would be
sent to subscribers not later than the end of April. About a year
passed, however, and on 5 January 1706 Defoe found it necessary
to devote a considerable part of a *Review* to placating his angry
subscribers and indignantly rebutting the charge that the sub-
scription had been only " a sham to get money in hand." The
poem was at last delivered to subscribers in the summer of 1706.
But Defoe's troubles were not yet over. Before long a piratical
publisher, Benjamin Bragg, was offering an octavo edition for
sale at half the price of Defoe's folio. In an advertisement which
he inserted in the *Review*, 3 August 1706, Defoe took the shortest
way with Benjamin Bragg:

Lately Publish'd,

JURE DIVINO, a Satyr in twelve Books, by the Author of the *True-
Born Englishman*, as it was printed in *Octavo* from the Author's
Edition in *Folio;* Price bound 5*s*. Being for the particular Accomo-

dation of the Reader printed upon extraordinary good ISSUE
PAPER,* adorn'd with above one thousand six hundred and ninety
Errors of the Press in Literals, Pointings, etc. and one hundred fifty
seven Errors in Sence, several Omissions of whole Lines, transposing
of Paragraphs, and inverting the Meaning. Whoever has a mind to
encourage such Robbery of other Men's Studies at their own Expence,
may be furnished with the said Book at Mr. *Benjamin Bragg*'s, Publisher in ordinary to the Pyrates.

Even Bragg was undercut in his turn by a cheap reprint issued
in parts, and then stitched together to form a chapbook.[28]

Such piratical activity points to the popularity of Defoe as
a writer. But it is hard to believe that anyone who bought *Jure
Divino*, whether in folio, octavo, or duodecimo, can have felt
that he was getting his money's worth, or that he hadn't heard
it all before. This "satire against tyranny and passive obedience"
goes over the old familiar ground so well covered by John Locke
in his *Two Treatises on Government* (1690). The gist of what
Defoe has to say is contained in a note to Book II of his poem:

Nothing in this book is design'd, or can be construed, to deny or
expose monarchy, or the sovereignty of government by kings; but to
prove that they have no powers immediately deputed from Heaven
superior and unsubjected to the good of those they govern; and that
when they assume such a right, they become tyrants, invaders of right,
and may be deposed by the people they govern.

Defoe's development of this thesis, as in his tracing the origins of
government to the desire for mutual defence against invasion
of property, is nearly all in Hobbes or Locke, and was by this time
accepted Whig doctrine. Such poetical excursions as his pindaric
digression on rebellion (VI), his examples from English history
(IX, X), and the inevitable panegyric of King William (XI),
offer less than his usual justification for writing in verse. Indeed,
wherever we have a chance of comparing his prose (in the notes)
with his verse, the advantage is almost always with the former. In
a note to Book III he tells his readers:

Reason is the test of law; for laws which are contradictory to reason
are void of their own nature, and not either to be made or regarded.

* A thin paper used in treating an "issue" or discharge of pus.

This has all the strong impact of his forthright prose; and when he puts the same, or similar, ideas into the often doggerel verse of *Jure Divino*, they lose rather than gain in effectiveness:

> The laws of God, as I can understand,
> Do never laws of nature countermand;
> Nature commands, and 'tis prescrib'd to sense
> For all men to adhere to self-defence:
> Self-preservation is the only law
> That does involuntary duty draw. . . .

There is little of the lively imagery that animated *The True-Born Englishman* and *A Hymn to the Pillory:* Defoe simply soldiers on through the twelve long books of his political testament, and leaves the reader replete rather than satisfied. Even allowing for an age in which verse was used for all sorts of discourse that would now normally be carried on in prose, *Jure Divino* is a sort of poetical Fonthill Abbey, liable to collapse by its own weight and the carelessness and indifference of its workmanship.[29]

"My harps are long since hung on the willows," Defoe wrote in the *Review* of 29 July 1708, "my brains have done crowing." In fact he continued to write verse into his old age, but after *Jure Divino* and *Caledonia* he never attempted anything so ambitious. "Cousin Swift," Dryden is reputed to have said, "you will never be a poet." If Defoe had never written better verse than he did in *Jure Divino*, the same might have been said of him. At its best, however, his verse has a rhetorical felicity different from that of his prose; and by balance and antithesis, repetition, concentration, satirical allusion, and audacious imagery he sometimes writes in verse what he could not have expressed so economically and with such emotional effect in prose. At its best, too, his verse writing is that of a man who is being carried along willingly and at times recklessly by the excitement of composition, and whose ideas come flying into his head as he sets them down on paper. Defoe the verse writer deserves more critical attention than he has yet been given.[30]

4

The Writer of Fiction (I)

W HEN DEFOE TURNED to writing fiction in 1719, his varied experience as an author had given him some preparation for this new venture. He had occasionally included short stories in the *Review* (usually in the form of letters from imaginary correspondents) that sometimes anticipate situations in his novels. On 14 April 1705, for instance, the Scandal Club dealt with a letter from a young woman whose husband had deserted her, and who was receiving advances from two admirers—what should she do? The situation is roughly similar to that in which Roxana was to find herself when her first husband the brewer disappeared for good one morning. As for the technique required for writing an autobiographical novel, Defoe had shown in *The Poor Man's Plea* and *The Shortest Way* that he could successfully adopt a *persona,* and write consistently from the point of view of someone other than himself. He had even written fiction of an unusual kind in *The Consolidator: Or, Memoirs of Sundry Transactions from the World in the Moon* (1705), which belongs to the genre of the imaginary voyage. This is narrative of a sort, but Defoe's main concern here is with allegorical-satirical allusions to contemporary England.

Later in the same year, however, he showed that he had little to learn in the art of telling a story by publishing *A True Relation of the Apparition of One Mrs. Veal, the Next Day after Her Death, to One Mrs. Bargrave at Canterbury.* This famous ghost story, once thought to be an early example of Defoe's fiction, is now known to be based on facts then circulating in Canterbury. Whatever Mrs. Bargrave saw, or thought she saw, on 8 September 1705, Defoe did not invent her story. There are several earlier accounts of Mrs. Veal's visit to the unsuspecting Mrs. Bargrave (who only discovered some time after her friend was gone that she had died the day before), and most of the facts in Defoe's *True Relation* appear in one or more of those accounts. We do not know whether Defoe went down to Canterbury and heard Mrs. Bargrave's story from her own lips, and we cannot tell whether he added anything of his own. But once or twice we may perhaps detect him contributing an extra touch of vivid detail. The important fact which any trained journalist would wish to focus upon was that all through Mrs. Veal's visit her friend was unaware that she was talking to a ghost. When Mrs. Bargrave opened her front door and saw Mrs. Veal standing there, she naturally offered to kiss ("salute") her. The three earliest accounts all mention this, and Mrs. Veal's rejection of the kiss:

(1) But Mrs. V. clapp'd her down in a Chair, by wch she concluded her not willing, & so forbore.

(2) . . . and went to salute her, but she rushed by her, and sat herself down in a great armed Chair, and fell into discourse of severall things y^t had hapned w^n they lived together at Dover.

(3) . . . asked her to Come in and offerd to salute her upon which she sat herself down in a Chair Saying she was very weary.

Defoe may have felt that this dramatic moment was so important that it deserved fuller treatment. At all events, he prolonged the suspense, and brought Mrs. Bargrave very close indeed to kissing a ghost:

Madam, says Mrs. Bargrave, I am surprized to see you, you have been so long a stranger, but told her she was glad to see her and offer'd to Salute her, which Mrs. Veal complyed with, till their Lips almost touched, and then Mrs. Veal drew her hand cross her own Eyes, and said, *I am not very well,* and so waved it.[1]

There are several other slight heightenings of this sort which seem to indicate that Defoe was writing up his story carefully— whether he was recalling what Mrs. Bargrave had told him or not. If you are telling a ghost story, or any story that is so unusual as to seem incredible, you will try to authenticate it by dwelling on factual details—so trivial that their very triviality will seem to vouch for their actuality. When Defoe came to write fiction, he used the same documenting method that he had used in *A True Relation* in order to convince the readers of *Robinson Crusoe* that what they were reading was actually and literally true. In his account of Mrs. Veal he had to give complete credibility to what was basically incredible; his problem in *Robinson Crusoe* was not essentially different—how to make us believe that a man who had lived twenty-eight years on a desert island could come through such an experience with his sanity unimpaired and without dying of starvation.

As narrative *A True Relation* owes something (not a great deal) to the casual and familiar conversation of Mrs. Veal and Mrs. Bargrave. Dialogue, as we have seen, was something that Defoe often introduced into the *Review*, and there are idiomatic snatches of conversation in many of his pamphlets. In 1715, however, in *The Family Instructor*, he showed for the first time what he could do in this way in an extended form. This work consists of a series of dialogues interspersed with short stretches of narrative and comment; it was followed by a second volume in 1718. Both volumes are examples of "guide literature"; and both, in the course of giving moral and religious instruction, tell several stories involving middle-class families. Most twentieth-century readers have a dislike of being "edified"; and it must be admitted that a story which turns upon the determination of a conscience-stricken father to give his family religious instruction, and to prevent his grown-up son and daughter from driving in the park on the Lord's day, or from reading plays, French novels, and modern poets like Boileau on *any* day of the week, is not likely to commend itself to the modern mind. Yet in his various dialogues Defoe not only puts before us credible characters, but he gives them words to speak that are often remarkably true to life. He is at his liveliest, as we might expect, with the bad characters— the disobedient children, the hot-tempered parents, the scoffing and stubbornly irreligious adults, and so on. In the fourth dialogue of Part I, for example, a younger brother, who is a good obedient boy, talks with his elder sister, who is resolved to have nothing to do with her father's new-found piety:

Sister. Prethee don't fill my head with all this *canting stuff*, I don't value it a farthing.

2nd Brother. Why, sister, have you no manner of inclination to live religiously, and *like a Christian,* or to listen to what your father may say to you?

Sist. I think I am religious enough in all conscience; and I don't intend to disturb my thoughts with any more religion than needs must.

2nd Bro. You talk wildly now; *I hope* you would be a good Christian?

Sist. A Christian! Why, what do you take me for, a Mahometan? I think I am a good Christian.

2nd Bro. Why, *suppose that too;* yet if it were no more than my father desires it, and says he resolves to have it so, you will hardly perswade yourself not to submit to him. *You know, besides,* that he is our father, and we ought in duty to obey him; for he has been the kindest, tenderest, obliging'st father in the world TO US; and it would be very ungrateful to show yourself rude to such a father, as it would be wicked to disobey him; I am sure you would not be a Christian if you should.

Sist. Don't tell me, I think my self as good a Christian as any of you, but I won't be made a fool of, *for all that;* I had as lieve you should think me *no Christian* as you should think me a fool; *sure* I am past my horn-book!

2nd Bro. And what, because you are past your horn-book, do you think you are past teaching? Have you nothing to learn but your A, B, C?

Sist. No, no, I'll learn anything too, but I won't be taught to be a hermit; if they have a mind to breed me up for an abbess, let them send me to a monastery; I'd as lief be in a real *cloister* as be *cloister'd up* at home; use none of your *new cant* with me; *I tell you, brother,* my mother may ruffle me as much as she will, I'll have my own way still.

This has the same ring of truth as the conversations of the Colchester family in *Moll Flanders:* Defoe had a good ear for the impertinence and pertness and wilfulness of his middle-class families. It may be added that in the passage just quoted Defoe is so far from allowing his moral disapproval to interfere with his stating of the girl's point of view that he in fact states it with unusual liveliness. In the first dialogue of the 1718 volume we meet with a husband and wife who bicker incessantly, their quarrel starting from the wife's "speaking slightly" of the way her husband conducts family worship. Again the subject may seem to promise little entertainment for the modern reader, but again the dialogue is almost painfully true to life, and the waspish and contentious wife (who finally goes out of her mind) is a character quite repellently real, and one who in the present century would be an ideal subject for psychoanalysis. Although Defoe never loses sight of his moral and religious purpose (and for the modern reader overdoes the tears and the swoonings), he always gives the bad characters a good run for their money; and if, at long last, they repent (and not all of them do), their conversion is usually convincing.[2]

That he had given careful thought to what he was doing in *The Family Instructor*, and to the problems involved in telling a story is apparent from some of the notes that he wrote for the various dialogues. Part II of the 1715 volume is concerned with a religiously-minded boy whose father has apprenticed him to a wealthy tradesman, a man who went to church on Sundays, but "troubled his head very little with anything that was religious all the week after." The boy, who is disappointed that his master has never invited him to take part in family prayers, has formed a habit of slipping out at six o'clock in the morning to attend family worship in the house of a godly clothier across the street. His master, who has noted his frequent absences, is convinced that he is up to no good, and taxes the boy with it; but the boy, without saying *why*, simply tells him that on each occasion he has been at the clothier's house. There follows a conversation between the master and the boy's father, and then one between the father and his son, in which the father, who knows why his son has been going regularly to the clothier's house, urges him to tell his master the whole truth. The boy, who is understandably reluctant to have to explain to his master that he thinks he should have been invited to take part in his family worship (it turns out later that there isn't any), nevertheless knows that he must obey his father, and in a subsequent conversation with his master the truth is dragged out of him. The master, however, is not yet convinced, and tells the boy that he will have to check his story "to be better satisfied." All this is perfectly natural; but Defoe appears to think that some at least of his readers may need reassurance, and he proceeds to give it:

There seems to be more circumlocutions in this dialogue than in any of the rest; but they will be found not useful only, but necessary, at least to preserve the cadence of things, and introduce the subject of the real story by necessary gradations: the boy's shifting off so many ways before he directly tells his master the whole of his business, is a mark of commendable modesty in a servant; his shyness of speaking what he knew touched his master's behaviour more than his own, may be very instructing to servants, if they please to mark it, in things where their master's character may be concerned: but above all it may be noted that all these things tend to bring the conviction home with the more energy and force upon the conscience of the master.[3]

In this explanatory passage Defoe takes us into his workshop, and shows us how he is constructing his story. It is true that his main concern is with the extent to which his mode of procedure will bring out useful moral lessons; but this is a cautionary tale, and such considerations would naturally be uppermost in his mind. On the other hand, when he writes of the protracted conversations between boy and master as being "necessary . . . to preserve the cadence of things, and introduce the subject of the real story by necessary gradations," he is thinking as a novelist rather than as a pure moralist. So, too, when he suggests that the gradual method—the long conversations that seem to be getting nowhere, the boy's hesitation to criticize his master—is the best way "to bring the conviction home with the more energy and force upon the conscience of the master," he is really thinking of what is best for the story he is telling.

Several of the dialogues deal with rebellious boys and girls, and with the great importance of children obeying their parents. In the 1718 volume there is a story of an irascible father whose tyrannical conduct leads to rebellion in his family. Later, one of his rebellious sons repents, and tells his sister: "I remember that terrible scripture with many a reproach to myself: *Cursed be he that setteth light by his father and mother.*" Some pages earlier a neighbor has observed, with reference to the disobedience of one of the other sons:

It is a certain rule, and all sober, religious children will adhere to and acknowledge it, that though the parent may fail of his duty to his child, yet that by no means dispenses with the duty of a child, because the child's obedience is not founded upon the father's conduct, but upon the laws of nature. . . . Obedience of children to parents is a natural law; neither humanity or Christianity can subsist without it.[4]

In view of the story which he was soon to write about a rebellious boy in the city of York who disobeyed the commands of his father and ran away to sea, such passages in *The Family Instructor* must be looked on as having a considerable bearing upon the most famous of all Defoe's works of fiction, *Robinson Crusoe*.

ii

As every schoolboy used to know, the prototype of Robinson Crusoe was a stubborn and refractory Scottish sailor, Alexander Selkirk (1676–1721), who while cruising on a privateering voyage under the command of William Dampier, quarreled with the captain of his ship, and had himself put ashore in 1704 on the uninhabited island of Juan Fernandez. After some initial difficulties, Selkirk managed to make a life of it, and when he was rescued in January 1709 from his self-inflicted exile by Captain Woodes Rogers, he was in good health and apparently quite satisfied with his island life. He consented, however, to sail with Woodes Rogers, who appointed him mate of his ship. Later he was given command of another ship, and returned at last to London in October 1711. Accounts of his life on Juan Fernandez were published in 1712 by Woodes Rogers and by Captain Edward Cooke, and on 3 December 1713 Steele devoted a whole paper to him in his periodical *The Englishman*. Defoe must have known some or all of these accounts, and it is odd that with his interest in voyages and pirates he made no reference to Selkirk in the *Review* or elsewhere. Steele claimed to have had frequent conversations with Selkirk when he came back to London in 1711, and although nothing is known of Defoe having ever met the Scottish sailor, it seems unlikely that he would not seek him out and learn his story from his own lips.[5]

At all events, *Robinson Crusoe* shares with most of Defoe's later fiction a firm basis in actuality: while his fiction *is* fiction, it often starts from, and in some cases stays very close to, a fact or series of facts. Selkirk's story gave Defoe the situation of a marooned mariner and a few accompanying circumstances—the

goats which he tamed, the goatskin clothing, the cats, etc. In
Steele's account it is related of Selkirk that he went through a
period of deep depression, "grew dejected, languid and melancholy," until gradually "by the force of reason, and frequent
reading of the scriptures, . . . he grew thoroughly reconciled to
his condition." Selkirk's progress from dejection to equanimity
is paralleled by that of Crusoe; but Defoe was quite capable of
imagining Crusoe's state of mind without having recourse to
Selkirk's. On the other hand, Crusoe's description of his religious
exercises may owe something to Steele's account of how Selkirk
had formed the habit of using "stated hours and places for exercises of devotion." On any count, however, Defoe's indebtedness
to the Selkirk narratives was small; and indeed it was essential for
him as a writer of fiction to conceal it as much as possible, since
Selkirk's strange experience was comparatively fresh in the public
mind, and had recently (1718) been recalled to memory by the
publication of a second edition of Woodes Rogers' *Cruising Voyage round the World*. Defoe's hero was not therefore marooned
on his island, but cast ashore by shipwreck; the imaginary island
was not off the west coast of South America, but off the east
coast. When Selkirk was put ashore on Juan Fernandez he lived
for some time on a diet of turtles until he could stomach them
no longer, but Crusoe doesn't mention his first turtle until he has
been on the island for the best part of a year. Selkirk was provided with some bedding, a musket, a pound of gunpowder, a
large quantity of bullets, a flint and steel, a few pounds of tobacco,
a hatchet, a knife, a kettle, a Bible and some other books, and his
mathematical instruments: Crusoe had at his disposal a more extensive collection of firearms and ammunition, and a much more
miscellaneous quantity of tools and other material which he had
saved from the wreck. And of course Crusoe lived for eight and
twenty years on his desert island, whereas the isolated existence
of Selkirk lasted for rather less than four and a half years.[6]

There were various other accounts of shipwrecked seamen,
real or fictitious, on which Defoe could have drawn, and he may
have taken a few hints from one or other of those, such as *A Relation of the Great Sufferings . . . of Henry Pitman* (1689). What
is not in doubt is the frequent use he made of Dampier's *A New
Voyage round the World*; and Professor A. W. Secord has drawn

particular attention to two other sources, Robert Knox's *Historical Relation of Ceylon* (1681) and Maximilien Misson's fictitious *Voyage of François Leguat* (1707). Although Knox's twenty-year captivity in Ceylon was very different from Crusoe's prolonged stay on his desert island, there are a number of resemblances in their activities, and (as Secord pointed out) Knox was much closer in character and personality to Crusoe than was Selkirk, and Defoe may even have known Knox and have used him as the model for Crusoe.[7]

In Defoe's own day readers of all classes—from Alexander Pope to every "old woman that can go to the price of it"—enjoyed *Robinson Crusoe* as a story of "strange, surprizing adventures." Twentieth-century critics have seen it as more than just that; but it is primarily as an adventure story that it still lives, and its continuing vitality is largely due to the skill and narrative confidence with which Defoe told it. In one of his less generous moments Dr. Johnson, who disliked Jonathan Swift, told Boswell that there was nothing especially remarkable about *Gulliver's Travels.* "When once you have thought of big men and little men," he said, "it is very easy to do all the rest." On the same grounds it might presumably be argued that once Defoe had thought of the desert island, his story of the shipwrecked Crusoe practically wrote itself. Defoe, however, showed a quite unusual ability to enter imaginatively into the situation he was developing, and to devise circumstances and events that would enable, and even compel, the reader to realize Crusoe's predicament and share vicariously in his difficulties. If we are to judge him as a novelist we have to admit that he had serious limitations; but he had in abundant measure one of the most essential gifts of the novelist, the ability to put himself in someone else's place, even to the extent of almost losing his own identity in that of a fictitious character—as he had done with such disastrous results to himself when he wrote *The Shortest Way with the Dissenters.* On the other hand, he is usually able to do this with only one character at a time, the hero (or heroine) who is the teller of the tale: the other characters are apt to be seen from the outside, and to have importance only in so far as they are involved in the life of the chief character. How far something of Defoe himself creeps into his heroes and heroines is a question that will be discussed later.[8]

In all his works of fiction Defoe was almost certainly invent-ing continuously as he went along. In *Robinson Crusoe*, for ex-ample, after twelve separate journeys to the wreck, during which Crusoe brings ashore all that he can lay his hands on and is able to move, a storm blows up, and in the morning the ship has disap-peared from view. A few pages further on, however, Crusoe enumerates a number of things that he had "omitted setting down before," including pens, ink, and paper, three Bibles, some mathe-matical instruments, etc. "And I must not forget that we had in the ship a dog and two cats, of whose eminent history I may have occasion to say something in its place." It is of course entirely natural that Crusoe should temporarily forget some of the things he had saved from the wreck, and their mention a little later cer-tainly does no damage to the credibility of the narrative. But any-one familiar with Defoe's casual mode of composition will be tempted to see this late introduction of the dog and the two cats as an afterthought. At this point in his narrative he may well have said to himself, "This is my last chance of letting Crusoe save anything more from the wreck. What else would be inter-esting or useful for him to have?" Later on, the pens, ink, and pa-per, the faithful dog, the two cats (one of which proves highly fertile), and above all the Bibles, all play their part in Crusoe's story.[9]

It is often possible to look over Defoe's shoulder in this way as he writes, and to watch him correcting or modifying some statement that he has just made. Like Shakespeare, he seems never to have blotted a line, and the stream of his writing merely flowed round any obstacle in its way. Near the end of *Robinson Crusoe*, when the Spaniard whom Crusoe has saved from the cannibals along with Friday's father, plans to return to the mainland and rescue his fellow countrymen and bring them to the island, he wisely suggests that before he makes the attempt it would be ad-visable to grow enough barley and rice to feed them. Accordingly they all set to work,

and in about a month's time, by the end of which it was seed time, we had gotten as much land cur'd and trim'd up as we sowed 22 bushels of barley on and 16 jarrs of rice, which was, in short, all the seed we had to spare; nor indeed did we leave our selves barely sufficient for our own food for the six months that we had to expect our crop, that is to say, reckoning from the time we set our seed aside for sowing, for it is not to be supposed it is six months in the ground in the country.

As Defoe was writing this passage, it looks as if he may have been thinking of the six months it would take *in England* from the time of sowing to the ripening and harvesting of a crop of barley; and then, or some time later, he remembered that conditions were very different on the island. Instead of canceling the "six months," however, he preferred to offer the rather lame explanation that he was reckoning from "the time we set our seed aside for sowing." If anyone should argue that the "six months" is not a slip at all, and that if it is, it is Crusoe's, and therefore another example of Defoe's verisimilitude, I cannot prove that he is wrong; but I would suggest that on the balance of probability it is Defoe's mistake rather than Crusoe's. But here, of course, the autobiographical form in which he chose to tell his various stories gives him a complete answer to those critical readers who may detect anomalies or contradictions or repetitions or other defects of composition. None of his heroes or heroines is a professional writer, and some of them have had little or no formal education. What more natural, therefore, for a Crusoe or a Singleton to make mistakes when he has a pen in his hand? Their very mistakes and awkwardnesses are a kind of guarantee of their authenticity: Defoe can't lose.[10]

At all events, he almost certainly wrote his various narratives in much the same way as an adult tells a serial bedtime story to a child, making up most of it as he went along. Anyone who has ever told such a story has probably made some slips which are instantly pounced upon by the vigilant young listener, who would be the first to object that Crusoe couldn't possibly have taken his parrot with him on board the ship that rescued him since he had already said that he left it on the island and that "poor Poll may be alive there still, calling after *Poor Robin Crusoe* to this day." Defoe made many such slips. "I must beg my reader's indulgence," he wrote in his old age, "being the most immethodical writer imaginable. It is true I lay down a scheme, but fancy is so fertile I often start fresh hints, and cannot but pursue them." He had undoubtedly laid down a scheme for *Robinson Crusoe,* but it is equally evident that many of his best things came to him on the spur of the moment. All creative writing is a compromise between the foreseen and the fortuitous. If the novelist foresees everything, we may lose the casual and disorderly and spontaneous impression made by real life; if everything is fortuitous, we have nothing but a chronological and unrelated series of events.[11]

That said, it should be added that the first part of *Robinson Crusoe* shows many indications of having been more carefully planned than most of Defoe's fictitious narratives. One small but significant sign of this is the extent to which he anticipates later developments. In the passage about the dog and the two cats already quoted, it will be remembered that Crusoe adds, "of whose eminent history I may have occasion to say something in its place." They duly reappear, but perhaps the "may" indicates that at this stage in the composition of *Robinson Crusoe* Defoe was not sure what he would do about them, and was therefore making no promises. But there are many phrases like "of which in its place" or "as will be observed hereafter" which indicate that Defoe was thinking ahead, and not just drifting along as his fancy took him. It is true that there are numerous repetitions (some perhaps conscious, others unconscious), loose ends, and contradictory statements; but these are in effect trivial, and due, no doubt, to Defoe's writing at odd times or in haste, and failing to revise his manuscript before publication. All this is very unlike Flaubert or Henry James, but it is not very unlike Sir Walter Scott. Some idea of the speed at which Defoe wrote may be seen from the appearance of *The Farther Adventures of Robinson Crusoe* slightly less than four months after the publication of the first part. At the conclusion of *The Life and Strange Surprizing Adventures* Defoe had dangled the prospect of a sequel before his readers, and had even given a brief forecast of its contents; but it is unlikely that he had written any of it before the success of the first part encouraged him to proceed.[12]

A more important indication of the way in which the first part of *Robinson Crusoe* was planned is to be found in Defoe's careful treatment of the first days on the island. It was wise of him to equip his hero with some tools, but it was still wiser not to give him too many. One of the strongest impressions made upon the reader of *Robinson Crusoe* is the sense of difficulty and frustra-

tion encountered by Crusoe in his attempts to create order out
of disorder and comfort out of privation. What this unfortunate
castaway hasn't got therefore becomes as important as what he
has. He has, for example, no needles, pins, or thread; to Crusoe,
who has a puritanical horror of going naked, and who keeps his
breeches and stockings on when swimming out to the wreck, this
was to prove a serious deprivation. When his supply of clothing
wore out, he "made but a very sorry shift indeed" to construct
breeches and drawers; and when at a later stage he ran together
a suit of goatskin, it was "wretchedly made." More serious was his
lack of either a pick-axe or a shovel. For the first of these some
iron levers proved to be a practical substitute, but the shovel had
to be painfully constructed from the wood of a tree "which in
the Brasils they call the Iron Tree," hacked and trimmed into
shape with his axe. With this primitive implement Crusoe was
able to till the ground that later produced his crops of barley and
rice, harrowing the freshly-dug soil by dragging "a great heavy
bough of a tree over it." Nature duly played her part, but more
frustration was to follow: when the corn was in the blade, goats
and hares broke in and ate it, and Crusoe was forced to tie his
dog to a stake, "where he would stand and bark all night long."
He managed to drive off the goats, but most of what was saved
in the blade was devoured in the ear when clouds of birds de-
scended on it. All through such trials the reader shares in Crusoe's
anxieties and rejoices with him in his little triumphs. "This want
of tools," he tells us, "made every work I did go heavily." Yet
we watch him making do with what he has, solving one problem
after another, and constructing his own clumsy equivalents of
chairs, tables, baskets, etc. In this way he contrived to make some
earthenware pots after a period of trial and error during which
many fell in and others fell out. As the ex-proprietor of a brick
and tile factory Defoe could have given Crusoe some useful advice, but he is left to think things out for himself, and do the
best he can. He is, as Coleridge said,

the universal representative, the person for whom every reader could
substitute himself. . . . And in what he does, he arrives at no excellence;
he does not make basket work like Will Atkins; the carpentering,
tailoring, pottery, etc. are all just what will answer his purposes, and

those are confined to needs that all men have, and comforts that all men desire.[13]

Crusoe's successes are nicely balanced by his failures. When he is returning on his raft after his first visit to the wreck, he accidently runs it on to a shoal, and has to use all his strength for the next half hour to keep the cargo from sliding into the water (another memorable picture of frustration), until the rising tide floats the raft level again. On a later journey from the wreck he is less fortunate, and loads the raft so heavily that it oversets and tips the whole cargo into the sea. What is needed for this sort of writing is something that Defoe had in full measure, a talent for make-believe. The process is seen in its purest form in the games played by children when they act out an imaginary situation or series of events. How near Defoe often came to reviving the memories of childhood may be seen from the numerous occasions on which Crusoe contemplates his little kingdom with a sort of naive and playful delight:

> It would have made a stoick smile to have seen me and my little family sit down to dinner. There was My Majesty, the Prince and Lord of the whole island; I had the lives of all my subjects at my absolute command. I could hang, draw, give liberty, and take it away, and no rebels among all my subjects.
>
> Then to see how like a king I din'd too all alone, attended by my servants. Poll, as if he had been my favourite, was the only person permitted to talk to me. My dog, who was now grown very old and crazy, and had found no species to multiply his kind upon, sat always at my right hand, and two cats, one on one side of the table, and one on the other, expecting now and then a bit from my hand, as a mark of special favour.

Similarly, in the *Farther Adventures* Crusoe tells us that his island dominion had been divided up in his absence into three colonies, and that his old habitation under the hill was now "the capital city."[14]

Simple make-believe and empathy may account for much of what Defoe has to give us in *Robinson Crusoe,* but occasionally they are accompanied by a psychological insight that may surprise us. When, for example, Crusoe fells with infinite labor a huge cedar tree and sets to work to hack out of it a periagua big enough to have carried twenty-six men, he has no thought of how he is going to get it to the sea. When he does begin to be conscious of this problem, he still refuses to face it: "I put a stop to my own enquiries into it by this foolish answer which I gave myself, *Let's first make it, I'll warrant I'll find some way or other to get it along when 'tis done.*" This looks very unlike the careful and provident Crusoe that we have come to know; but his normal canniness has given way to the excitement of finding a means to leave the island, and with this *idée fixe* controlling his thoughts he can think of nothing else. "This was a most preposterous method," he admits; "but the eagerness of my fancy prevail'd, and to work I went." The ordinary process of make-believe has here been transformed by the perception of a creative writer who is interested, as Wordsworth was, in "the manner in which we associate ideas in a state of excitement."[15]

"I had never handled a tool in my life," Crusoe tells us, "and yet in time by labour, application, and contrivance, I found at last that I wanted nothing but I could have made it. . . . ." When Defoe was writing, the division of labor was already well advanced, and skills which were common even in the Elizabethan age had now become specialized, or had been supplanted by the machine. Even the earliest readers of *Robinson Crusoe*, therefore, were able to find pleasure in Crusoe's primitive carpentry, pottery, bread-making, basket-weaving, etc., with which the growing specialization of industry had begun to make them unfamiliar. If this was true of Defoe's contemporaries, it is still more so today. As Professor Ian Watt has said, the extent to which we have been deprived by economic specialization "is suggested by the way our civilisation has reintroduced some of the basic economic processes as therapeutic recreations: in gardening, home-weaving, pottery, camping, woodwork and keeping pets, we can all participate in the character-forming satisfactions which circumstances force on Defoe's hero. . . ."[16]

Ultimately, much of the power of *Robinson Crusoe* lies in its appeal to the permanent feelings and essential interests of the human race. In this story Defoe achieved a drastic simplification of society and social relationships, and by stripping life of its inessentials he got down to the roots of human experience. This return to the essential can hardly have been difficult for him: he was never far from it in his own life. He had none of the artificiality and little of the sophistication of the polite writers of the day; he habitually wrote plain English, called a rogue a rogue, and a whore a whore, and continually reduced moral and religious problems, political issues, and economic policies to the simplest terms. So much is this sharp dichotomy between good and bad, right and wrong, true and false inseparable from his normal way of thinking, that when, for example, Moll Flanders tells us her story she never pretends that the life she is living is anything but wrong, and the title-page informs us that she was "twelve year a whore" and "twelve year a thief." Defoe's black-and-white view of things undoubtedly leads at times to oversimplification (however effectively it enabled him to make his points as a controversialist), but in *Robinson Crusoe* it tends rather to clear the way for an uncomplicated vision of life lived on its simplest and most essential terms.

In some ways Defoe was the most unpoetical soul alive, and in all his stories we are conscious of the background of the counting-house, of profit and loss and periodical stock-taking. Yet in this famous story, in which he has succeeded in transporting us into a closed world of his own imagining, he comes nearer to being a poet than he had ever been before or would ever be again. It was the belief of Wordsworth that the passions and thoughts and feelings of the poet were essentially those of all men. And with what, he asked, are they connected?

Undoubtedly with our moral sentiments and animal sensations, and with the causes which excite these; with the operations of the elements, and the appearances of the visible universe; with storm and sunshine, with the revolution of the seasons, with cold and heat, with loss of friends and kindred, with injuries and resentments, gratitude and hope, with fear and sorrow. These, and the like, are the sensations and objects which the Poet describes, as they are the sensations of other men, and the objects which interest them.

There is little in this catalogue that we do not find in *Robinson Crusoe;* and as for "loss of friends and kindred, gratitude and hope, fear and sorrow," we find them on every other page. When, for example, Crusoe has suffered a change of heart as a result of his experiences on the island, and has learned to depend upon

God's providence, he looks back on the days of despair before the grace of God had entered his soul:

Before, as I walk'd about, either on my hunting, or for viewing the country, the anguish of my soul at my condition would break out upon me on a sudden, and my very heart would die within me, to think of the woods, the mountains, the desarts I was in, and how I was a prisoner lock'd up with the eternal bars and bolts of the ocean, in an uninhabited wilderness, without redemption. In the midst of the greatest composures of my mind this would break out upon me like a storm, and make me wring my hands, and weep like a child.

This moving passage (it might be described in Wordsworthian terms as one of emotion recollected in tranquillity) has the large simplicity of Bunyan, and may indeed owe something to the author of *The Pilgrim's Progress*. At all events, the general level of emotion is higher in *Robinson Crusoe* than in any other of Defoe's works of fiction; and to meet with any comparable expressions of feeling we must go to his *Appeal to Honour and Justice*, and to his private correspondence with Harley and others in hours of personal crisis and distress, i.e. to his autobiographical writings. In *Serious Reflections . . . of Robinson Crusoe* he hinted that the whole story was really an allegory of his own life; and however we may judge this claim, the impression remains that he is more deeply involved in the story of his shipwrecked mariner than in any other of his works of fiction. The frequent poignancy of feeling in *Robinson Crusoe*, and the intensity with which Defoe realizes the loneliness and anguish of his hero, are compatible with some kind of self-involvement on the part of the author in the vicissitudes and sufferings that he describes.[17]

As a story, *Robinson Crusoe* has the firm and satisfying structure of a man triumphing over difficulties, creating his own little cosmos out of what, if he had been merely idle and despondent, must have remained chaos. In most of Defoe's fiction the situation is that of the hero or heroine alone against the world, surviving by dint of perseverance and ingenuity and sheer native energy; but nowhere is that situation brought home to us more forcibly than in *Robinson Crusoe*. The hero has his moments of self-pity and even despair, but these have the effect of intensifying our awareness of his desperate plight. If all Defoe's heroes and heroines give the impression of being solitaries, even when they are

living in crowded cities, the physical isolation of Crusoe is for
many years complete, and, for all he can see, likely to be permanent. Some form of companionship is provided by the faithful
dog, the cats, the parrot, the goats, and later by the arrival of
Friday on the island. But although Friday provides him with a
human companion, and is more useful to Crusoe than his now
defunct dog was, he remains essentially a more versatile, articulate, and amusing dog, and Crusoe is still left alone to wrestle
with his own thoughts and problems. As Professor Watt notes,
his relations with Friday are egocentric: he "does not ask his
name, but gives him one"—in the same way in which one names
a pet animal. It is not until the arrival of the Spaniards that the
spell of loneliness is broken and Crusoe can resume his place in
human society which has been for so long in abeyance.[18]

This isolation of a human soul would normally provide the
conditions usually associated with tragedy. The story of Crusoe's
fight for survival certainly arouses both pity and fear, and in
his indomitable struggle with dangers and difficulties he comes
near at times to heroic stature. But Defoe avoids the tragic implications of Crusoe's position. Crusoe's very virtues perhaps in-
capacitate him for being a tragic hero. For one thing, his usual
response to the vicissitudes of fortune is not some grand gesture
or defiant utterance but immediate practical application. There
is something almost ant-like in his activity as he goes to and from
the wreck during his first two weeks on the island, carrying back
hatchets, Dutch cheeses, bottles of cordial waters, bags of nails,
fowling-pieces, and the rest. We expect action from a tragic
hero, but not this sort of action, at once so detailed, dispersed, and
miscellaneous: when the tragic hero strikes back it is normally
with one great blow of gathered strength that brings down the
pillars of the temple, and characteristically, too, he enables us to
realize his tragic situation by the eloquence and imaginative power
of speech. Defoe seems to be almost committed to avoiding such
moments of revelation. After his twelfth visit to the wreck Crusoe
experiences some difficulty in reaching the shore again, for a sudden storm has made the water rough. None the less, carrying
several razors, a pair of large scissors, some ten or a dozen knives
and forks, and about £36 of gold and silver coins, all wrapped up
in a piece of canvas, he swims back through the choppy seas:

... I was gotten home to my little tent, where I lay with all my wealth about me very secure. It blew very hard all that night, and in the morning when I look'd out, behold no more ship was to be seen. I was a little surpriz'd, but recover'd my self with this satisfactory reflection, *viz.* that I had lost no time, nor abated no dilligence to get every thing out of her that could be useful to me, and that indeed there was little left in her that I was able to bring away if I had had more time.

Behold, no more ship! It is just here that nine out of ten great writers would have chosen to make the reader feel the full impact of Crusoe's now complete isolation. As long as the wrecked ship was still there it was a link of sorts with civilization and with Crusoe's past; but now that it had disappeared, Crusoe had nothing to look upon but a waste of waters. Yet so far is Defoe from dwelling on the finality of this event that he seems to go out of his way to belittle it: Crusoe was "a little surprized." The practical reflection and self-congratulation that follow are typical of Crusoe, and no doubt of Defoe himself. To deny heroism to Crusoe, however, is perhaps to take too histrionic a view of the heroic. Crusoe has the heroism of London's wartime firemen and air-raid wardens digging in the rubble for survivors after an "incident," or of the blitzed shopkeeper "carrying on" as usual the next morning. This is the heroism of the practical and the imperturbable; it lives in an atmosphere, not of cloud-capped towers, but of unemotional comment and habitual understatement.[19]

Is *Robinson Crusoe* a simple story of adventure, or has it a deeper significance? In recent years critics have tended to concentrate attention on the character of Crusoe, and to interpret his story in accordance with his ruling passion. More especially, they have dwelt upon that "original sin" about which Crusoe himself expatriates at some length:

I have been in all my circumstances a *memento* to those who are touch'd with the general plague of mankind, whence, for ought I know, one half of their miseries flow; I mean that of not being satisfy'd with the station wherein God and nature has plac'd them; for not to look back upon my primitive condition, and the excellent advice of my father, the opposition to which was, as I may call it, my ORIGINAL SIN, my subsequent mistakes of the same kind had been the means of my coming into this miserable condition; for had then Providence, which so happily had seated me at the Brasils as a planter,

bless'd me with confin'd desires, and I could have been contented to
have gone on gradually, I might have been by this time (I mean, in
the time of my being in this island) one of the most considerable
planters in the Brasils.

To Professor Watt, Crusoe is a characteristic embodiment of economic individualism. "Profit," he assures us, "is Crusoe's only vocation," and "only money—fortune in its modern sense—is a
proper cause of deep feeling." Watt therefore claims that Crusoe's motive for disobeying the commands of his father and leaving home was to better his economic condition, and that the
argument between himself and his parents in the early pages of
the book is really a debate "not about filial duty or religion, but
about whether going or staying is likely to be the most advanta-
geous course materially: both sides accept the economic motive as
primary." We certainly cannot afford to ignore those passages
in which Crusoe attributes his misfortunes to an evil influence
that hurried him on to "the wild and indigested notion of raising
my fortune," and into "projects and undertakings beyond my
reach, such as are indeed often the ruine of the best heads in
business," and that drove him "to pursue a rash and immoderate
desire of rising faster than the nature of the thing permitted."
These are among the very errors and temptations that Defoe was
to enlarge upon in *The Complete English Tradesman,* and that
had proved fatal to him in his early years as a merchant. But
surely the emphasis here is not on the economic motive as such,
but on the willingness to gamble and seek for quick profits beyond
what "the nature of the thing permitted."[20]

Crusoe's father wished him to take up the law as a profession,
and if Crusoe had done so and had prospered he might have become a very wealthy man indeed. Professor Novak seems to come
nearer to the truth when he attributes Crusoe's failure to accept
his father's choice for him to his personal characteristics: "his
lack of economic prudence, his inability to follow a steady profession, his indifference to a calm bourgeois life, and his love
of travel." On the very first page Crusoe tells us that he could
"be satisfied with nothing but going to sea"; his inclination in
that direction was so strong that "there seem'd to be something
fatal in that propension of nature tending directly to the life of

misery which was to befal me." The modern reader may miss the true force of the word "fatal": Defoe almost certainly intended it to suggest that Crusoe's longing to go to sea was decreed by destiny, and therefore beyond his power to resist. Elsewhere Crusoe tells his father that his thoughts were "so entirely bent upon seeing the world" that he could never bring himself to settle down at home; and looking back on his highly favorable prospects as a planter in the Brasils, he reflects that all his miscarriages had come about "by my apparent obstinate adhering to my foolish inclination of wandring abroad and pursuing that inclination," when he might so easily have prospered by a "plain pursuit of those prospects and those measures of life which nature and providence concurred to present me with, and to make my duty." Back in England after his adventures, he married and settled down, but the old restlessness returned on the death of his wife: he was "inur'd to a wandring life," and "had a great mind to be upon the wing again." In the *Farther Adventures* he tells us again of his "native propensity to rambling" and of his inability to resist "the strong inclination I had to go abroad again, which hung about me like a chronical distemper." He even states expressly that his motives were *not* economic, "for I had no fortune to make, I had nothing to seek: if I had gain'd ten thousand pound, I had been no richer." His subsequent travels in the *Farther Adventures* were due to nothing but "a deep relapse into the wandring disposition, which, as I may say, being born in my very blood, soon recover'd its hold of me, and like the returns of a violent distemper, came on with an irresistible force upon me."[21]

Unless we are to say—and we have no right to say it—that Crusoe did not know himself, profit hardly seems to have been his "only vocation." Instead, we are presented with a man who was driven (like so many contemporary Englishmen whom Defoe either admired or was fascinated by) by a kind of compulsion (a "strong inclination") and a fever in the blood ("a chronical distemper," "a violent distemper") to wander footloose about the world. As if to leave no doubt about his restless desire to travel, Crusoe contrasts himself with his partner, the very pattern of the economic motive and of what a merchant ought to be, who would have been quite happy to go on trading on the same route, and "to have gone like a carrier's horse, always to the same inn, backward and forward, provided he could, as he call'd it, *find his account in it.*" Crusoe, on the other hand, was like a rambling boy who never wanted to see again what he had already seen. "My eye," he tells us, "which like that which Solomon speaks of, was *never satisfied with seeing,* was still more desirous of wand'ring and seeing." Here it seems to be reasonable to detect an auto-biographical element in *Robinson Crusoe:* if Defoe had seen a good deal less of the world than Crusoe, he was none the less an inveterate traveler. He may have made several visits to the con-tinent of Europe in his earlier years, and although the extent of his travels is not certainly known, they have been plausibly pieced together by Professor Moore. In his preface to *A Tour thro' the Whole Island of Great Britain* he claimed to have gathered his material in "seventeen very large circuits, or journeys" and "three general tours over almost the whole English part of the island," besides having "travell'd critically" over most of Scotland. Such tourism was quite exceptional in the early eighteenth century; and as for countries which he had been unable to visit in person, he was still an eager mental traveller, poring over atlases and maps and the accounts of voyagers gathered together by Hakluyt and Purchas, or written by such of his contemporaries as Dampier and Woodes Rogers. At all events, no one was better fitted than Defoe to understand Crusoe's wanderlust.[22]

The refusal of Crusoe to follow the "calling" laid down for him by his father has, as Professor Novak has suggested, religious implications. Those implications have been investigated in greater detail by Professor G. A. Starr, who has shown convincingly how the various stages in Crusoe's religious development—from orig-inal sin to spiritual hardening (during the eight years of "seafaring wickedness" when he conversed only with sinners like himself, "wicked and profane to the last degree") to a gradual repentance and ultimate conversion—follow closely the established pattern of seventeenth-century spiritual autobiography. Starr points out that the writers of those autobiographies show the same sort of concern as Crusoe with omens and portents, and with the appar-ently direct intervention of providence in the life of the indi-vidual; and that the imagery by which they seek to express their spiritual travails is often paralleled by the actual physical suffer-ings and vicissitudes of Crusoe. When all such evidence is taken into account (together with that offered by Professor J. Paul Hunter in a similar study), the religious element in *Robinson Crusoe* is seen as the common property of English Protestantism; and it is clear that otherworldly concerns do a great deal more than merely punctuate the narrative with what Professor Watt calls "comminatory codas." If Crusoe is not the Platonic pattern of a converted sinner, his life history is at least a progress from the careless self-indulgence of the natural man, without forethought or reflection, to a life of reason and introspection and ultimately of faith; and it is in this progress towards repentance and moral stability that Professor Starr finds the structural unity of *Robinson Crusoe*. Defoe's hero never shows the least signs of becoming a saint—he remains a man like ourselves—but he ceases to be a mere sinner.[23]

So much do we tend to think of *Robinson Crusoe* as a desert-island story that most readers probably forget that almost a quarter of the book is taken up with other matters—Crusoe's early voyages, his capture by the Sallee rover, his subsequent escape with his boy Xury, his rescue by the Portuguese merchantman, his life as a tobacco-planter in Brazil, and finally, when he leaves the island, his return to Europe and his journey across the Pyrenees in winter. The Pyrenees episodes, in which Friday demonstrates his unexpected expertise with a bear and in which the whole party is nearly devoured by ravenous wolves, have the sort of narrative interest that Defoe could always impart to adventures by land or sea, and enable him to give his readers another view of Friday, translated from his native tropics to "the severest winter all over Europe that had been known in the memory of man." But perhaps the real reason for this journey over the mountains in the depth of winter is that Defoe's publisher had told him he needed a few more pages to make up the volume; and Professor Moore is almost certainly right in his suggestion that the account of the wolves and the deep snow was based on a paragraph in *Mist's Weekly Journal*, no doubt written by Defoe himself, describing severe conditions in the Pyrenees the year before.[24]

That he had at least planned a sequel to *Robinson Crusoe* may be seen from the last pages of the book, where he gives a brief outline of his second visit to the island in 1694 and the developments that had taken place in his absence, concluding with a

promise that he might give an account of "all these things, with
some very surprizing incidents in some new adventures of my
own" in a future volume. This (with some divergences from the
original plan) he proceeded to do in *The Farther Adventures of
Robinson Crusoe.* More than half of this sequel is given to recording the troubled history of the island community since he had
left it eight and a half years before; the rest of the book recounts
his adventures on the way to the island, his subsequent wander-
ings to Brazil, Madagascar (where the sailors massacre the natives), and China, his profitable trading ventures, and then his
journey overland from Peking to Archangel, and ultimately by
land and sea to London, which he reaches on 10 January 1705. All
this makes for a very different sort of story. The extended
account of the no longer deserted island is given mainly in a third-
person narrative, for Crusoe is now dealing with events in which
he was not personally involved. Defoe was faced with a stylistic
problem here, and decided that the best method was to "collect
the facts historically":

I shall no longer trouble the story with a relation in the first person,
which will put me to the expence of ten thousand *said I's*, and *said
he's*, and *he told me's*, and *I told him's*, and the like; but I shall collect
the facts historically, as near as I can gather them out of my memory
from what they related to me, and from what I met with in my conversing with them, and with the place.

This was no doubt the right decision to make in view of the
extended account to which he was now committed; but we lose
the sense of intimacy that we had with Crusoe in the first part,
and we realize how much we were under the spell of the mariner
and his serious, measured narrative. With the sense of immediacy
we have also lost the powerful effect of Crusoe's solitude.[25]

All this was perhaps inevitable; but Defoe might have reconciled us better to the changed circumstances if he had made more
of the new situation on the island. What had been happening,
after all, was the birth of a new society—the sort of development
that Locke had envisaged in his *Two Treatises of Government,*
when men living in a primitive state band together to protect
their property and choose a king or leader. It is true that Defoe
describes some of the birth throes of a nation, notably the per-

sistent attempts of Will Atkins and his English comrades to over-throw the Spaniards and seize possession of the island, and the eventual reconciliation of the two European races when they are compelled to combine forces against the savages. Yet one is left with the feeling that an opportunity has been missed. Perhaps Defoe's Calvinistic attitude to human nature kept him from expecting very much of his voluntary islanders. When Crusoe came to consider them individually, he found that some were doing well, and others badly. "The diligent liv'd well and com-fortably, and the slothful liv'd hard and beggarly; and so I believe, generally speaking, it is all over the world." The latest information Crusoe received about his colonists was that "they went on but poorly, were male-content with their long stay there; that Will Atkins was dead; that five of the Spaniards were come away," and that the rest wanted to leave the island. This depressing upshot may be a proof of Defoe's sense of reality; but we are left won-dering why, with his great interest in schemes for English settle-ments, he went out of his way to show such a scheme failing miserably. It is true that the English colonists on Crusoe's island were of thoroughly unpromising stock, insubordinate, lazy, law-less, and without any sense of religion. (In one of his more acid comments Crusoe tells us that "they pretty often indeed put one another in mind that there was a God, by the very common method of seamen, viz. swearing by his name.") Little was to be expected of such men; but when in due course they became reformed characters and married their native mistresses, it might have been thought that now Defoe intended to show his settlers creating a prosperous and model commonwealth. But either he felt that "you can't make a silk purse out of a sow's ear," or he was himself skeptical about their change of heart. The conversion of Will Atkins in particular is inadequately motivated, and hap-pens much too suddenly. Nor does it apparently have any effect on later developments.[26]

A curious and interesting episode in the *Farther Adventures* concerns the French Roman Catholic priest who arrives with Crusoe on the island. Defoe goes out of his way to establish the religious sincerity and innate goodness of this man, who (Crusoe admits) had everything against him, "as first, that he was a Papist; secondly a popish priest; and thirdly, a French popish priest."

None the less, he was "a grave, sober, pious, and most religious person," who set a fine example in almost everything he did. There was clearly a Shavian streak in Defoe; he enjoyed shocking the beliefs and attitudes of the conventional, and indulging a love of what, to his good Protestant readers, could only seem to be paradox. As a member of the merchant class, accustomed to coming into contact with men of various nations, he would of course have learned to be more tolerant of religious differences than most of his fellow countrymen, and as a nonconformist he had had ample experience of intolerance. What he looked for among the religious, and rarely found, was charity; his criticism was frequently directed against ecclesiastical hierarchies, and against the professional clergy as a body. Crusoe had even found priestcraft amongst "the most blinded, ignorant pagans," and had met with the same determination to make a mystery of religion "in order to preserve the veneration of the people to the clergy." When he set about teaching Friday the rudiments of the Christian religion, he followed the principle of John Locke and taught him only the doctrine of salvation by Christ, "so plainly laid down in the word of God," which "the bare reading of the Scripture made me capable of understanding." To have perplexed Friday with doctrinal niceties would have been a waste of time or worse, even if Crusoe had been able to understand them himself.

As to all the disputes, wranglings, strife and contention which has happen'd in the world about religion, whether niceties in doctrines, or schemes of church government, they were all perfectly useless to us; as for ought I can yet see, they have been to all the rest of the world.[27]

For some of the fictionalized facts in the *Farther Adventures* Defoe drew again upon Dampier. For Crusoe's adventures in China he took material from Louis Le Comte's *Memoirs and Observations Made in a Late Journey through the Empire of China* (translated from the French in 1697, and several times reprinted); and for the long homeward journey from Peking he was heavily indebeted to E. Ysbrants Ides, *Three Years Travels from Moscow Overland to China*, which had been translated from the Dutch in 1706. In using Ides, Defoe of course reversed the direction of the journey from east to west. It should be remembered that by 1719 he had built up an extensive collection of travel literature, and without moving out of his library at Stoke Newington had all the facts he needed at his command.[28]

iii

The episodic form of the *Farther Adventures* was to be repeated by Defoe in a number of seafaring stories and biographies which he wrote over the next few years. (The dividing line between biography and fiction in this context is almost impossible to draw.) In December 1719 he published a 90-page pamphlet, *The King of the Pirates*, a fictitious or semi-fictitious account of a real pirate, Captain John Avery, "in two letters from himself." Defoe's constant endeavor to impart an air of authenticity to his fictitious narratives comes out in the Preface, where he contrasts the extravagant and incredible accounts of Avery hitherto available with this reliable account from the Captain himself. "There is always a great difference," he observes sagely, "between what men say of themselves, and what others say of them." As a general statement this is unexceptionable; but as a statement intended to justify the authenticity of the "two letters from himself" it leaves us where we were. Defoe reinforces his point, however, by offering several examples of the "romantic" and exaggerated statements made by earlier writers, who are now shown by Avery himself to be unreliable. In the end, his conscience appears to have pricked him slightly, for he half withdraws his claim to the authenticity of the letters, and concludes with his tongue in his cheek:

But this may be said without any arrogance, that this story, stripped of all the romantic, improbable, and impossible parts of it, looks more like the history of Captain Avery than anything yet published has done; and if it is not proved that the Captain wrote these letters himself, the publisher says none but the Captain will ever be able to amend them.

Since the Captain had disappeared from view many years before, there was little danger of his reappearing in 1719 to challenge the veracity of the letters attributed to him. *The King of the Pirates* anticipates at several points Defoe's next story of piratical adventure, *Captain Singleton*: Avery, like Singleton, tells us that he was resolved to make reparation to those persons he had wronged; and when he finally abandons the life of a pirate he makes his way (again like Singleton) from Basra to Bagdad. We actually meet him again in *Captain Singleton*, and in both stories the island of Madagascar is an important base for the action.[29]

The Life, Adventures, and Piracies of the Famous Captain Singleton appeared in the summer of 1720. Unlike Avery, the Captain Bob Singleton who tells us his story was a pure creation of Defoe's. The account of his life is given in two parts. In the first and shorter of these he recounts his adventures at sea as a young man, and describes how, after an abortive mutiny, he is set ashore on the coast of Madagascar along with five Portuguese sailors, to be joined shortly afterwards by twenty-three more who leave the ship at their own request. In due course they succeed in reaching the east coast of the African continent, and from there set out on a prolonged and hazardous journey across central Africa to the west coast, from which Singleton eventually returns to London, enriched by his share of the gold dust that he and his comrades have collected in Guinea. For the Madagascar adventures Defoe drew again upon Misson, but also made use of Mandelslo's "Voyages and Travels," from which he obtained some of his information about the natives and their customs. For the journey across Africa he had to rely for the most part on his own invention. Little was known of the dark continent in Defoe's day, but the map-makers had already recorded, or invented, lakes, rivers, and mountain ranges, and the journey of Singleton and his companions was based on existing knowledge, or belief, or hypothesis about the largely unexplored interior. Defoe, however, was still free to invent his own deserts, lakes, and rivers, and to bring his travelers from a region well grown with oaks, cedars, and fir trees to a wilderness that had "a kind of thick moss upon it, of a blackish dead colour." (In the whole long journey there is no mention of anything resembling jungle country.) In the same liberal spirit he was able to people the continent with a fauna half authentic and half fabulous: lions, tigers, elephants, a creature that "seemed to be an ill-gendered kind, between a tiger and a leopard," other creatures "that seemed to be between a kind of buffalo and a deer" (the wildebeest?), hares "of a kind something different from ours in England," and "an ugly, venemous, deformed kind of a snake or serpent in the wet grounds near the lake, that . . . would raise itself up, and hiss so loud that it might be heard a great way off." Such vaguely defined creatures as those last three seem to indicate that Defoe is walking warily in unknown territory. Among the phenomena to which he recurs again and again for the delight of his wondering and simple-minded readers is the nudity of the savage tribes, an un-European state of affairs which was often recorded by the English voyagers ("some naked women ran and fetched us great quantities of roots"; "They were all stark naked as they came into the world"; "most of them, of both sexes, stark naked"). This nudity theme reaches its climax when Singleton and his companions come upon a naked Englishman—"a gentleman, not an ordinary-bred fellow, seaman, or labouring man."Another simple appeal of a less sensational kind comes from the constant barter with the natives of worthless trinkets in exchange for cattle and other kinds of food, a circumstance to which Defoe was to return in *A New Voyage round the World,* and which he had found in Dampier and some of his other sources. Natives, hostile and friendly, keep appearing fairly frequently on Singleton's trans-African journey, and considering the fact that none of the Europeans knows a word of any language they speak, the degree to which successful communication takes place is frankly incredible. In *Captain Singleton,* as in *Robinson Crusoe,* apparently elaborate conversations are carried on by a sort of sign-language. Defoe can be very off-hand about this, but he counts on the willing cooperation of his readers, who can be trusted to enjoy the miming and not to worry about the limited possibilities of such communication.[30]

In all Defoe's stories it is his common practice when he has exhausted one episode or series of adventures to make a very perfunctory, not to say abrupt, transition to the next. It takes only half a page for Singleton to tell us that in London he fell into bad company, squandered most of his money, and was cheated out of the rest. His good-time friends soon let him know that "as my money declin'd, their respect would ebb with it, and that I had nothing to expect of them farther than as I might command it by the force of my money." All Defoe's heroes and heroines live in a tough world in which it is a case of *pecuniae obediunt omnes*: poverty—"necessity"—is nearly always dogging their footsteps; they have few illusions, and most of their time and energy is devoted to the business of survival. Stranded in London without money or a means of livelihood, Singleton ships himself on a voyage to Cadiz, and before long has become the leader of a band of pirates. The rest of his story is concerned with his piratical expeditions in many parts of the world (at one time in company with Captain Avery); but there are several stories inset, such as that of the thirteen Englishmen who had reached Japan by way of the north-west passage, and the account of Robert Knox's captivity in Ceylon.[31]

The interest of such a book depends largely on what happens next; on dangerous situations, difficulties overcome, escapes, surprises, and discoveries, and, no doubt, on the steady accumulation of loot which ultimately makes Singleton a very wealthy man. As Singleton is not only the hero but the narrator, we have at least an intellectual interest in his progress, but he never becomes interesting as a man. No doubt, as a single-minded pirate, he is not the sort of person who can easily become endearing, although he makes some bid for our sympathy by being against unnecessary cruelty. But Defoe has succeeded in humanizing what would otherwise be a mere sequence of rough and callous actions by the introduction of the Quaker William. This unexpected character is a casuist of the first order, a rogue with a dry humor whose moral sensitivity is active in certain areas, but completely anesthetized in others. As a Quaker, William refuses to take any part in shedding blood, but he has no scruples about being the friend and companion of pirates who do, and is on most occasions the willing accomplice of Singleton and his crew. Characteristically, however, he asks for a certificate from Singleton that he has been taken aboard by force as a prisoner, and Singleton (who has already sized him up) goes through the pantomime of having him pinioned and dragged aboard the frigate, and draws up and signs the certificate. William, who is an educated man and the real brains of the whole party, does most of the planning for each enterprise, but maintains a tone of admirable gravity and moral rectitude. He has the detachment of a man who believes that if something is to be done it had better be done the right way. What in other writers might have been a harsh and satirical portrait of hypocrisy is in Defoe a comic creation of undeniable attractiveness. Defoe was a puritan, but a highly atypical one, who is always apt to surprise us with his moments of moral non-involvement and of pure creative sympathy.[32]

In comparison with most of his other stories *Captain Singleton* is in fact surprisingly free from moral comment; the reader tends to lose all sense of right and wrong, and simply to follow Singleton from one piratical success to the next. Defoe appears to have conceived his hero as a natural leader of men, but essentially uneducated, and therefore incapable of much discrimination. Singleton was, as he tells us himself, "a kind of charity school-boy," and he took to piracy as Colonel Jack says *he* took to picking pockets—naturally and unreflectively, and with no "reproaches upon [his] mind for having done amiss." As a young man, Singleton had been impressed by the gunner's warning that "to be ignorant was to be certain of a mean station in the world"; but although he resolved to make up for his lost education when he returned to England, he had done little or nothing about it. In his complete lack of formal education beyond the primary stage he differs from Crusoe, Moll Flanders, and Roxana, and from Colonel Jack in his later years; and he is touchingly dependent on the one educated man he knows, the incorrigible Will. It could therefore be said that for the greater part of his career Singleton is hardly a moral agent at all. When, near the end of his story, he has something like a change of heart, his repentance for his past life is neither convinced nor convincing. He steals away from his crew with a lion's share of the accumulated booty, and although he tells us several times that he has no real pleasure in the possession of his ill-gotten wealth, he shows little disposition to disgorge any of it. When his conscience is troubling him on one occasion, William is at hand to allay his qualms:

To quit what we have, and do it here, is to throw it away to those who have no claim to it, and to divest our selves of it, but to do no right with it; whereas we ought to keep it carefully together, with a resolution to do what right with it we are able; and who knows what opportunity Providence may put into our hands to do justice at least to some of those we have injured?

William's advice that they should go on to some place of safety where they might await God's will is "very satisfying" to Singleton, although he continues for some time in a troubled state of mind. It is true that he sends a present of £5,000 to Will's widowed sister in England, but even this charitable act is accompanied by what almost amounts to an apology for his quixotic behavior ("You may think, perhaps, that I was very prodigal of my ill-gotten goods, thus to load a stranger with my bounty, and give a gift like a prince to one that had been able to merit nothing of me, or indeed know me . . .").[33]

A few pages earlier, however, this good woman has been the occasion for one of the most touching episodes in all of Defoe's fiction. When Singleton and Will, now men of immense wealth, are living together incognito in Venice, Will writes to his sister in London, and about five weeks later he has a reply from her:

> It was a very moving letter he receiv'd from his sister, who after the most passionate expressions of joy to hear that he was alive, seeing she had long ago had an account that he was murthered by the pirates in the West Indies, she intreats him to let her know what circumstances he was in; tells him she was not in any capacity to do anything considerable for him, but that he should be welcome to her with all her heart; that she was left a widow with four children, but kept a little shop in the Minories, by which she made shift to maintain her family; and that she sent him five pound, lest he should want money in a strange country to bring him home.
>
> I could see the letter brought tears out of his eyes as he read it, and indeed when he shewed it me, and the little bill for five pounds upon an English merchant in Venice, it brought tears out of my eyes too.

Coming where it does, almost at the end of a story in which goodness and kindness and gentleness have been at a minimum, this sudden revelation of natural human feeling is extraordinarily effective. It is perhaps characteristic of Defoe that the situation he describes so well has something to do with money; and it is a splendid irony that *this* money has been sent to a brother who is immensely rich by a widow who is hard put to make ends meet. In such moving passages as this Defoe often has at the back of his mind some phrase or event in the sacred story, and on this occasion he may well be recalling the poor widow who threw her two mites into the treasury, and of whom Christ said that "she of her want did cast in all that she had, even all her living." It is also characteristic of Defoe that, as on many other occasions (e.g. the footprint in the sand in *Robinson Crusoe*), the effect depends upon a visual image—"the little bill for five pounds upon an English merchant in Venice."[34]

It is easier to believe Singleton's assurance that the widow's letter and its pathetic enclosure brought tears to his eyes than to believe in his penitence when he ceases to be a pirate. How are we to account for his apparently uncharacteristic behavior? Quite simply, it looks as if Defoe had decided that his story was to have a happy ending, and therefore some form of repentance was necessary. To have Singleton return to England, be recognized, arrested, and hanged at Tyburn would have made a more natural conclusion to the life he had been leading; but apart from the fact that in those circumstances he could hardly have told us his own story, such an ending would have cheated the expectations of Defoe's readers. Singleton's career had been one of almost unbroken success; and to let it all end in final disaster—however much that might have reinforced the moral lesson—would have destroyed the buoyant effect of what had gone before. Nor, apparently, could Defoe bring himself to contemplate Singleton giving his vast fortune away, either because such an action would have been untrue to his pirate's acquisitive character, or because it would have been difficult to accomplish without betraying his identity, or perhaps because the author himself took a dream-like pleasure in contemplating the accumulation of wealth and was reluctant to think of it being dissipated. So Singleton keeps hold of his treasure, and there is just enough talk of repentance to allow Defoe to bring his hero back to England incognito, where he may safely settle down and marry William's sister. This last event is given to us at the end of a long sentence in the penultimate paragraph of the book. It is a characteristically huddled conclusion to a book that had to be brought to an end. From first to last *Captain Singleton* is an adventure story, and little else.

In writing his tales of pirates and adventures on the high seas Defoe was not so much creating a new taste as satisfying a literary appetite that already existed. Exquemelin's *Buccaniers of America*, translated from the Dutch in 1684, had been a highly popular book. William Dampier's *New Voyage round the World* (1697) was in its fourth edition before the end of the century, and Robert Knox's *Historical Relation of the Island of Ceylon* (1681) was reprinted in 1705 in one of several popular collections of voyages published in the early eighteenth century. England had been a great naval power since the days of Queen Elizabeth at least, and the Dutch wars of the seventeenth century, and more recently the Thirty Years War, had accustomed Englishmen to follow the exploits of their seamen with the deepest interest, and often (although not always) with pride and admiration. These exploits were often barely distinguishable from acts of piracy; but in war-time, if the captain of a ship had been granted letters of marque, they had official sanction, and even without that sanction they were likely to be accorded patriotic approval. When Defoe gave the public what it wanted, this was almost always something that he also wanted himself. With his life-long interest in trade and commerce went a corresponding interest in the ships that carried the merchandise and the sailors who manned them; and as one who had sustained serious losses through the capture of ships in which he had an interest, he had a feeling of involvement in the risks run by merchant vessels in war-time, or in the more perma-nent risks they faced from the depredations of pirates. When he no longer had any personal stake in the danger from "land-rats and water-rats" or "the peril of waters, winds, and rocks," he still retained his interest in adventures and misadventures at sea. Indeed, the subject appears to have fascinated him more and more as he grew older, and he continued to write about pirates and buccaneers almost to the end of his life.

When he wrote about pirates, as in *An Account of the Conduct and Proceedings of the late John Gow* (1725), he almost in-variably mixed some fiction with his facts. Sometimes an account which appears to be solidly based on fact may be entirely ficti-tious. In *The Four Years Voyages of Capt. George Roberts* (1726), which is said to be "written by himself," he tells the story of a seaman who was set adrift along with a boy and a child on one of the Cape Verde islands, where he remained for two years until he "built a vessel to bring himself off," and in due course returned to England in the summer of 1725. Roberts has his own modest entry in the *Dictionary of National Biography* (based on this 458-page account "written by himself"), but Professor Moore believes him to be another of Defoe's fictitious characters, and his Crusoe-like adventures the fabrication of Defoe. Other schol-ars, while not questioning that Defoe had some hand in the work, have preferred to believe that it must have been based on the journal or the spoken account of an actual Captain Roberts—of whom nothing else, however, appears to be known. Professor Moore perhaps dismisses too lightly the postscript at the end of the book, which he thinks can have had no real value in substantiating the narrative:

N.B. *The little boy so often mention'd in the foregoing sheets now lives with Mr. Galapin, a tobacconist, in Monument Yard, and may be referred to for the truth of most of the particulars before related.*

This little boy was either to be seen or not to be seen at the shop of Mr. Galapin the tobacconist. If he was not there, the interested inquirer would want to know why not; if he was there, and could be questioned, it would not have been difficult for any intelligent lawyer to walk round to Monument Yard from the Inns of Court and find out by examining the boy if he had ever been anywhere near the Cape Verde islands. Defoe took risks in his constant practice of authenticating the fictitious; but would he have taken this risk?[35]

A similar problem confronts us with *Madagascar: Or, Robert Drury's Journal, during Fifteen Years Captivity on That Island.* For about a century and a half after its publication this work was believed to be an authentic narrative, and was frequently cited as such by historians of Madagascar; but towards the end of the nineteenth century various scholars began to suspect that Defoe had a hand in the composition, and by 1939 Professor Moore claimed that it was almost wholly his work. So far from his being the writer of an authoritative account of Madagascar, the very existence of Robert Drury was now suspect. When the work was first published in 1729 it was stated in the preface that "the original was wrote by Robert Drury," but at such length that "the transcriber" had to contract it, and "put it in a more agreeable method." This transcriber admitted that he was responsible for adding some reflections on religion and on the origin of government, but insisted that he had not altered any of Drury's facts or introduced any fiction of his own. At the close of the work, to substantiate its authenticity, there appeared a statement signed by Drury which bears some resemblance to the statement at the end of *The Four Years Voyages*:

I am every day to be spoken with at Old Tom's Coffee-house in Birchin Lane, where I shall be ready to gratify any gentleman with a further account of anything herein contained, to stand the strictest examination, or to confirm those things which to some may seem doubtful.[36]

What are we to make of this? The patient researches of Professor Secord have not merely confirmed the existence of Robert Drury, but have shown that a considerable number of the statements he made about himself and about others (or that were made for him) can be verified from contemporary documents. There seems to be no longer any reason to doubt that many of the facts in *Robert Drury's Journal* were supplied by Drury himself, although whether he had written down those facts in the form of a journal, or merely communicated them orally to the "transcriber," is an open question. That the transcriber was Defoe, few, if any, would nowadays seek to deny: the point at issue is whether he was, as Secord believed, no more than the editor of Drury's manuscript, or whether, as Moore has argued, he was the virtual author. The answer is still to be found; but *Robert Drury's Journal* may contain less of Defoe than Moore believes it does, and more of him than Secord was prepared to admit.[37]

The great interest shown by English readers of the 1720s in the careers of pirates was reflected in the popularity of *A General History of the Robberies and Murders of the Most Notorious Pyrates . . . By Captain Charles Johnson* (2 vols., 1724, 1728). Like Captain Roberts, Captain Charles Johnson has his place in the *Dictionary of National Biography*, but nothing whatever is known about his life, and it would appear that he is another of those ghost authors who occasionally find their way into biographical dictionaries. Some thirty years ago, after making a detailed critical examination of *The History of the Pyrates*, Professor Moore advanced the claim that Captain Johnson was no other than Daniel Defoe, and this attribution is now generally accepted. The two Johnson volumes were for long looked upon as the main source of information about English pirates in the late seventeenth and early eighteenth centuries. Some sort of authority Captain Johnson may still be, for where his statements can be checked they usually prove to be true: Moore has shown that some of the facts come from Dampier and Woodes Rogers and from printed accounts of the trials of pirates, and he suggests that Defoe may also have obtained information from Thomas Bowrey, John Atkins the naval surgeon, and others. But often Defoe's facts cannot be checked for the simple reason that a number of his pirates are no more real persons than are Crusoe and Singleton, and even when he is dealing with actual pirates he records conversations and speeches which are clearly fictitious. By 1724, indeed, he had become so accustomed to living in a twilight world between fact and fiction that the two mingle imperceptibly in his mind. To some extent he may have become the victim of his own narrative technique. Early in the nineteenth century a writer in the *Gentleman's Magazine* defended the authenticity of *Robert Drury's Journal* by claiming that it had "all that simplicity and verbiage . . . expected in narratives of the illiterate, but none of the artifices of fiction." But by 1729 Defoe was expert at imitating the simplicity and verbiage of illiterate narrators. Much earlier than that, a hostile journalist had made a sneering reference to "the little art he is truly master of, of forging a story, and imposing it on the world for truth." When a man has some outstanding skill he seeks opportunities to use it, and in time perhaps he comes to use it almost unconsciously. At all events it is a remarkable tribute to Defoe's technique in "forging a story" that the true identity of Captain Charles Johnson should have remained unsuspected for almost two hundred years.[38]

In 1724, still working the same vein, Defoe published *A New Voyage round the World*. Why he should have chosen to give this story the identical title of Dampier's first book (1697) is difficult to determine, even though the title-page carried the additional words, "By a Course never sailed before." In this *roman à thèse*, as it has been called, Defoe was doing several different things. A ship chartered by some English merchants sets out on 2 January 1714, with a French captain and a partly French crew, on a trading voyage which is also to be a voyage of exploration. The war with France and Spain had been brought to an end some months earlier by the Peace of Utrecht, but if a Spanish ship was met with, the intention was to attack it, for then "we were English cruisers, had letters of mart from England," and "had no account of the peace." The reason for having a French captain and some French seamen was that the French were allowed to trade with the Spanish possessions in South America and else-where, and "when on the coast of New Spain we sought to trade, we were French men." Since those activities might "be liable to some exceptions, and perhaps to some inquiries," the narrator thinks it best for the present to conceal his name, and that of the ship.[39]

The voyage proceeds more or less as planned. The respectable trading vessel becomes a pirate when occasion offers, having 46 guns mounted and a crew of 356 men; and diversity is given to the voyage by a mutiny on board ship, by an encounter with some treacherous natives of Ceylon, by the discovery of non-existent islands, where the usual bartering of baubles and trinkets for gold takes place and the sailors spend several days finding valuable pearls in oysters, and by a good deal else. At the beginning of his account the narrator had criticized those earlier navigators whose published reports contained little more than facts about sandbars and creeks and the depth of channels, and what latitude the ship was in, and how hard the wind blew. We have very few descrip-tions, he complains, of "their landings, their diversions, the acci-dents which happen'd to them, or to others by their means; the stories of their engagements, when they had any scuffle either with natives or European enemies, . . . the storms and difficulties at sea or on shore." All these the narrator supplies in *A New Voyage round the World*, which, to this extent, is only another tale of trading and adventure.[40]

Defoe, however, had two much more serious reasons for writing this book: he wished to offer a new method for trading with the Spaniards in South America, and he wanted to outline a scheme that had long been in his mind for settling two new Eng-lish colonies. His trading innovation was to steer a course east to the Philippines, where the ship, flying the French flag, came to anchor off Manila. Here permission was sought to trade with the local merchants, but the request was met with a polite refusal. The following day, however, the French captain sent the Gov-ernor a handsome present, and after some further exchange of courtesies he was given to understand that although the Governor could not permit an open and avowed trade he would wink at some exchange of goods, provided it was carried on in secret. As a result the English ship disposed of its entire cargo at an immense profit in exchange for silks, China ware, nutmegs and cloves, and even diamonds, and sailed away to the west coast of South America to repeat the same clandestine and profitable process with the Spanish merchants there. The moral of those underhand activities for Defoe was that with merchants the world over, trade and profit come first: laws were laws, no doubt, and they could not be openly flouted, but every man loves a bargain, and a little quiet smuggling does no one any harm. Robinson Crusoe certainly thought so, for, as Professor Moore reminds us, he met with his final shipwreck "in an illegal expedition to the Guinea coast to bring slaves to the Brazilian planters, so as to avoid the high prices charged by the licensed Portuguese slave-traders." Similarly, Colonel Jack was not above carrying on some clandestine free trade with the Spanish merchants at Havana.[41]

Trade, then, could proceed profitably even in places where it was prohibited, always provided you went about it in the right way. But Defoe's main purpose in writing *A New Voyage* was to realize in imagination a dream that had haunted him for many years. About a quarter of a century earlier he had submitted a plan to King William for the planting of two English colonies in Patagonia and the southern part of Chile, where the Spaniards were very thin on the ground. In July 1711, after the formation of the South Sea Company, he had forwarded the same scheme to Robert Harley. Chile, he explained, was admirably suited for an English colony, having "a climate so tempered both for the constitution of English bodies and the production of the necessary fruits of life, . . . especially in the southern parts"; it had a great deal of gold, exceeding what could be found on the Guinea coast of Africa, and since the natives hated the Spaniards they could easily be won over. The best place for a capital city would be Valdivia, which has an excellent harbor. To supply this colony it would be advisable to plant another on the southeast coast between the Rio de la Plata and the Straits of Magellan. The territory of Patagonia was especially good cattle country, and was also very suitable for growing corn, "being a plain country covered well with good grass, vast downs and valleys for feeding, and rich marly ground for plowing"; and ships coming from England could provision there before going on the long voyage round the Straits of Magellan to Chile. But communication between the two colonies could also be effected overland across the Andes, the distance being about 360 miles, as opposed to nearly 2,000 miles by sea. Harley duly filed Defoe's memorandum, but did nothing about it; and now in 1724, only a few months after Harley's death, Defoe gave to the whole world what had begun as a secret draft to King William, which might well have been implemented if the King had lived a little longer. In *A New Voyage round the World* he followed almost exactly his original proposal, and he sought to demonstrate the practicability of his overland route between the two colonies by setting ashore a party of fifty men, who succeeded in crossing the Andes and making their way to the coast, where the ship was waiting to pick them up.[42]

The *New Voyage* has many of the features of Defoe's other adventure stories: the same autobiographical and episodic narrative (although there are more signs of planning than is usual with him); the same dwelling on detail and fact, and the facts given an air of complete authenticity. Defoe's methods of convincing his reader that the story is true from start to finish are remarkably various. Much of this authentication in his autobiographical narratives takes the obvious form of "I remember" and "I saw," but he can often do better than that. In *A New Voyage*, when the ship puts in at the island of Juan Fernandez, and the surgeons set some of the men to gather medicinal herbs, Defoe tries a new gimmick. "They gave me the names of them," the narrator tells us, "and 'tis the only discovery in all my travels which I have not reserv'd so carefully as to publish for the advantage of others, and which I regret the omission of very much." Presumably Defoe's sources were silent about medicinal herbs on Juan Fernandez, and as this island was by no means *terra incognita* he did not feel free to be more specific about a flora whose existence could be checked. But it is characteristic of him that he should turn his ignorance to advantage by making his narrator assure the reader that apart from this one little lapse all the other observations recorded were carefully documented.[43]

One reader of *A New Voyage* has found it to be "remarkably well written." Leaving aside the implication that some of Defoe's other stories are not well written, this seems to be a tribute, not to Defoe's ability on at least one occasion to write good English, but to his ability to suit the style to the narrator, and to the occasion.

The narrator here is an educated man, who naturally tells his story in a more "correct" and less colloquial way than, say, Moll Flanders. But the occasion, too, affects the style of writing; for in *A New Voyage,* as we have seen, Defoe is putting forward serious suggestions for trading and for settling new colonies, and he hopes to attract more thoughtful readers than those who would enjoy *Captain Singleton* or any other tale of mere adventure. He therefore writes here in much the same style as he used to write to Robert Harley; without pomp and circumstance, but with rather more than his normal care to shape his sentences, and with a less colloquial and more educated vocabulary.[44]

iv

Defoe's stories of shipwrecked mariners, pirates, explorers, and merchant venturers account for about half the fiction he wrote between 1719 and 1728. But during those years he also wrote autobiographical narratives of several other kinds. In 1720, only a few days before the appearance of *Captain Singleton,* a group of publishers brought out another full-sized volume by Defoe which has some claims to be considered as the first historical novel in English: *Memoirs of a Cavalier: or A Military Journal of the Wars in Germany, and the Wars in England.* The Cavalier's memoirs, covering the years from 1632 to 1648, were said on the title-page to have been "written threescore years ago by an English gentle-man." With his usual willingness to make his readers believe that what he was offering them was not fiction but authentic historical fact, Defoe gave his book careful, if intentionally vague, documentation. The manuscript, we are told in the Preface, was found "by great accident" among the papers of one of King William's secretaries of state; and although "no small labour" had been expended in trying to discover the name of the author, the only clue to his identity was contained in a memorandum found with the manuscript:

Memorandum.—I found this manuscript among my father's writings, and I understand that he got them as plunder at, or after, the fight at Worcester, where he served as major of ——'s regiment of horse on the side of the parliament.

I.K.

The Battle of Worcester was fought in August 1651, when presumably the Cavalier had again taken up arms on the side of the royalists during Charles II's abortive attempt to recover the throne of England. If it may seem odd that the Cavalier should be carrying his memoirs around with him in the middle of a military campaign, it is still odder to find that the last few pages contain several references to events which took place after the date on which the manuscript was said to have been captured, notably the restoration of Charles II in 1660. Defoe's left hand did not always know what his right hand was doing. His meticulous attempt to authenticate the *Memoirs* coupled with this elementary carelessness about dates is so strange that one might be tempted to suppose the discrepancy was not due to carelessness at all, but that Defoe's conscience was troubling him and that he had decided to present his readers with the necessary means of realizing that the *Memoirs* were actually fictitious. Yet this supposition would be more convincing if there were not so many other such discrepancies scattered about his fiction which can be due to nothing but rapid and careless writing and the failure to revise what he had written.[45]

At all events Defoe's ruse appears to have succeeded with early readers of the *Memoirs*. About the middle of the eighteenth century his cavalier was confidently identified with a Shropshire gentleman, Andrew Newport, whose father became the first Baron Newport in 1642. Professor Secord, who has made the most detailed study of the sources of *Memoirs of a Cavalier*, believed that Defoe undoubtedly had the Newport family in mind, but noted that Andrew Newport was born in 1623, and was therefore too young to have taken part in the campaigns of Gustavus Adolphus, when he would have been not yet ten years of age. But, as he went on to point out, Defoe almost certainly found in Clarendon's *History of the Rebellion* the account of a gentleman "of very good extraction . . . who lived within four or five miles of Shrewsbury," and who presented Charles I with £6,000 and was made a baron, and on those facts based the Cavalier's statements about his birth and family. From that point on, Defoe could proceed with his usual technique of authenticating the narrative by making the events personal to the narrator. In this way the Cavalier tells us that he can give a more particular description of the crossing of the River Lech than is to be found in other accounts, "having been an eye-witness to every part of it"; and in almost identical words he vouches for the truth of what he has to tell us about the storming of Leicester during the Civil War. So, too, when the parliamentary forces took Shrewsbury by surprise he had "a particular loss in this action; for all the men and horses my father had got together for the recruiting my regiment were lost and dispersed."[46]

So apparently authentic is the Cavalier's narrative of his military adventures in the service of Gustavus Adolphus that some of his modern biographers have clung to the belief that it must be based on an actual manuscript or manuscripts. Even Professor Moore, who is usually well aware of Defoe's imaginative manipulation of printed sources, has suggested that for the earlier part of the narrative he "could make full use of the manuscripts he mentioned many times, some of which must have been written by the Scottish soldiers of Gustavus." Perhaps he did have access to some manuscript material. Perhaps, too, he picked up some of his information from sources similar to those of Colonel Jack, who tells us that he was "always upon the inquiry" when he was a boy:

I lov'd to talk with seamen and soldiers about the war, and about the great sea-fights, or battles on shore, that any of them had been in; and as I never forgot any thing they told me, I could soon, that is to say in a few years, give almost as good an account of the Dutch War, and of the fights at sea, the battles in Flanders, the taking of Maestricht, and the like, as any of those that had been there, and this made those old soldiers and tars love to talk with me too, and to tell me all the stories they could think of, and that not only of the wars then going on, but also of the wars in Oliver's time, the death of King Charles I, and the like.

It is just possible that in this passage Defoe was recalling his own childhood in London; he was certainly "always upon the inquiry," and he was the sort of man who "never forgot any thing they told me." But we would do well to remember a claim Defoe made in 1700 to have read "all the histories of Europe that are extant in our language, and some in other languages"; and it is unlikely that he did not keep this sort of reading up to date in later years. At all events, Secord was convinced that the *Memoirs of a*

Cavalier is "essentially a compilation based on previously printed biographies, memoirs, and histories," with Du Fossé's *Memoirs of the Sieur de Pontis* (1676; trans. 1694) as a possible literary model. For the Cavalier's brief campaign with the French in Savoy Defoe used Jean Le Clerc's *Life of Richelieu* in the English translation of Tom Brown (1695); and for his adventures under Gustavus Adolphus his authority throughout was the semi-annual publication of Nathaniel Butter, *The Swedish Intelligencer* (1632–3). Sometimes Defoe ascribed to his hero a part in some action which was in fact played by a historical character; and at other times he fabricated some vivid circumstance of his own to add detail to the historical events his cavalier was describing. Secord's most interesting example of this fictional development is to be found in the account of how the soldiers of Gustavus crossed the River Lech on a makeshift bridge of planks, and launched their attack on Tilly's army. At this point the Cavalier tells us that Gustavus had first of all to learn the depth of the river, and offered fifty dollars to anyone who could give him the necessary information. A sergeant of dragoons disguises himself as a ploughman, and carrying a long pole in his hand "comes boldly down to the bank of the river, and calling to the sentinels which Tilly had placed on the other bank . . . pretended he wanted to come to them." Having reached the point where Gustavus was hoping to construct the bridge, the dragoon

stands parlying with them a great while, and sometimes pretending to wade over, he puts his long pole into the water, then finding it pretty shallow he pulls off his hose and goes in, still thrusting his pole in before him, till being gotten up to his middle, he could reach beyond him, where it was too deep, and so shaking his head comes back again. The soldiers on the other side laughing at him, asked him if he could swim. He said, "No." "Why, you fool you," says one of the sentinels, "the channel of the river is 20 foot deep." "How do you know that?" says the dragoon. "Why, our engineer," says he, "measured it yesterday."

If Defoe had a source for this lively episode it was not the account of the engagement given in *The Swedish Intelligencer*, which has nothing to say about a dragoon-ploughman; and unless he was using some unknown manuscript source he seems to have been drawing upon his own invention. (The sentinel's phrase, "Why, you fool you," may be found several times in dialogue passages by Defoe, but I cannot recall meeting with it anywhere else.) Secord was able, however, to suggest a possible source in an earlier passage in the *Intelligencer* where Gustavus gives a sergeant a hundred dollars for going forward to reconnoitre the enemy lines. For the Cavalier's account of the Civil War and the various actions he claims to have taken part in, Defoe appears to have relied almost exclusively on Clarendon's *History of the Rebellion,* Bulstrode Whitelocke's *Memorials of the English Affairs,* and Edmund Ludlow's *Memoirs,* all three published long after "the fight at Worcester," and well-known to English readers in 1720. Defoe moves easily from one source to another, and it is a tribute to his remarkable power of assimilating and refashioning his material that the extent of his borrowings should have remained for so long unsuspected. In view of his almost complete dependence on Clarendon and his other printed sources it is ironical to find him stating in the Preface that there is no need to doubt the authenticity of the *Memoirs of a Cavalier*, since "the actions here mentioned have a sufficient sanction from all the histories of the times to which they relate." But when he goes on to claim for his Cavalier that "many accounts recorded in his story are not to be found even in the best histories of those times," and that "this work is a confutation of many errors in all the writers upon the subject of our wars in England, and even in that extraordinary history written by the Earl of Clarendon," he reaches a pitch of confident audacity that is remarkable even for Defoe. In fact, to establish the authenticity of his own spurious memoirs he is prepared to question the veracity of the contemporary sources on which those memoirs were based.[47]

What does Defoe add to the histories and memoirs already in print? When he is dealing with historical actions he may, as has been suggested, add some vivid circumstances or incidents of his own invention. When he is not so closely tied to well-known historical events he has obviously more freedom to fabricate his own episodes, as he quite clearly does in the Cavalier's adventures following upon the battle at Marston Moor, where the characters with whom he is involved are "three country fellows on horseback" and some other rustics. Those episodes are interesting enough, but more interesting are the occasional glimpses which Defoe is able to give us of the mind of a professional soldier, and more especially what it felt like for such a man to be fighting against his own countrymen in a civil war. The Cavalier was already well experienced in military service when he took up arms for Charles I, and when the King hastily collected a volunteer army to intimidate the Scots, the Cavalier found himself among a body of untrained and easily frightened cavalry who were ready to take to their heels at the first sign that the Scots army was approaching. "Hereupon," he says, "we made a halt, and indeed I was afraid 'twould have been an odd sort of a halt; for our men began to look one upon another, as they do in like cases when they are going to break; and when the scouts came galloping in, the men were in such disorder, that had but one man broke away, I am satisfied they had all run for it." Was Defoe drawing upon his experience as a young trooper at the battle of Sedgemoor? Again, the Cavalier tells us that when the war broke out he never troubled himself "to examine sides"; he was a soldier, and here was a chance to practice his profession. He knew, of course, what was likely to happen to a country that was fought over, for he had seen the full havoc of war in Germany; but in the first excitement of being back in uniform he forgot all that:

I went as eagerly and blindly about my business as the meanest wretch that listed in the army; nor had I the least compassionate thought for the miseries of my native country, 'till after the fight at Edgehill.

In Germany he had been among strangers, and when a town was sacked and the citizens were slain it was a German town and the inhabitants were Germans:

But I found a strange secret and unaccountable sadness upon my spirits to see this acting in my own native country. It grieved me to the heart, even in the rout of our enemies, to see the slaughter of them; and even in the fight, to hear a man cry for quarter in English moved me to a compassion which I had never been used to; nay, sometimes it looked to me as if some of my own men had been beaten; and when I heard a soldier cry, "O God, I am shot!" I looked behind me to see which of my own troop was fallen. Here I saw myself at the cutting of the throats of my friends, and indeed some of my near relations. My old comerades and fellow-soldiers in Germany were some *with us*, some *against us*, as their opinions happened to differ in religion.

It is in such passages that the *Memoirs of a Cavalier* comes near to being a historical novel. We are not just reading about historical events, but sharing in the thoughts and feelings of an imaginary character who has lived through them; and how that person felt and thought is as important as what he did or saw. Yet if we are to think of the *Memoirs of a Cavalier* as a historical novel, it must be with considerable reservations. This story of a young man setting out to make his way in the world can hardly be said to have a plot; and the Cavalier himself is the only character to be given any prominence. Nor has he any fully developed relationship with anyone else who crosses his path; his world is almost entirely masculine, and his activities almost exclusively military. Defoe has given us another autobiographical narrative (this time based fairly closely on historical fact), and he was to repeat this formula several times with varying success.[48]

In March 1722 he published what was undoubtedly his most remarkable example of this genre, *A Journal of the Plague Year*. This was preceded in February by a shorter volume, *Due Preparations for the Plague as Well for Soul as Body*. Both books had a topical interest for the English reader of 1722. Although the Great Plague of 1665 was the last serious visitation of bubonic plague in England, there had been serious outbreaks on the continent of Europe from time to time, and in 1720 a disastrous epidemic broke out in Marseilles, spread through Provence, and continued to be a grave menace for the next two years. Early in 1721 the government of Sir Robert Walpole, anxious to take preventive measures, had passed a Quarantine Act "to enable her Majesty effectually to prohibit commerce (for the space of one year) with any country that is or shall be infected with the plague." This Act, which prescribed the death penalty for anyone who refused to go into quarantine, or who escaped from it, was unpopular in the country, and more especially among the merchants whose ships might be laid up for an indefinite period and their cargoes spoiled. Defoe, who was now writing regularly for *Applebee's Weekly Journal*, had followed closely the progress of the plague in France, and had

Daniel Defoe

commented on it from time to time. As an ex-merchant he knew how serious the Quarantine Act was for trade, but as a writer for the government, and as a responsible citizen, he must have felt bound to support the measures now being taken to prevent the plague spreading to England. On 29 July 1721, in a long letter signed "Quarantine," he criticized severely those men who would "risk themselves, and the lives of a whole city, nay, a whole nation, for their present profit"; and on several occasions during the next few months he returned to the same subject, partly to suggest precautions, and partly to allay unreasonable fears in the minds of the public. In *Due Preparations* he produced a kind of vade-mecum for the London citizen, instructing him how to behave and what measures to take if the plague (which God forbid!) should reach England. The little book was advertised as "very proper to give given away," and being a duodecimo it could easily be carried in the pocket. Defoe had done his duty by the government, and as a good journalist had seized his chance to write on a matter of topical interest.[49]

Due Preparations was didactic in tone and intention; but by introducing two long narratives describing the precautions taken by several London families during the Great Plague Defoe was able to provide some human interest. It may now have occurred to him that he had much other material at his disposal which could be used for an account of the terrible Plague of 1665, and that if he were to compile such an account he could not do better than throw it into his usual form of autobiographical narrative. The narrator in this case was one H. F., a saddler living in the parish of St. Botolph, Aldgate, who remained in London all through the Plague. Since we know that Defoe had an uncle, Henry Foe, a saddler, of St. Botolph without Aldgate, and since there is evidence that he stayed on in London during the plague months of 1665, the conclusion that H. F. was Defoe's uncle appears to be inescapable. But it by no means follows that he was the first literary member of the Foe family, or that his brilliant nephew merely edited *A Journal of the Plague Year* for publication from his manuscript. If there was a manuscript at all, it may have contained little more than brief jottings about the pestilence and such pious ejaculations as the godly of those days were apt to commit to paper. We are told by H. F. that in his spare time he wrote down his memorandums of what occurred to him every day, and that from these he had compiled "most of this work, as it relates to my observations without doors." He also tells us that he wrote down his private meditations, but that he doesn't want those to be made public "on any account whatever." On the face of it, it seems not improbable that Defoe's uncle might have done the two things that H. F. is made to say that *he* did; but it is perhaps more probable that he merely told his nephew some of the anecdotes that appear in the *Journal*. This he could easily have done, for he lived on until February 1675, when Defoe was a boy of fourteen. During the months that the plague was raging in London the chances are that Defoe's father was living in the country with his family (as H. F. says that his brother was), and in that case Defoe could have had no first-hand knowledge of what was going on. But when James Foe brought his family back to London his young son would inevitably hear a good deal about what must for some time have been an absorbing topic of conversation, and he could visit the sites of the burial pits, look at the houses that were still shut up, and "snatch a fearful joy" from those and other signs of the dreadful visitation.[50]

We certainly cannot rule out the possibility, and even the likelihood, that some of Defoe's information about the plague year came to him from survivors with whom he had conversed—either Londoners whom he knew as a boy, or (as he puts it) "antient persons still alive" in 1722, who had not been, like Defoe himself, in their nonage in 1665, but fully adult. Yet when due allowance is made for such oral evidence, it still remains true that for most of his historical facts, and for some of the opinions expressed by his narrator, he relied as usual upon printed sources. He made use of *Orders Conceived and Published by the Lord Mayor and Aldermen of the City of London concerning the Infection of the Plague*, which had originally appeared in 1665, and had been reprinted, very conveniently for Defoe, in 1721, along with several other pieces on the Plague which the renewed threat of infection in that year had encouraged a London bookseller to republish. Defoe took his statistics for the spread of the plague from one parish to another from *The Weekly Bills of Mortality*, compiled by the Company of Parish Clerks. He was also able to draw some facts and ideas from a few contemporary accounts of the Great Plague, notably Nathaniel Hodges' *Loimo-logia* (1672), written in Latin, but translated (again conveniently for Defoe) in 1720. The scholarly hunt for Defoe's sources has probably led to the impression that he used more than he actually did. He was usually writing at speed, and the notion that on this or on similar occasions he consulted a large number of authorities is almost certainly erroneous.[51]

How much he simply invented in *A Journal of the Plague Year* can never be certainly known. The tendency of modern scholars, rendered cautious, no doubt, by the recollection that such apparent inventions as *The Apparition of Mrs. Veal* have turned out to be almost pure fact, is to suggest that he invented very little. To claim, however, that the *Journal* is almost entirely based on actual fact, and that although there must be some residue of invented detail it is "small and inessential," is surely to go much too far. The passages we are most likely to remember are usually those for which no source has been found or suggested, and which appear to have no other source than the visualizing and dramatizing mind of Defoe himself: the visit of H. F. to the burial pit in Aldgate, where he sees the poor distracted husband "go to and again, muffled up in a brown cloak, and making motions with his hands under his cloak, as if he was in a great agony," and where he hears him cry out aloud, unable to contain himself, as the bodies are "shot into the pit promiscuously"; the mother who undressed her daughter and put her to bed, and who, "looking upon her body with a candle immediately discovered the fatal tokens on the inside of her thighs"; the man at the post-house who picked up with a pair of red-hot tongs a small purse "with two keys hanging at it." If we were to classify the *Journal* as history, such facts would undoubtedly be "small and inessential"; if we read it as a work of imaginative literature which has to be made to seem factually true, they are of the first importance.[52]

The incident at the post-house just referred to is a good example of how Defoe went to work on his factual material. He could have read in several printed accounts how unwilling people were in times of plague to touch anything that might have come into contact with an infected person, and how ready they were to adopt elaborate means to avoid contamination; but the episode of the purse appears to have had at least a nucleus of hard fact. Writing some eighteen months earlier in the *Commentator* about the plague of 1665, Defoe had remarked "how grass grew in the streets of London, and in the Exchange; how the most frequented places were abandoned; how all commerce was interrupted, and few shops in London were kept open: how a purse of money lay on the pavement in the Post-House-Yard, and no body durst take it up for some hours, till a man that had the plague, and was recovered, came with a pail of water, and a pair of red-hot tongs, and took it up, and burning the purse dropped the money into the pail." Here, if anywhere, Defoe may be indebted to the reminiscence of Uncle Henry. At all events, when the purse reappears in *A Journal of the Plague Year* the whole episode has become much more circumstantial:

It pleased God that I was still spar'd, and very hearty and sound in health, but very impatient of being pent up within doors without air, as I had been for 14 days or thereabouts; and I could not restrain my self, but I would go to carry a letter for my brother to the post-house. Then it was, indeed, that I observ'd a profound silence in the streets. When I came to the post-house, as I went to put in my letter, I saw a man stand in one corner of the yard, and talking to another at a window; and a third had open'd a door belonging to the office. In the middle of the yard lay a small leather purse, with two keys hanging at it, and money in it, but no body would meddle with it. I ask'd how long it had lain there; the man at the window said it had lain almost an hour, but that they had not meddled with it, because they did not know but the person who dropt it might come back to look for it. I had no such need for money, nor was the sum so big, that I had any inclination to meddle with it, or to get the money at the hazard it might be attended with; so I seem'd to go away, when the man who had open'd the door said he would take it up, but so, that if the right owner came for it, he would be sure to have it. So he went in and fetched a pail of water, and set it down hard by the purse; then went again and fetch'd some gun-powder, and cast a good deal of powder upon the purse, and then made a train from that which he had thrown loose upon the purse; the train reached about two yards. After this he goes in a third time, and fetches out a pair of tongs red hot, and which he had prepar'd, I suppose, on purpose; and first setting fire to the train of powder, that sing'd the purse, and also smoak'd the air sufficiently. But he was not content with that; but he then takes up the purse with the tongs, holding it so long till the tongs burnt thro' the purse, and then he shook the money out into the pail of water; so he carried it in. The money, as I remember, was about thirteen shillings, and some smooth groats and brass farthings.[53]

Defoe sets this little scene with all the care that he usually takes with significant incidents. To make his point about the reluctance of people to touch infected objects, the man with the red-hot tongs would be enough; but we are told that there were two other people there—a man standing in one corner of the yard talking to a second man at a window. Those two men have some importance merely as spectators; they help to frame the incident simply by watching, as H. F. is also watching, the whole odd process of fumigation. But the main justification of their presence is that they are expendable; their very irrelevance is a sort of guarantee that they must have been there, and that the whole incident is literally true; for why mention them at all unless they were an actual part of a recollected experience? "I am sensible," Wordsworth once went so far as to admit, "that my associations must have sometimes been particular rather than general"; and in his poetry of recollected experience we occasionally meet with factual details which are in the poem only because they were accidentally attached to the incident and therefore mixed up with the feelings it aroused. But what may be a defect in poetry is a powerful adjunct to credibility in Defoe's world of make-believe. In his account of the purse the effect of actuality is sustained by the precise measurement of time ("almost an hour"), of length ("the train reached about two yards"), and of money ("about thirteen shillings, and some smooth groats and brass farthings"). The groats (small silver coins not minted after 1662) are said to be smooth, i.e. worn thin by use, because Defoe is no doubt recollecting the deplorable state of the unmilled silver coins of the late seventeenth century, which led to the calling in of all silver money, and the great recoinage of 1696. From the snatches of reported dialogue, such as that of the man with the tongs, who said that he would take up the purse, "but so, that if the right owner came for it, he would be sure to have it," we get the impression that each of the four individuals in the post-office yard would have been willing to make off with the purse if no one else had been looking. When the contents are finally shaken out into the pail of water we have been so absorbed with the whole fascinating process of retrieving them that we probably never stop to ask ourselves how H. F. could possibly have known before the money in the purse had been tipped out of the pail and counted that the sum was not "so big."[54]

Enough has now been said about Defoe's constant endeavor to create in his reader's mind a belief in the absolute veracity of the narrator. Yet this much may be added: nowhere else is this authenticating process carried so far as in *A Journal of the Plague Year*. Here he frequently goes beyond a simple "I remember" to such a claim as "I remember, and while I am writing this story I think I hear the very sound of it . . . ," and so on to an account of the shrieks of a distracted mother. Sometimes, again, the narrator is made to express some uncertainty; and by his admission on such occasions that he is not quite sure, or does not know, he reinforces our belief in his absolute veracity on all other occasions. In this way H. F. remarks of the red-hot tongs that it had been "prepared, I suppose, on purpose"; and in his story of the mother who discovered the fatal tokens on her daughter he tells us that the mother, the daughter, and the maid had just returned from some little outing, "I do not remember what," and that he *believes* the mother died not long after her daughter, although "it is so long ago that I am not certain, but I think the mother never recovered, but died in two or three weeks after."[55]

In all Defoe's stories we are conscious of the isolated human being contending with circumstances. This impression is no doubt partly the result of the autobiographical form, which preserves an unbroken contact between the narrator and the reader, and by means of which every happening and every circumstance are seen from the narrator's point of view. But in the *Journal*, as in the first part of *Robinson Crusoe*, the circumstances themselves are such as to deepen the impression of isolation and loneliness. Shut up in his own house H. F. is cut off from his fellow men, and walking about the streets of the plague-stricken city he makes as few contacts as possible; he is the withdrawn spectator, sharing his experiences with few or none, and driven back into solitary contemplation. Most of Defoe's stories are concerned with a concatenation of events which are either discrete or not strictly

sequential, and these may stretch over the greater part of a lifetime. The reader's attention is held by his interest in the individual
episodes, and only to a limited extent by his concern for the ultimate fate of the hero or heroine, or by any strong feeling that
what happens is the inevitable result of what has gone before. In
stories like *Moll Flanders* and *Colonel Jack* there is a sort of
progress from youth to age, innocence to experience, poverty to
wealth, and so on. There is also some correlation between character and circumstance, and there is to some extent a development
of character, although any advance towards moral virtue is usually
accompanied by a good deal of compromise and backsliding. But
the emphasis is still upon change of scene, altered circumstances,
new characters, fortune and misfortune, adventures and misadventures; the one unifying factor is the hero or heroine to
whom everything happens, and whose voice is for ever in our
ears. The effect of *A Journal of the Plague Year* is very different.
However haphazard Defoe's arrangement of his materials may be,
he is pursuing one theme from start to finish. Instead of dispersal
we have concentration; the action takes place in a single great
city, and is limited in time to a few months of continuous crisis.
Instead of variety we have repetition; but here both repetition
and monotony have the effect of fixing our minds inescapably on
the one appalling circumstance which is the subject of the *Journal*.
We move with Defoe's saddler about the silent and deserted
streets, we hear the rumble of the dead carts at night and see the
lurid light of the torches. For all the grave manliness of H. F., we
are in the grip of a terrible fear, and the plague is never for one
moment out of our thoughts. Here, too, the religious element in
Defoe's narrative has an important effect in deepening the impression of gloom, and inducing a feeling akin to the supernatural: the
plague was a "visitation," a judgment, it was "the hand of God."
Whatever we may think of Defoe's religious comments on some
other occasions, there can be little reason to doubt their sincerity
here, or to question their literary effectiveness.

It would be easy to exaggerate his art in the *Journal*, and to give
him credit for something he never intended. The work is a hodge-
podge of statistics, proclamations, medical data, anecdotes, and
reflections of one sort or another; it also contains the very long
and abruptly introduced digression of the three men from Wap-

ping, which, it has been plausibly suggested, Defoe may originally have intended to form part of *Due Preparations* and now frugally inserted in the *Journal*. It might be argued that H. F.'s unmethodical and repetitious narrative is exactly what we should expect from a saddler turned author; and certainly the frequent accounts of men and women shrieking from windows or falling down dead in the street only tend to reinforce the nightmare impression that the *Journal* makes on the mind of the reader. But to suppose that the lack of method and the repetitions were all part of Defoe's conscious art, and were intended to suit the character of the narrator, is surely to go wide of the mark. The saddler is, in fact, a highly methodical person, and if his narrative is unmethodical it is not his fault but that of his creator. Defoe took great pains to establish a basis of formal realism in all his narratives; but what he gave so convincingly with one hand he was liable to take away with the other. It is astonishing how little it seems to matter. Professor Watt, who is not especially kind to Defoe's shortcomings as a novelist, ends by weighing very fairly his achievements against his limitations:

Very few writers have created for themselves both a new subject and a new literary form to embody it. Defoe did both. In his somewhat monocular concentration on making his matter seem absolutely convincing, there was much he did not see. But what is left out in probably the price for what is so memorably and unprecedentedly put in.[56]

In the *Journal* exception may be taken to what he occasionally puts in rather than to what he leaves out. But although he sometimes interrupts the chronological sequence with digressions, and moves inconsequentially from one topic to another, he does succeed in giving us an unforgettable impression of what life must be like in a plague-stricken city. As with Crusoe's life on the island, too, so here in the London of 1665, the very nature of the events imposes an order on the narrative. H. F.'s story has a beginning in the first weeks of uncertainty when plague breaks out in the parishes of St. Giles in the Fields and St. Andrews, Holborn; a middle, when it spreads eastwards across the City and rages in one parish after another; and an end, coming almost suddenly and apparently miraculously, when "it pleased God . . . to cause the fury of it to abate, even of it self." There follows a

brief but moving passage on the joy of the citizens when the bills
of mortality reveal a sharp decrease in the number of deaths. " 'Tis
all wonderful," one of them cries, " 'tis all a dream!" Characteristically enough, however, H. F. goes on to record how quickly
most of his fellow citizens, like the Children of Israel who had
been delivered from the host of Pharaoh, forgot to give thanks to
God. If anything should persuade us to believe that Defoe was
making at least some use of memoranda kept by his Uncle Henry,
it would be the words with which H. F. brings his story to an end:

I shall conclude the account of this calamitous year, therefore, with a
coarse but sincere stanza of my own, which I plac'd at the end of my
ordinary memorandums, the same year they were written:

> *A dreadful plague in London was,*
> *In the year sixty five,*
> *Which swept an hundred thousand souls*
> *Away; yet I alive!*

If a saddler were driven by a traumatic experience to write verse,
this looks very like the sort of verse he would have written. But
of course that idea may also have occurred to Defoe.[57]

In 1728 there appeared *The Memoirs of an English Officer*,
attributed on the title-page to Captain George Carleton. This
work has had some distinguished admirers, including Dr. Johnson,
who came across it late in life, and was "so much pleased with it,
that he sat up till he had read it through." Doubts about its
authenticity, however, began to grow in the nineteenth century;
and finally, after a detailed examination, Professor Secord showed
that many of the statements in Carleton's narrative were "based
on materials gathered painstakingly from Boyer's *William III* and
Queen Anne, Freind's *Account [of the Earl of Peterborough's
Conduct in Spain]*, the D'Aulnoy *Letters*, and the *London
Gazette*." The gathering together of those materials, he was convinced, was the work of Defoe.[58]

The Memoirs of an English Officer presents a problem roughly
analogous to that of *Robert Drury's Journal*. There was, in fact,
a Captain George Carleton, and what we learn about him from
the *Memoirs* corresponds to such facts as have been recovered.
Unlike *Robert Drury's Journal*, however, Carleton's narrative is
not marked by "all that simplicity and verbiage . . . expected in

narratives of the illiterate."* The style varies from one section to another, but there are some passages of pompous and highfalutin writing, utterly different from anything that Defoe normally wrote, that appear to be the expression of a man who has had some education, but not enough to keep him from trying to show it off. Thus Carleton tells us that, little as he admired a life of inactivity, "there are some sorts of activity to which a wise man might almost give supineness the preference." However, he adds, "my better planets soon disannulled those melancholy ideas." When the English forces marched in the reign of Queen Anne "to the support of the tottering empire," it was not his good fortune "to participate in those glorious appendages of the English arms in Flanders," but he was recommended to the Earl of Peterborough by Lord Cutts, who, "returning with his full share of laurels for his never to be forgotten services at Venlo, Ruremond, and Hochstet, found his active genius now to be reposed under the less agreeable burthen of unhazardous honour, where quiet must provide a tomb for one already past any danger of oblivion. . . ." Those unlovely statements all occur within a few pages, together with the lofty assertion that "these Memoirs are not designed for the low amusement of a tea-table, but rather of the cabinet," and they read like the Captain's attempts at fine writing. It may be argued, of course, that such passages only serve to show how cleverly Defoe could imitate the style of a pompous military man; but for Defoe to write like this, even in imitation, would have been almost a masochistic exercise, and in any case the greater part of the *Memoirs* is written in a quite different style, simple and forthright, and very like the staple of Defoe's narrative writing. It would seem, therefore, that on this occasion Defoe had some sort of manuscript placed at his disposal, that he obtained at least the framework of the narrative from it, and that occasionally he retained some passages of the Captain's own composition. There is, indeed, some evidence that Carleton foisted in a few paragraphs of his own while the book was printing, including those with which the *Memoirs* conclude.[59]

Whatever the truth may be here, the attribution of the *Memoirs* to Defoe adds little to his reputation. It is difficult to see why this

* Cf. page 153.

work should have kept Johnson reading into the small hours, or why it so interested Sir Walter Scott that he persuaded Constable to reprint it in 1808, even though the Peninsular War had given it a topical appeal. The most interesting passages are certainly those dealing with the remarkable exploits of the Earl of Peterborough in Spain; but there is much impertinency mixed with the matter, and the digressions become more and more frequent. Towards the end, when Carleton turns into a sort of tourist in Spain and describes Montserrat, a bull fight, Madrid, the Escurial, and other Spanish places and customs, Defoe is either adapting information obtained from the Baroness D'Aulnoy and other writers, or perhaps drawing on his own memories of a visit to the peninsula. Contemporary readers appear to have shown little interest in Captain Carleton's memoirs: in 1740 the unsold sheets of the 1728 edition were re-issued with a new half-title, and they were offered to the public again in 1743 with a new title-page.[60]

5

The Writer of Fiction (II)

UP TO THE BEGINNING OF 1722 Defoe's various works of fiction had all dealt with an almost exclusively masculine world. That he should now, with the publication of *The Fortunes and Misfortunes of the Famous Moll Flanders*, produce an autobiographical narrative in which life is seen through the eyes of a woman was for him a distinct innovation, but one that was not, in view of some of his earlier writings, particularly surprising. Among the writers of his period he held unusually liberal ideas about women. As a sex they were at a grave disadvantage legally and economically, and the girls in a family normally received an education inferior to that of their brothers. On these matters Defoe had long since made up his mind, and in his own day he must have appeared to be a formidable champion of the rights of women. As early as 1697 in *An Essay upon Projects* he had outlined a scheme for an Academy of Women. There they would be taught the graces of speech and conversation, and learn music and dancing; but they would also be instructed in languages, such as French and Italian, and brought to read books, especially of history, so that they might be able to understand the world and "to know and judge of things when they hear of them." Indeed, there was no sort of learning unfit for women if their genius led them to it. Most of those accomplishments were acquired by Moll Flanders while she lived in the Colchester household, although we hear nothing more about her ability to dance and speak French in later life. At all events, Defoe had a strong preference for the woman who was intelligent and well educated:

A woman well bred and well taught, furnish'd with the additional accomplishments of knowledge and behaviour, *is a creature without comparison*. . . . She is every way suitable to the sublimest wish; and the man that has such a one to his portion has nothing to do but to rejoice in her, and be thankful. . . . I cannot think that God Almighty ever made them so delicate, so glorious creatures, and furnish'd them with such charms, so agreeable and so delightful to mankind, with souls capable of the same accomplishments with men, and all to be only stewards of our houses, *cooks and slaves*. Not that I am for exalting the female government in the least; but, in short, *I wou'd have men take women for companions, and educate them to be fit for it*.[1]

A woman's estate became her husband's after marriage, although provision could be made in a pre-nuptial contract to enable her to retain control of it. Since careers open to women were normally limited to such economically unrewarding employments as domestic service (unless they were widows and were able to carry on their husbands' business, e.g., as printers or publishers), a successful marriage was a woman's greatest hope of happiness. But if she wished to "marry well" she had to have a fortune of her own, or at least be able to bring her husband a sizable dowry. In the late seventeenth and early eighteenth centuries the marriage of convenience had spread from the upper class down to the middle classes, as Moll was to learn to her cost when she had to find a replacement for her spendthrift draper husband, who simply took off one morning and fled from his creditors to France. The man she eventually found was less well off than he had given her to understand; but Moll, who had passed herself off as a well-to-do widow, had only about £500, and not the £1,500 he had been led to expect. Both, however, were good-natured, and the marriage was a success until it was brought to an end by the unforeseen and unforeseeable circumstance that the man she had married was her own brother. The problem of marriage from a woman's point of view bulks large in the early pages of *Moll Flanders*: Moll soon discovered that "the market run all on the men's side," and that although a man chose a mistress because she was handsome and well-shaped, with "a good mien, and a graceful behaviour," he was moved by quite different considerations when it came to choosing a wife. Then "the money was the thing," and "the money was always agreeable, whatever the wife was." In a world in which "the wars, and the sea, and trade, and other incidents have carried the men so much away, that there is no proportion between the numbers of the sexes," Moll realized that a woman had to use her wits, and if necessary indulge in a little deception, to secure a good husband.[2]

In the pages of the *Review* Defoe had offered a good deal of sensible advice on the problems of marriage, and now in *Moll Flanders* he showed those problems affecting the life of his heroine from youth to middle age, and with what varying success she solved them. When her Bath lover became a reformed character and brought their irregular connection to an end, Moll found herself thrown on her own resources again and took stock of her now worsening situation:

I knew what I aim'd at, and what I wanted, but knew nothing how to pursue the end by direct means; I wanted to be plac'd in a settled state of living, and had I happen'd to meet with a sober good husband, I should have been as true a wife to him as virtue it self could have form'd. If I had been otherwise, the vice came in always at the door of necessity, not at the door of inclination; and I understood too well, by the want of it, what the value of a settl'd life was, to do any thing to forfeit the felicity of it; nay, I should have made the better wife for all the difficulties I had pass'd thro', by a great deal; nor did I, in any of the times that I had been a wife, give my husbands the least uneasiness on account of my behaviour.

A little earlier she has explained the nature of her relationship with the married man she met at Bath:

It is true that from the first hour I began to converse with him I resolv'd to let him lye with me, if he offer'd it; but it was because I wanted his help, and knew of no other way of securing him.

Those two statements are crucial to an understanding of Moll, and of the regular-irregular life she has been living. We can agree with Professor Watt that she is an example of economic individualism: the world being what it was for women in Defoe's day, and Moll being determined to capitalize her physical assets while they lasted, her career is entirely intelligible. It is true, indeed, that it was not inevitable: Moll could have scraped an honest, if unattractive, living by plying her needle, or (worse still) by accepting some form of domestic service. Like Roxana, however, she was not content just to keep the wolf from the door; ever since, as a little girl, she was playfully referred to by visitors as "the little gentlewoman," she had been determined to live the life of a lady, and not to go out to work. For Moll "necessity" was a relative term; it meant not being able to go on living the easy sort of life to which she had become accustomed, both as a wife and a mistress. There is a significant passage in the *Review* which seems to cover her case:

Men rob for bread, women whore for bread; necessity is the parent of crime. Ask the worst high-way man in the nation, ask the lewdest strumpet in the town, if they would not willingly leave off the trade if they could live handsomely without it—and I dare say, not one but will acknowledge it.

As Professor Shinagel has pointed out, the key word in this passage is "handsomely"; and it is also the word that Moll uses on several occasions to describe her own way of living when things are going well with her. When her banker husband dies and leaves her all but destitute, she is faced—at the age of around fifty—with what in the common acceptance of the term is genuine necessity. At this point Defoe recalls, through the mouth of Moll, one of his favorite biblical quotations—"the wise man's prayer, *Give me not poverty lest I steal.*" If only (Moll reflects) the settled life she had lived with her banker husband could have lasted, how happy she would have been! But she had been left helpless and friendless to shift for herself, and had "fallen into that poverty which is the sure bane of virtue." By selling her possessions and "eeking things out to the utmost," she had managed to keep her head above water for almost a year, but in the end she was driven desperate, and on a sudden impulse she committed her first theft.[3]

The thefts that follow immediately upon this one may be said to be caused by Moll's continuing economic necessity; but she proves to be such an intelligent and adroit thief that in time she becomes comparatively rich, and if she had been content to leave off, as her "governess" advised her to do, she might have retired from her new profession in at least modest affluence. That she went on from one "purchase" to another until she was finally caught at it, was partly due to the natural pleasure she took in the exercise of her professional skill (as, say, Defoe himself took in writing a political pamphlet, or Yehudi Menuhin takes in playing the violin), but mainly to her desire to live handsomely, and to an acquisitiveness that is an essential element in almost all Defoe's heroes and heroines.

The story of Moll Flanders is therefore one that traces the effects of economic necessity and economic individualism. It might equally well, however, be considered as our first sociological novel. Defoe is interested not only in marriage and extramatrimonial relationships, but in the effects of education or the lack of it, in the problems presented by illegitimate children, in the habits of the criminal class and the way in which one form of delinquency leads to another. He touches the life of the day at many of its sore points, and he clearly intends to draw the attention of the reader to various social problems and abuses. Since it is Moll who is telling her story, Defoe has to express his criticism of society by way of the comments she makes as she looks back on her past life. Yet although he sees to it that Moll makes the necessary gestures of disapproval or shame when she has described some morally unacceptable action or situation, the over-all impression made by her story is one of frank reminiscence rather than of didactic intention. And the chief reason why we have this impression is that in *Moll Flanders* Defoe has not just written a cautionary tale embodying his own views on economic and social problems, but has created a heroine who holds our attention and retains a large measure of our sympathy.

Moll has had many distinguished admirers, including Virginia Woolf, who thought that *Moll Flanders* stood "among the few English novels which we can call indisputably great," and E. M. Forster, who discussed it as "a novel in which character is everything and is given freest play." What delights most readers of *Moll Flanders* is partly Moll's irrepressible vitality, the determination to survive which she shares with Crusoe and with other of Defoe's heroes and heroines. But she has not merely the will to live; she gets, being Moll, a great deal of pleasure out of life, she is gay and good-humored and lively. We are given one especially memorable glimpse of Moll having fun when her gentleman-draper husband takes her to Oxford in a magnificent hired equip-

age, and passes himself off as a lord and Moll as his countess.
"Give him his due," Moll remarks humorously, "not a beggar alive
knew better how to be a lord than my husband." But the fun was
only beginning:

We saw all the rarities at Oxford, talk'd with two or three fellows of
colleges about putting a nephew that was left to his lordship's care to
the University, and of their being his tutors; we diverted our selves
with bantering several other poor scholars with the hope of being at
least his lordship's chaplain and putting on a scarf; and thus having
liv'd like quality indeed as to expence, we went away for Northamp-
ton, and in a word, in about twelve days' ramble came home again, to
the tune of about £93 expence.

Moll was still a young woman when this escapade occurred, but
she never lost her *joie de vivre*. When she returned to England
from Virginia after her disastrous marriage to her half-brother,
she had the misfortune to lose most of her goods at sea, and her
capital was reduced to about £250. But what of it? "I took the
diversion of going to the Bath, for as I was still far from being
old, so my humour, which was always gay, continu'd so to an
extream." If her cargo had only come home safe, she "might have
married again tollerably well"; but that was now out of the
question. Yet Moll had a way of going with the stream and
adapting herself to changed circumstances; and this time she was
able to secure a very eligible lover, an intelligent middle-aged
husband who was living apart from a lunatic wife, and with him
she continued to cohabit very handsomely for several years.[4]

A husband, however, was what Moll wanted and what she
approved of. Like the Wife of Bath, this volatile, persistent
woman could have said, "Housbondes at chirche-door I have had
fyve"; and from what she tells us, she was a good wife to all of
them. So far as being in love is concerned, she seems to have been
physically attracted by her first lover, the young man who
seduced her and then coolly passed her on to his younger brother
for a wife; and she had also a genuine feeling for her Lancashire
husband, the highwayman who reappears towards the end of the
book and shares with her an Indian summer of prosperity. The
appeal of both of those men was at least partly due to the fact
that they were "gentlemen." When she has married the Lan-

cashire husband in the belief that he has a substantial estate, and then finds that he is penniless, she reflects that it might have been much worse: " 'Tis something of relief even to be undone by a man of honour rather than by a scoundrel." This man of honor, as we learn much later, was already a highwayman when he married Moll, and therefore (one would have supposed) something of a scoundrel; but in Moll's rather muddled morality that fact would not have lessened her admiration for a man who had the air of a gentleman, and who was handsome and open-handed. Moll is certainly susceptible to attractive men, but she never strikes one as being oversexed, and indeed goes out of her way several times to tell us so. When she first settles in Bath she says that she resisted "some casual offers of gallantry," since she was not "wicked enough to come into the crime for the meer vice of it": if she had had any "extraordinary offers," *then* she might have been tempted. She is all for permanent relationships if she can have them, but it is a necessary condition of marriage that a husband should be able to support her. Some time after she has taken a passionate leave of her Lancashire husband, who "had made such impressions on me that I could not bear the thoughts of parting with him," and has given birth in secret to the child of this brief marriage, she hears again from the amorous banker who has been courting her that his whore of a wife has "destroyed herself," and that he is therefore free to marry her. Since her Lancashire husband is unable to keep her, Moll is now resolved to have the banker, and within a few months they are married. So far as the banker is concerned, he may be only the next best thing; but he is solvent, and she quickly accepts the new situation and enjoys it. Of her honeymoon at Brickhill she tells us, "I never liv'd four pleasanter days together in my life; I was a meer bride all this while, and my new spouse strove to make me easie in every thing. O, could this state of life have continu'd!" In fact it continued "in the utmost tranquillity" for five years, during which Moll "minded" her family and "obliged" her husband; and this domestic idyll was only broken by a financial disaster and the consequent death of the banker.[5]

Sexually, at any rate, Moll has the characteristics of a normal woman. When, after she has become a thief, a gentleman who has been drinking rather heavily picks her up and carries her in a

coach to a house "where they made no scruple to show us up
stairs into a room with a bed in it," Moll, with her eye on his
purse and gold watch, lets him have his way with her. "As for the
bed etc.," she explains, "I was not much concern'd about that
part." It was only a necessary preliminary to more important
business. Once more in the coach, she strips the now sleeping
gentleman of all his valuables, and when the coach is held up in a
narrow street she steps softly out and moves off quietly with her
loot. Her reflections on this episode may seem to be an instance
of Defoe intruding on the story with his own moral comment,
but they are such as come quite naturally from Moll herself:

There is nothing so absurd, so surfeiting, so ridiculous as a man heated
by wine in his head, and a wicked gust in his inclination together; he is
in the possession of two devils at once, and can no more govern himself by his reason than a mill can grind without water; vice tramples
upon all that was in him that had any good in it; nay, his very sense
is blinded by its own rage, and he acts absurdities even in his view;
such is drinking more when he is drunk already; picking up a common
woman, without any regard to what she is, whether sound or rotten,
clean or unclean, whether ugly or handsome, old or young, and so
blinded as not really to distinguish; such a man is worse than lunatick;
prompted by his vicious head he no more knows what he is doing
than this wretch of mine knew when I pick'd his pocket of his watch
and his purse of gold.

This last observation of Moll's may remind us that among her
other virtues she has a robust intelligence. Living by her wits, she
has had occasion to bring her mind to bear on her various relationships with men, and to adapt her tactics to suit each new
situation. Later she applies her mind with equal success to the
technique of theft, in which she shows not only skill and quickness
of reaction, but judiciousness in knowing when to venture and
when to hold her hand. Since the reader stays with Moll from
beginning to end, he learns to appreciate her liveliness of mind
and the shrewd practical comments that she bases on her experience. However little Defoe may approve of Moll's activities, his
natural preference for intelligent women and his admiration of
efficiency clearly affect his attitude to his errant and erring
heroine, and he ends, however reluctantly, by being the first of
her admirers.[6]

Those critics who have reservations about Moll as a fictitious character have based their objections on two main grounds. It is suggested, in the first place, that she is sometimes no more than the mouthpiece of her creator, as when, for example, she expresses a moral disapproval of actions that it is thought she would be unlikely to feel; and secondly, her behavior is held to be occasionally inconsistent. There is some substance in both objections, but less than is sometimes supposed.

It is true that Defoe had no intention of writing a story in which vice would be rewarded and allowed to go unpunished; and it is clear that in all his works of fiction there were opinions that he wanted to express—moral, religious, social, economic— and that perhaps his main reason for writing fiction was to get those opinions expressed. It is equally clear that the autobiographical form in which he chose to tell his stories presents special difficulties for a writer who can't keep his own views out of his fiction and has no intention of trying to do so. But what is remarkable in *Moll Flanders* is the degree to which Defoe was able to find expression for his own point of view without seriously damaging the impression made by his heroine. To some extent his success was due to a compromise: he was willing to meet his heroine half way, but she had to be punished, and she had to show an awareness of her immorality and at least some signs of repentance. No author, of course, can be sure that his attitude toward any character will be shared by his readers, as Richardson found to his cost when giddy young females fell in love with the handsome betrayer of Clarissa; and Moll's rather superficial repentance in Newgate is a triumph for Defoe's realism rather than for his morality. On this occasion Moll may be said to have got the better of her creator. At all events her attack of morality proves to be a comparatively mild one, and she is soon starting a new and prosperous life in Virginia with the proceeds of her twelve years of successful theft. Yet just as Dr. Johnson saw to it that "the Whig dogs should not have the best of it," so Defoe brought Moll's career as a thief to an end with a genuinely traumatic experience when her fate hung in the balance, when she experienced all the horrors of Newgate, and when her name was even included in the "dead warrant." As for the moral observations that are strewn through the narrative, it should be remembered that it is the penitent Moll, writing in her old age, who is telling us her story, and a certain amount of moralizing on the sins of her sprightly youth and unregenerate middle age is in order. Accordingly Moll moralizes, but not too much. The account given of her old age in Defoe's editorial preface seems to tally perfectly with the woman we have come to know:

> She liv'd, it seems, to be very old; but was not so extraordinary a penitent as she was at first; it seems only that indeed she always spoke with abhorrence of her former life, and of every part of it.

This is what we should expect of the protean and adaptable Moll, who was spending her old age in very comfortable circumstances, and had again assumed that mantle of respectability which she was always ready to wear when things were going well with her. If we are determined to look for authorial interference in *Moll Flanders*, we are more likely to find it in those passages in which Moll warns the reader against the tricks of thieves—a point which is spelled out in the preface. In this respect *Moll Flanders* is in the tradition of Thomas Harman's *Caveat or Warning for Common Cursetors* or Robert Greene's "conny-catching" pamphlets.[7]

As for Moll's supposed inconsistency, much of it is surely due to the fact that inconsistency is a part of her character. In spite of all that has been happening in literature over the past two hundred years, some critics are still apt to discuss characters in fiction in the rigid terms of classical decorum. So far as character was concerned, the theory of decorum called for typical behavior on the part of the old and the young, of men and women, of lawyers, soldiers, and so on. Old men, Horace tells us, are peevish, querulous, given to praising the old days and to finding fault with the younger generation; young men are fond of sport, impatient of advice, prodigal, improvident, high-spirited, and apt to change with every fancy. Classical drama is full of such type characters who invariably behave in accordance with established expectation, and who rarely display more than a few well-known traits. With the growth of prose fiction in the eighteenth century the presentation of character was free to develop and to become much more complex than it had usually been in the old drama, and this new complexity made it possible to present men and women acting and thinking and feeling in different ways on different occasions and in altered circumstances. The process has continued ever since; and although we may still expect a character to be recognizable and to act "in character," we have a much more open mind about what a person might do or feel in any given circumstance, and a fuller realization of the conflicting motives that may lie behind his actions.[8]

  Not all of this can be applied to *Moll Flanders*, for Defoe was writing in the grey dawn of modern fiction. Yet the heroine of *Moll Flanders* strikes most readers as being not only exceptionally alive, but as responding naturally to the various situations in which she finds herself. From what Moll says about herself and from what she does there emerges a character who is both warm-hearted and hard-headed: the warm heart remains in spite of the buffetings of life, the hard head was there from the first and has enabled her to survive. The two can scarcely be expected to function simultaneously, but that one or the other should be uppermost alternately is natural enough. Indeed, some of the most interesting passages in her story occur when the heart and the head are in conflict, as they are in Moll's intricate relationship with her Lancashire husband, where her affection struggles with her acquired prudence while she strives in vain to persuade him to settle with her in Virginia.[9]

  With Moll's ability to feel goes a corresponding capacity to forget and to move on to a new relationship. That she should be blissfully happy with her banker husband so soon after she has lost the Lancashire husband from whom she could not bear the thought of parting will seem inconsistent only if we fail to take account of two of her most persistent characteristics, her powers of recuperation and her ability to live for the moment. I find it difficult to believe that this rapid transference of her affections was not contemplated ironically by Defoe; but although I find rather more conscious irony in *Moll Flanders* than Professor Watt is apparently prepared to admit, I would agree with him that "there is no consistently ironical attitude present in *Moll Flanders*," and that what may appear to be highly ironical to the twentieth-century reader may not have seemed so to Defoe. For the most part I think that Defoe simply followed Moll around;

and having a perfectly clear idea of her character he was chiefly
concerned to show her acting and feeling in every situation as he
believed she would.[10]

At all events, the woman he was portraying was full of in-
consistencies, and Defoe knew it. When she is able to respond to
life freely—i.e. when she is not in the grip of economic necessity
—Moll can be gay, warm-hearted, impulsive; but with each new
economic crisis she becomes calculating again, and in the old
phrase proceeds to "take care of number one." Indeed, a lifetime
of uncertainty has made prudential calculation almost habitual
with her. It is this necessity for a woman alone in the world to
look after herself first that presumably accounts for Moll's treatment of her children, who are little more than the debris of her
various marriages to be jettisoned along the way as opportunity
offers. Of the two she had by her first marriage she tells us that
they were "taken happily off my hands by my husband's father
and mother, and that was all they got by Mrs. Betty." The Bath
gentleman provided for an illegitimate son she bore him, and the
"brave boy" she had by her Lancashire husband was farmed out
to "a country woman from Hertford or thereabouts"; but Defoe
takes some pains to mitigate the impression of Moll's indifference
by making her express some reluctance at her abandoning of those
two infants. Although she says of the Bath gentleman's son that
"it was death to me to part with the child," she adds that when she
considered how she might be left without the means to support
him she resolved to let him go. When the banker renews his over-
tures soon after the birth of her son by the Lancashire husband,
she reflects what an "inexpressible misfortune" it is to have a
newly-born child on her hands, and takes the necessary steps to
get rid of it. "It touch'd my heart so forcibly," she tells us, "to
think of parting entirely with the child, and, for ought I knew, of
having it murther'd, or starv'd by neglect and ill-usage, which was
much the same, that I could not think of it without horror." But
if she is ever to marry her banker the child must be disposed of,
and after some further scruples she is convinced by her "governess" that it will be well looked after by one of those women
"who, as it is their trade, and they get their bread by it, value
themselves upon their being as careful of children as their own
mothers."

In all this there is admittedly a good deal more of the head than of the heart: the renewed prospect of poverty has hardened Moll's feelings, and it is part of Defoe's intention to show that it inevitably does so. "Give me not poverty lest I steal" has become "Give me not poverty lest I become an unnatural mother." Moll has once again embarked on a struggle for survival, and in such circumstances children, whether legitimate or illegitimate, are an embarrassment, and for the mode of life that Moll has adopted an impossible encumbrance. No doubt they also proved an embarrassment to the author, who must have wanted to get rid of them as much as Moll did. At the same time (let us face it) Defoe used the situation to ventilate a social problem which was much on his mind and to which he was to return in *Colonel Jack*: the widespread practice of farming out illegitimate children on professional foster-mothers. In consequence he had to make use of Moll on this occasion and show her taking part in an inhumane practice; but at the same time he does what he can to preserve her image as a good-natured woman by letting her dwell upon her natural feelings ("O mother, says I, if I was but sure my little baby would be carefully look'd to, and have justice done it, I should be happy"), and prolonging her scruples to the point that she nearly gives up her friend at the bank.

> Can a woman's tender care
> Cease towards the child she bare?

Yes, says Defoe the realist: what Moll does with her child other women are doing all over the England of our day, and it is a practice that must be utterly condemned. But *this* woman, he wants us to feel, abandoned her child only with the utmost reluctance, and only when driven to it by a kind of necessity. The foster-mother that she found was "a very wholesome-look'd likely woman" who lived in a pleasant cottage and had "very good cloaths and linnen," and so—but "with a heavy heart and many a tear"—Moll was reconciled to letting the woman have her child. With this difficult business settled she is ready to begin life again:

And thus my great care was over, after a manner, which, tho' it did not at all satisfy my mind, yet was the most convenient for me, as my affairs then stood, of any that could be thought of at that time.

Magna est necessitas et praevalebit. At all events, Defoe has done the best he can to salvage his heroine's reputation.[11]

Moll's spells of hard-heartedness do not make her a less credible character. Nor, as already suggested, do they conflict with her sudden outbursts of maternal feeling when there is nothing to prevent her from indulging in such feeling. When she returns to Virginia as an elderly woman she contrives, without being recognized herself, to see the son that she had left there as a child. "Let any mother of children that reads this consider it," she says, "and but think. . . . what yearnings of soul I had in me to embrace him, and weep over him; and how I thought all my entrails turn'd within me, that my very bowels mov'd, and I knew not what to do, as I now know not how to express those agonies." When he had passed by she stood there trembling, gazing after him as long as she could see him, and then lay on her face and wept, and "kiss'd the ground that he had set his foot on." This extravagant behavior has worried some of Defoe's readers, who find it difficult to reconcile Moll's sentimental fervor on this occasion with the comparative unconcern with which she has abandoned several of her other children. Professor Watt offers two possible explanations for this apparent contradiction. We ought not, he suggests, to interpret Moll's behavior in terms of psychological understanding, but of literary technique:

In reading Defoe we must posit a kind of limited liability for the narrative, accepting whatever is specifically stated, but drawing no inferences from omissions, however significant they may seem.

Alternatively, he continues, we ought to take into account the fact that "the criminal individualism which Moll pursues in her later days tends to minimise the importance of personal relationships." While both of those explanations are ingenious, and the first has considerable relevance to the way in which Defoe wrote all his fiction, they are hardly necessary here. Moll's emotional reaction on seeing her son is in keeping with her character. What she has just seen, after all those long years, is not the infant she had left behind in Virginia but "a handsome comely young gentleman in flourishing circumstances"—a sight that would have quickened Moll's heartbeat at any time, but that overwhelms her with emotion when she knows that this attractive and wealthy young man is her own son.[12]

A more serious objection to the credibility of Moll's character is her apparent immunity from the normal consequences of a life of crime. Could she do all that she has done and at the same time experience, at least intermittently, feelings of tenderness and compassion, and be troubled by a still active conscience? In view of the life she has led we might surely expect her to have become completely selfish and callous, with nothing but an eye for the main chance. To a certain extent this is just what Defoe shows us to have been happening. The young girl who was seduced by the elder brother in the Colchester household was comparatively innocent, and very much in love. It is true that the golden guineas her lover lavished so freely on her had a good deal to do with his conquest, but in her innocence she genuinely believed him when he promised to marry her "as soon as he came to his estate."[13] Of all the other men with whom Moll later became involved, the only one she seems to have fallen deeply in love with was, as I have already suggested, her Lancashire husband. But by this time she was a very different person, experienced in the ways of the world and walking much more warily. This particular love affair began in mutual deception, and ended with Moll concealing some of her assets from her impecunious husband. Even so, she came near to giving him everything she had. Defoe, it may be thought, is again having it both ways: he knows that Moll can't have lived the life she has lived without becoming hardened and selfish, and yet he cannot allow her to make this impression too strongly on the reader. Why?

Before answering this question we may look at another episode in which Moll's conscience is functioning normally, and in which she displays all the emotional reaction we should expect from a woman who has done something wrong for the first time. When she becomes a thief Moll crosses a sort of moral divide. Up till now she has lived a life which is in many ways immoral, and which has embraced fornication, adultery, and bigamy. (She cannot be blamed for the incest, which was none of her choosing.) After the death of her banker husband she is left "in a dismal and disconsolate state indeed," and only manages to keep herself from

starving by selling off her possessions one by one, until she reaches
a point where she imagines that every time she buys a sixpenny
loaf of bread it will be the last she can afford. Moll's condition, in
fact, is like that which Roxana was to experience on the break-up
of her first marriage, when she was compelled to send out her
maid Amy "to pawn or sell my *pair of stays*, to buy a breast of
mutton, and a bunch of turnips." But there was one great difference in their respective situations: Roxana was still young and
attractive, but Moll, who was now almost fifty, realized that she
was "past the flourishing time" and had little or no hope of
becoming some man's mistress again. She is now really desperate,
and is about to do something she would have shrunk from before,
and even now contemplates with horror: she is driven by necessity to steal. For Defoe, as for Moll, this is a deeper plunge into
immorality than any she has so far taken, even though her past
life has been largely a preparation for it. Defoe therefore gives
to her first theft that full circumstantial treatment which as a
writer of fiction he has always at his command. Brought, as she
says, almost to the last gasp, and distracted in her mind, Moll
goes out one evening with no settled purpose and just wanders
about the streets.

Wandring thus about I knew not whither, I pass'd by an apothecary's
shop in Leadenhall-street, where I saw lye on a stool just before the
compter a little bundle wrapt in a white cloth; beyond it stood a maid
servant with her back to it, looking up towards the top of the shop,
where the apothecary's apprentice, as I suppose, was standing upon the
compter, with his back also to the door, and a candle in his hand,
looking and reaching up to the upper shelf for something he wanted,
so that both were engag'd, and no body else in the shop.

This has all the accuracy of a Dutch painting. Time stands still as
Moll gazes fascinated at the little bundle wrapped in a white
cloth, and eternity seems to hang on the event. But we know
what is going to happen. Even so, Defoe underlines the importance of this crisis in Moll's life by making her hear a voice—"I
remember, and shall never forget it, 'twas like a voice spoken over
my shoulder"—the voice of the Devil saying to her, "Take the
bundle; be quick; do it this moment." Moll yields to the temptation, and makes off with the bundle without being noticed. Everything that now follows reinforces the impression that she has

taken an irretrievable step on the downward path. She is filled with horror at what she has done, she wanders away in a kind of dream, with no heart at first to run or even to walk quickly, and not feeling the ground she treads on. Safely home in her lodging at last, she opens the bundle, but she is still filled with terror, and she bursts into tears as she thinks of how she is sure to be found out and taken to Newgate and tried for her life. Next day the theft is still preying on her mind:

> . . . I was impatient to hear some news of the loss; and would fain know how it was, whether they were a poor bodie's goods, or a rich; perhaps, said I, it may be some poor widow like me that had pack'd up these goods to go and sell them for a little bread for herself and a poor child, and are now starving and breaking their hearts, for want of that little they would have fetch'd; and this thought tormented me worse than all the rest, for three or four days.

All this is marked by that psychological understanding that some critics of Defoe have been so unwilling to grant him. The pathetic bundle that Moll had purloined, with its silver porringer, silver mug, six teaspoons and miscellaneous clothing, was only one of many such possessions stolen every day in eighteenth-century London, and was hardly likely to be the subject of much comment or enquiry. But for Moll, filled with a sense of guilt, it had assumed enormous importance; it was something that people were sure to be talking about, it must be in the news. The sentimental supposition that it may have belonged to "some poor widow like me" who might now be starving is again entirely natural in the circumstances: Moll's feelings have been so completely shaken up by her first theft that she is capable of any extravagance. Moll has now taken the plunge. Her second theft, when she takes a necklace worth about twelve or fourteen pounds from a child, leaves her a good deal less concerned, and this too is what we should expect. But again Defoe gives us an interesting glimpse into Moll's mind; she has already become sufficiently hardened to attempt some self-justification, her old buoyancy is returning:

> As I did the poor child no harm, I only thought I had given the parents a just reproof for their negligence, in leaving the poor lamb to come home by it self, and it would teach them to take care another time.

In her need to blame somebody else for what she knows she ought not to have done Moll is like some one who has been caught stealing from a supermarket, and who complains that such places oughtn't to be allowed to put temptation in the way of honest folk. Even "the poor lamb" sounds right: Moll is expressing the conventional feeling of an adult towards an unprotected child, regardless of the fact that it was herself that the child required to be protected from. Having paid this tribute to Defoe's knowledge of human behavior, we should face the fact that Moll's comment on the negligence of the child's parents was one that he wanted to make on his own account. In his preface to *Moll Flanders* he makes the point that Moll's various thefts are "so many warnings to honest people to beware of 'em," and he cites her robbing of the child in particular as "a good memento to such people hereafter."[14]

From now on, at all events, Defoe shows us a woman who becomes progressively indifferent to the moral implications of what she is doing, and who turns in due course into a highly professional thief. As part of her general moral degradation, too, she gives way to a certain amount of casual prostitution. Every now and then she expresses some compunction (although, as Professor Watt points out, it is not always easy to decide whether she felt it at the time, or is merely looking back on her past actions from a penitent old age), and there is frequently a background of fear, and the ultimate dread of Newgate. The fear is intelligible enough, but is the compunction in character? It may be admitted that no one is going to make a successful thief unless he has enough fear to keep him from being foolhardy; but if his conscience troubles him every time he commits a theft he had better try some other profession. Yet in *Moll Flanders* this is not really what happens. As Moll tells us the story of her life in the twelve years she was a thief, she proceeds for the most part buoyantly in her account, recording her escapades and her various "purchases" almost in the picaresque manner. From time to time, however, comes the moment when she reflects on the life she is living: she never quite forgets—or, more precisely, Defoe never allows her (and therefore us) to forget—that what she is doing is morally wrong. It could be argued that however far she had advanced in a life of crime Moll might still have those moments of contrition, and that therefore her behavior is not inconsistent. But it is perhaps nearer the truth to interpret her still active conscience as a device deliberately adopted by Defoe to bring home to his readers the situation in which she now finds herself. To do this he is prepared to sacrifice some psychological realism; but if he had failed to give her those twinges of conscience Moll's account of her life as a thief would have been only a picaresque story, with the emphasis falling on her ingenuity and her hairbreadth escapes, and everything taking place in a moral vacuum. Because Moll is made to express compunction and even horror we are the better able to realize just what it is she is doing; but because she none the less does it, and does it very successfully, we are also able to take an intellectual pleasure in her ingenuity and resourcefulness, and to have an intellectual sympathy with her success. Defoe, as usual, is having it both ways. He gives us what he calls in the preface "abundance of delightful incidents," but he sees to it that "all of them [are] usefully apply'd"—or at least enough of them to preserve the moral significance of the story.[15]

The notion, then, that Moll's intermittent twinges of conscience and her moral reflections are only so many crude interventions of the author into her story does less than justice to Defoe's artistry. Since he had elected to tell her story in the form of autobiography, he had no alternative if he was to satisfy *his own* conscience. If, as a consequence, Moll's scruples sometimes seem to be inconsistent with her conduct, that was a risk that Defoe was no doubt prepared to take. What he did in *Moll Flanders* (and later in *Roxana*) has an analogy with what Robert Bridges considered that Shakespeare had done in *Macbeth*. The hero of that tragedy is a sensitive and imaginative man who recoils from villainy, but who also behaves with the utmost cruelty. Without the sensitiveness and the imagination Macbeth would be no more than a bloody-minded villain, although not the less real for that reason; *with* the sensitiveness and the imagination he becomes psychologically almost impossible in view of what he does, but he retains our sympathy, he enables us to realize the depth of his crimes, and he "raises his villainy beyond common meanness." Not all of this can be applied to *Moll Flanders*, but on its more pedestrian level it shows the same sort of psychological inconsistency consciously accepted by the author for the same sort of reasons. That it is also accepted by the average reader who is not going out of his way to look for objections is due to the fascination exerted by the personality of Defoe's heroine. What Bridges wrote about the reaction of an audience to *Macbeth* is equally true for the readers of *Moll Flanders:* "It is when their minds are preoccupied by his personality that the actions follow as unquestionable realities." The writer who can cast this sort of spell over our minds has little need to worry about an occasional inconsistency in the thoughts or actions of his characters.[16]

In *Moll Flanders* Defoe follows his usual practice of constructing his story in a more or less disconnected series of episodes, of varying length and importance. Some approach to a plot, however, is obtained by the reappearance of Moll's Lancashire husband when she is in Newgate, and by her subsequent return to Virginia, where her second husband and their son are still living on their plantation. It is also through her marriage to her brother that Moll discovers who her mother is. Apart from such links between the past and the present, Moll's story moves, by a combination of character and circumstance, in a downward moral curve, culminating in her imprisonment in Newgate. From that climactic experience her fortunes begin to improve, and Moll ends her long and checkered career in the condition of economic and social stability to which she has always aspired. If we cannot say that virtue has been rewarded we can at least see her eventual rehabilitation as the triumph of toughness and persistence. Since we are always conscious of Moll's character, and therefore of what she is likely to do and feel, her story arouses expectations which are duly gratified; but since Defoe endlessly varies her circumstances, the element of surprise is equally strong and persistent. This mixture of the foreseen and the fortuitous is to be found, in different proportions, in all Defoe's fiction.

ii

Although Moll's life as a thief occupies only about a quarter of the whole novel, it must have been one of the most interesting sections to the contemporary reader, as indeed it is to the reader of today. In the years during which Defoe was writing his fiction the sensational acts of highwaymen, and the ingenious activities of thieves and pickpockets, were among the most frequent topics in the newspapers. The death penalty for comparatively minor offences apparently did little to discourage the criminal population, but it undoubtedly increased public interest in the lives of the criminals. The publication eight times a year of the Sessions Papers (*The Whole Proceedings of the Sessions of the Peace, and Oyer and Terminer for the City of London and County of Middlesex*) provided the public with shorthand reports of trials, which frequently included some racy dialogue of defendants and witnesses. Some months after the publication of *Moll Flanders* a report appeared in *Mist's Weekly Journal* of the apprehension of a notorious thief who might well have been the prototype of the "comrade" who taught Moll the art of "taking off gold watches from the ladies' sides":

Moll King, a most notorious offender, famous for stealing gold watches from the ladies' sides in the churches, for which she had been several times convicted, being lately return'd from transportation, has been taken, and is committed to Newgate.

Less than two years later, the remarkable exploits of Jack Sheppard in breaking out of Newgate roused the public interest to a new height. Defoe characteristically took advantage of the popular excitement to write two pamphlets on the life of this young criminal, and he followed them up with two more on the notorious Jonathan Wild, who had at last been caught red-handed and hanged at Tyburn in 1725.[17]

When therefore he was casting about in 1722 for a story that would repeat the success of *Moll Flanders*, it was not surprising that he should think of writing about another pickpocket. *The History and Remarkable Life of the Truly Honourable Col. Jacque, Commonly Call'd Col. Jack* is dated 1723, but was published in December 1722. The title-pages of Defoe's stories do not always correspond very closely with their contents. Robinson Crusoe was rescued from his island by the captain of an English merchantman, but the title-page says that he was "strangely deliver'd by Pyrates." It is true that there had been a mutiny on board ship, but this had been put down by Crusoe, the captain, and some of his men; and unless Defoe was equating mutineers with pirates (which is of course possible) it looks as if at some point he had changed his mind about how Crusoe was to be rescued. But with *Colonel Jack* the discrepancies between the title-page and the contents are much more marked. Jack is said to have been "six and twenty years a thief", but this statement is in striking conflict with the facts: although in this novel Defoe is unusually vague about the passage of time, there seems no reason to suppose that Jack's life as a thief extended much beyond his boyhood. After working for his Virginia master not less than seven years Jack becomes a planter himself, and some years after this he was (or so he says) "above thirty year old." Defoe's chronology is in fact so imprecise that the less notice taken of it the better; but the statement on the title-page that he was a thief for twenty-six years points unmistakably to a change of plan at some point during the composition of the story. Again, the closing words of the sub-title tells us that Jack "fled with the Chevalier, and is now abroad completing a Life of Wonders, and resolves to dye a General." Here again the statement on the title-page is not borne out by what Defoe actually wrote. An explanation of this second discrepancy is offered by Professor Moore, who points out that the book was published while Bishop Atterbury was in the Tower awaiting trial for conspiracy in a Jacobite plot to restore James Stuart, the Old Pretender (the "Chevalier"), and that Defoe would not have represented a successful Jacobite as a hero. This is a plausible suggestion; but it leaves unanswered a much harder question—why Defoe, who had been in such serious trouble in 1713 for supposedly writing three Jacobite pamphlets, should ever have entertained the idea of making his hero become a successful Jacobite. Apart from this, rumors of a plot were in circulation at least as early as May 1722, when Defoe could have been planning his story; Atterbury had been arrested four months before *Colonel Jack* was published, and another of the conspirators, Christopher Layer, was condemned to death in November. Since late August, at all events, when the government began to arrest the Jacobite conspirators, Defoe must have known that a book with a Jacobite hero would be political dynamite. Is this, then, yet another example of Defoe the journalist taking a dangerous risk for the sake of being topical? If it is, he must at some point have allowed more prudent considerations to prevail, and provided the story with a less provocative ending. Perhaps he always intended to satirize this part of Jack's career, and there are signs elsewhere in the novel that his attitude to his hero is comical-satirical; but if so, he did well not to pursue the Jacobite theme any further, in view of the sort of misunderstandings that some of his previous ventures into satire had occasioned. Yet why, having made the necessary adjustments and shown his hero repudiating his former Jacobite connections, did he not have the original title-page canceled?[18]

In this case I am prepared to believe that the most startling explanation is probably the true one. Defoe, who was obviously writing at speed, was probably feeding the printer with the copy of *Colonel Jack* in instalments, and as each section of the manuscript left his hands, that was almost certainly the last he saw of it. If this seems highly improbable, it is not very different from the way in which Dickens wrote *Pickwick Papers* or Thackeray wrote *Vanity Fair*, except that their work was not only written but *published* serially, whereas *Colonel Jack* was not published until the last piece of copy had been received and set by the printer. If this explanation is accepted, it means that the first page that Defoe sent to the printer contained the long descriptive title of the book he had now started to write. Although there must have been some occasions (e.g. with many numbers of the *Review*) on which Defoe never read his work in proof, there is no need to suppose that he did not read and receive proofs of *Colonel Jack*. But if, as I suggest, those proofs came back to him in instalments while he was still writing the book, he almost certainly read them as they came in, returned them to the printer, and then was finished with them for good and all. We have little information about Defoe's dealings with his printers; but a surviving letter of 10 September 1729 to John Watts, who had started printing *The Complete English Gentleman* for him, shows that on this occasion at least the printer had begun to set the book before he had received all the copy. "I here return the first sheet and as much copy as will make near 3 sheets more," Defoe told Watts. "You shall have all the remainder so as not to let you stand still at all." If we had a letter from Defoe to the printer of *Colonel Jack* it might well be couched in similar terms.[19]

The discrepancies and contradictions in *Colonel Jack* are far from being confined to the title-page. Even for Defoe this novel is carelessly written, showing signs of haste, uncertain construction, and changes of direction. Not only is the time-scheme indeterminate, but statements made by Jack are often contradicted within a few pages. On one page, for example, he tells us that his money "abated a-pace"; on the next he says, "I had not much diminished my stock of money," but he adds, in the very next sentence, "I was not so anxious about my money running low, because I knew what a reserve I had made at London." What, again, are we to make of the following passage, in which Colonel Jack relates an early escapade of the Captain?

There was it seems some villainous thing done by this gang about that time, whether a child was murther'd among them, or a child otherwise abus'd; but it seems it was a child of an eminent citizen, and the parent some how or other got a scent of the thing, so that they recover'd their child, tho' in a sad condition, and almost kill'd; I was too young, and it was too long ago for me to remember the whole story, but they were all taken up, and sent to Newgate, and Capt. Jack among the rest. . . .

In such a passage as this Defoe's creative powers seem to be grinding to a halt. The initial uncertainty about what happened to the child is surely not in the mind of Colonel Jack, but in that of his creator: Defoe seems to be feeling his way along, and when he *has* made up his mind about what occurred, he does not trouble to cancel the vague "some villainous thing done by this gang" or the expression of uncertainty as to whether the child was murdered or only "otherwise abus'd." The repetition, too, of "it seems" is the work of a tired writer. One is tempted to apply to *Colonel Jack* the uncompromising words that Swinburne used to characterize the plays of Thomas Dekker—"reckless and sluttish incoherence." The chief fault that Swinburne found in Dekker, his want of a fixed and steady purpose, seems to have beset Defoe when he wrote *Colonel Jack*. At all events, this novel is an amalgam of all the genres he had so far tried, dealing in turn with the criminal classes, life on a Virginia plantation, marriage problems, military adventures in the mode of *Memoirs of a Cavalier*, and trading adventures which recall those of *The Farther Adventures of Robinson Crusoe* and anticipate those of *A New Voyage round the World*.[20]

If Defoe was a tired man when he wrote *Colonel Jack* he had good reasons for being so. For several years now he had been turning out in rapid succession a series of long works of fiction, besides publishing numerous pamphlets on political, religious, and other subjects, long historical works on Charles XII of Sweden and Peter the Great of Russia, and such books as *Religious Courtship*. All this time, too, he was contributing to *Mist's Weekly Journal*, *Applebee's Weekly Journal*, and various other periodicals, besides writing his own essay-journal, *The Commentator* (1720). So large and so varied an output would be hard to parallel in any other great writer, and Defoe may have brought himself to the verge of a breakdown. It is at least significant that in 1723 the flow of books and pamphlets suddenly dried up; and for the whole of that year only one pamphlet can be safely attributed to him. Yet if he had really overtaxed his strength he must have made a complete recovery, for 1724 was another vintage year.

In one respect *Colonel Jack* is characteristic of most of Defoe's fiction: it has passages of the greatest interest alternating with stretches of comparatively commonplace writing. Like Dekker, Defoe trusted to his moments of inspiration, and in between those he simply went through the motions of continuing the story. The opening section of *Colonel Jack*, in which he deals with the boy-thief, is as good as anything he ever wrote, not only for the much-praised episode of the hollow tree in which Jack hides and loses his money, but for Defoe's understanding of the mind of a child. Little Jack has grown up in a state of nature; no one has taught him what he must or mustn't do, and (as with all young children) it is some time before he develops a moral sense. Speaking of his early experiences as a pickpocket, he explains to us that it was a good while before he came to realize that he was committing any offence. "I look'd on picking pockets as a kind of trade, and thought I was to go apprentice to it." Later, after he has become proficient, he goes out of his way to emphasize that the course of life on which he had embarked seemed entirely natural to him, and that he was quite unconscious of doing anything wrong:

Nothing is more certain than that hitherto, being partly from the gross ignorance of my untaught childhood, as I observ'd before, partly from the hardness and wickedness of the company I kept, and add to these, that it was the business I might be said to be brought up to, I had, I say, all the way hitherto, no manner of thoughts about the good or evil of what I was embark'd in; consequently, I had no sense of conscience, no reproaches upon my mind for having done amiss.

This state of innocence was not to last much longer, but at this early stage Jack was not a moral agent, and had no means of knowing (as Moll Flanders always knew) that every fresh theft was another step in the downward path. To Jack it was simply another job well or badly done. In his account of his hero's childhood Defoe is concerned to show the importance of education in early years, and to emphasize, as he does in the Preface, "the miserable condition of multitudes of youth, many of whose natural tempers are docible, and would lead them to learn the best things rather than the worst." But although Defoe has this didactic intention, Jack's account of his amoral childhood is beautifully told, and is based throughout on sound psychology. His passionate burst of grief when he believes that he has lost his money in the hollow tree and his extravagant delight when he recovers it are entirely natural. Among the starkest tragedies in the life of a child is the loss of some beloved possession—as Wordsworth saw when he told the story of Alice Fell, "insensible to all relief" after her cloak became entangled in the wheel of a post-chaise and was reduced to a miserable and unrecognizable rag. "When I was a child, I spake as a child, I understood as a child, I thought as a child. . . ." I have already suggested that in moments of intense feeling Defoe's mind turned naturally to the words of the Bible; and here, in seeking to express his little hero's joy at recovering the money he had wrapped in "a foul clout," he seems to be recalling that passage in 1 Corinthians. "I was but a child," Jack tells us, "and I rejoic'd like a child. . . ." It is notable how many of the most passionate moments in Defoe's fiction are moments of intense joy, which on the whole he handles more movingly than the moments of sorrow.[21]

Emotionalism of one kind or another is far from uncommon in Defoe's fiction, from Friday's transports of gratitude to Moll's extravagant behavior at the sight of her son Humphrey in Virginia. But there is a sentimental note in *Colonel Jack* which, if not new to Defoe (for it had certainly been present in *The Family Instructor*), had not yet appeared so insistently in his novels. It may therefore be significant that Steele's highly successful sentimental comedy, *The Conscious Lovers*, was produced at Drury Lane on 7 November 1722, rather less than two months before the publication of *Colonel Jack*. If Defoe was present at an early performance, and if (as seems probable) he was still writing *Colonel Jack* during November and December, he may well have been influenced by Steele's play. In any case it had been a topic of conversation long before it had been brought upon the stage. As early as 1720 Steele had given some account of the play in his periodical *The Theatre*, and there was a reference to it—conceivably written by Defoe—in *Mist's Weekly Journal*, 18 November 1721. Defoe could not have failed to approve of Steele's merchant, Mr. Sealand, who says to Sir John Bevil, in words that Defoe might have used himself, "We merchants are a species of gentry that have grown into the world this last century, and are as honourable, and almost as useful, as you landed folks." ("Why 'almost'?" Defoe might have asked.) One of the innovations in Steele's comedy occurs when young Bevil, provoked and challenged by his friend Myrtle, declines to fight a duel. The circumstances are quite different in Defoe's novel, but Colonel Jack also declines to give satisfaction to an irate gentleman, although when further provoked by having his nose tweaked he throws the man to the ground and "had certainly stamp'd him to death" if a constable had not intervened. Later, when he has learned to use a sword, he uses it very effectively on a French marquis who has been too free with his wife, and whom he runs through the body. Here, too, however, we are reminded of Steele's attitude to duelling. When the marquis says he must have satisfaction, Colonel Jack tries to pacify him by pointing out that it is his wife who is the offender, and if she is willing to be a whore *she* is the one who ought to be punished:

I told him . . . that the injury was mine in having a bad woman to deal with; that there was no reason in the thing, that after any man should have found the way into my bed, I, who am injur'd, should go and stake my life upon an equal hazard against the men who have abus'd me.[22]

This realistic attitude is very similar to that of Steele, who had several times pointed out in his periodical, *The Tatler*, the folly of duelling. In the number for 7 June 1709 he told his readers an anecdote designed to expose the false notions of honor which induced men to accept a challenge:

An honest country gentleman had the misfortune to fall into company with two or three modern men of honour, where he happened to be very ill treated; and one of the company, being conscious of his offence, sends a note to him in the morning, and tells him, he was ready to give him *satisfaction*. "This is fine doing," says the plain fellow; "last night he sent me away cursedly out of humour, and this morning he fancies it would be a *satisfaction* to be run through the body."

Whether Defoe was influenced by Steele or not, *Colonel Jack* has fairly been described as the most lachrymose of Defoe's novels, and Professor Monk claims to have counted thirty-three instances of weeping in it, and at least two swoonings. Even when he has reached manhood Jack is easily moved to tears, and one such outburst of feeling has an important result on his subsequent career. When the rich Virginia planter for whom he is working takes occasion to talk "mighty religiously" to a transported pick-pocket and to impress upon him the chance he now has to live an honest life, Jack, who has been listening, is "exceedingly mov'd at this discourse of our master's," and the planter, noticing that Jack has been crying while he spoke to the pickpocket, is curious to know the reason for this unexpected emotion. As a result of their conversation Jack is made an overseer, and some time later obtains his liberty from his generous master, and becomes in time a prosperous planter himself. It is all too good to be true: we are in the same world as that of Steele's sentimental drama. Again, Jack's kindly treatment of Mouchat the slave is heavily charged with that unashamed and at times mawkish emotionalism that Defoe seems to reserve for primitive people and children; and the scene near the end of the novel in which Jack's first wife falls on her knees before him in abject repentance and begs his forgiveness while Jack trembles "like one in an ague" provides yet another example of Defoe deliberately plucking at our heart-strings.[23]

What is more unusual for Defoe, and what gives a theme to even this chaotic story, is the fact that its hero has a natural propensity to goodness. Normally Defoe had little belief in man's natural benevolence; his view of human nature was nearer to that of Calvin than of the third Earl of Shaftesbury. He believed that "the imagination of man's heart is evil from his youth," and that "if we say that we have no sin, we deceive ourselves, and the truth is not in us." With such convictions went a belief in the need for a moral and religious education, and this is indeed one of the secondary themes in *Colonel Jack*, as it is the main theme of *The Family Instructor*. But although Jack gradually works out his own salvation, and ends by becoming at least moderately religious, he is not shown undergoing any form of repentance like that of Crusoe and Moll Flanders, and we are left with the impression that in his case there is not the same need for it. After the statement already quoted that he had no notion there was anything wrong in picking pockets for a living, Jack goes on to say:

Yet I had something in me, by what secret influence I knew not, kept me from the other degree of raking and vice, and in short, from the general wickedness of the rest of my companions. For example, I never us'd any ill words, no body ever heard me swear, nor was I given to drink, or to love strong drink.

Jack himself accounts for the "secret influence" that worked for good in him by telling us that he was the illegitimate son of a man of quality and a gentlewoman, and that when his father left him in the charge of a nurse he made the woman promise that

she should always take care to bid me *remember that I was a gentleman;* and this, he said, was all the education he would desire of her for me; for he did not doubt, he said, but that sometime or other the very hint would inspire me with thoughts suitable to my birth, and that I would certainly act like a gentleman, if I believed myself to be so.

It is true that when Moll Flanders was a little girl she was set on being a lady, and the results were very different. The circumstances, however, were not the same: Moll's mother was certainly not a gentlewoman, and no mention is made of her father. It is equally true that from *The True-Born Englishman* to *The Complete English Gentleman*, written near the end of his life, Defoe had made many sarcastic observations about the hereditary upper class; yet he continued to believe in the hereditary principle. When he went to the races at Newmarket he knew that the thoroughbred filly was more likely to win than the horse with no pedigree at all; and in the same way he was prepared to accept the importance of good blood in men and women. This, to be sure, could largely be nullified by lack of education, and there was always the danger of original sin destroying all the virtues of good breed; but the hereditary gentleman did start with all the advantages of his race. In *The Complete English Gentleman* Defoe even issued a warning (one must suppose seriously intended) about the danger of ladies not suckling their own children, but turning them out to nurse, and exposing them "to suck in the life blood of a dairy wench or a wooll comber, nay of a cook maid of the family marry'd perhaps to a carter or other slave, people but a few degrees above beggars." Why go to all the trouble to keep the breed pure if you proceed to contaminate it, since " 'tis certain, and physitians will tell you so and explain it too, that a child's temper is more influenc'd by the milk he sucks in than by all the other conveyances of nature"? At all events, whether he sucked in his mother's milk or that of the nurse, Jack was the son of gentle folk; and whether that made any difference or not (and Defoe seems to have thought it did), Jack's conduct was certainly influenced by the *belief* that he was by heredity a gentleman. This was no substitute for a virtuous education and a settled way of living, but it acted as a kind of guiding light in the darkness.[24]

Colonel Jack is noticeably unlike Defoe's other heroes and heroines. Crusoe, Singleton and the Cavalier, Moll and Roxana, however they may differ, are all resolute, self-reliant, and possessed by a tireless energy and resourcefulness. Jack is a much less positive character, never very sure of himself, tentative, more sinned against than sinning, frequently unsuccessful, and at times oddly unheroic. As a boy, he tells us, he had the reputation of being bold and resolute, but whenever possible he avoided fighting, and on several occasions he talked himself out of trouble. When in later life he was confronted by the angry bully who presented him with a bill for £30 drawn by his wife and he refused to honor it, he confesses that he was "frighted to the last degree"; and when the maidservant rescued him by fetching a constable and three or four of his neighbors, he tells us that he "took courage while the constable was there, for I knew that he would keep us from fighting, which indeed I had no mind to. . . ."

His matrimonial history is one of almost unmitigated failure, in which he is either duped or made to look ridiculous; and his military career, although not without honor, has its unheroic moments, and appears to have been partly motivated by a desire for his share in the spoils of war. His bravery at Cremona leads to his being commissioned Lieutenant-Colonel by Louis XIV, and in several subsequent skirmishes he gains the reputation of being a good officer; but (he says) he gained something that he "lik'd much better, and that was a good deal of money." Colonel Jack, in fact, has more of the picaro in him than Defoe's other heroes; he knocks about the world, engaging in a series of miscellaneous and unrelated adventures, and his failures are given as much prominence as his successes. His story, if not quite "a novel without a hero," anticipates to some extent the twentieth-century comic novel of Kingsley Amis and John Wain, in which the protagonist is at once passive, blundering, and frustrated.[25]

iii

If *Colonel Jack* shows signs of disintegrating into the loose form of a picaresque narrative, *The Fortunate Mistress* (published early in 1724, and generally known as *Roxana*) is the most elaborately constructed of all Defoe's novels. There are more links than usual between the past and the present, and some of these are highly important in the development of the events and of the situation in which Roxana finds herself. Her improvident first husband turns up again in Paris, a trooper in the service of Louis XIV, but futile as ever; and, more important, the Dutch merchant who helped her to sell her jewels and later to escape to Holland becomes more deeply involved with her, and eventually, after an absence of many years, comes to England and marries her. All this time Roxana's faithful maid Amy is either with her or working for her. At first a fairly neutral character, Amy ends by becoming something a good deal more significant than a female Man Friday.

Most important of all (for this is a novel in which retribution becomes the dominant theme) is the reappearance of the children of Roxana's first marriage. When in the later pages her past begins to catch up with her and a daughter that she had conveniently forgotten about for many years begins her relentless pursuit of her, a tension is engendered that is unlike anything in Defoe's other stories. The special effect of the concluding section of *Roxana* is a strongly aroused expectation, a sense of impending discovery and consequent disaster, just when the heroine appears to be set at last on a prosperous course and to have real hopes of living down that notorious past which is quite unknown to her kindly and honorable husband. It seems only a matter of time till the blow will fall; yet when the situation has become desperate and is moving towards a complete exposure and a tragic ending, the narrative comes to a sudden stop, leaving Roxana's story manifestly unfinished. As the book ends, Roxana, now a countess, has retired with her husband to Holland. "Here," she tells us,

after some few years of flourishing and outwardly happy circumstances, I fell into a dreadful course of calamities, and Amy also; the very reverse of our former good days; the blast of Heaven seem'd to follow the injury done the poor girl by us both; and I was brought so low again that my repentance seem'd to be only the consequence of my misery, as my misery was of my crime.

From the first Defoe had been apt to bring his stories to a rather perfunctory conclusion, but here there is no conclusion at all. So obvious was this, that some years after Defoe's death someone gave *Roxana* a new ending in about 30,000 words, in which Roxana is found out, loses her fortune, is imprisoned for debt, and dies in an Amsterdam jail, while her maid Amy (who must by this time have been well over sixty) apparently expires in a hospital as the result of venereal disease.[26] Why, then, did Defoe fail to finish his own novel in his own way? The crudest explanation would be that the book he had written was already longer than *Moll Flanders* or *Colonel Jack*, and that his publishers had cried, "Hold, enough!" But such an explanation is surely implausible: an experienced writer like Defoe had no need to leave the outcome of Roxana's life history hanging in the air when two or three more paragraphs would have brought it to a genuine conclusion. It is hard to resist the assumption that *Roxana* had got out of hand, and that Defoe didn't know how to finish his own story; or, alternatively, that he knew what must be done but couldn't bring himself to do it. His general pattern in the fiction he had previously written was for a hero or heroine to pass through various adventures and vicissitudes, and at the end to achieve stability and prosperity. This happy ending was some- times achieved only with a certain amount of moral compromise on the part of the author, who allowed his Captain Singleton and his Moll Flanders to retain their ill-gotten gains, but at the same time indicated that they had turned over a new leaf and attained at least some measure of repentance. It looks as if he had intended a similar rehabilitation for Roxana; for she too shows signs of repentance, and after her marriage to the Dutch merchant appears to be heading for a respectable old age. Yet, when it came to the point, Defoe may have felt unable to ignore the moral conse- quences.

King David and King Solomon led rich luxurious lives,
They spent their money freely on concubines and wives;
But when old age came creeping on, then both of them felt qualms,
And Solomon wrote the Proverbs, and David wrote the Psalms.

Those lines represent pretty well the moral situation of Captain Singleton and Moll, although Defoe might have repudiated any such suggestion indignantly. Why, then, does he make an excep- tion of Roxana? For one thing, he almost certainly drew a distinc- tion between the prosperity attributable to successful theft or piracy (wrong, of course, but *comparatively* speaking respect- able), and that due to successful whoring. That he made such a distinction is suggested by the behavior of Roxana when she marries her faithful and honorable Dutch merchant. She cannot bear to think (she says) that the wealth her husband had gained by honest trading should be mixed up with her own tainted possessions:

Unhappy wretch, said I to myself, *shall my ill-got wealth, the product of prosperous lust and of a vile and vicious life of* whoredom and adultery, *be intermingled with the honest well-gotten estate of this honest gentleman, to be a moth and a caterpiller among it, and bring the judgments of Heaven upon him, and upon what he has, for my sake! Shall my wickedness blast his comforts! Shall I be fire in his flax! and be a means to provoke Heaven to curse his blessings!* God forbid! *I'll keep them asunder, if it be possible.*

It is Roxana who is speaking, but she is probably expressing Defoe's feelings as much as her own. The fact that her statement is set in italic type is obviously meant to draw the reader's particular attention to it, and the biblical overtones seem more natural to Defoe than to Roxana.[27]

Quite apart, however, from Defoe's own attitude to a life of luxury and lucrative whoring, he had embarked in the later pages of his novel on a course that could only lead to disaster for his heroine. Once he had brought her daughter upon the scene he was committed to a process of retribution, and there was now no escape for Roxana so long as this troublesome girl was still alive. At some point in the course of composition (possibly with a view to achieving even yet some sort of happy ending for Roxana) Defoe seems to have decided that her daughter must be removed from the scene. She could conceivably have died a natural death or have met with a fatal accident; but Defoe chose to have her murdered by the too faithful Amy. The statement in the final sentence of the novel already quoted, that "the blast of Heaven seem'd to follow the injury done the poor girl by us both" refers to the fate of this daughter; but it is symptomatic of the ambiguous nature of the concluding pages that Defoe never states quite clearly that the girl was in fact murdered. The first time that Amy threatens to make away with her, Roxana says that if she ever does such a dreadful thing she will personally see that she hangs for it, and would even cut Amy's throat herself. Some time later Amy tells Roxana that her daughter has found out about her marriage to the Dutch merchant, and that she knows his name and will certainly seek her out. "In the middle of all my amazement," Roxana tells us,

Amy starts up, and runs about the room like a distracted body; I'll put an end to it, that I will; I can't bear it; I must murther her; I'll kill her, B——,* *and swears by her Maker, in the most serious tone in the world. . . .*

But again she is rebuked by Roxana who forbids her to hurt a hair of her daughter's head, but ends by saying rather feebly, "Well, well, be quiet, and do not talk thus, I can't bear it." Later

* This is the reading of the first edition. I take B—— to stand for "By God!". Some later editions read: "I'll kill the B——" [bitch].

still, when Roxana has become convinced that her identity (and her past life) are known to her daughter, and is upbraided by Amy for not having allowed her to kill the girl, she says, "I was not for killing the girl yet." This undoubtedly looks ominous; but "yet" almost certainly carries the meaning of "nevertheless," especially as she goes on to say, "I cou'd not bear the thoughts of that neither." At last, when Amy recurs once more to the pressing need to do away with the girl, Roxana finally breaks with her terrible maid, and tells her she will never see her face again.[28]

Defoe has been so careful, on one occasion after another, not to implicate Roxana in the death of her daughter and to make her recoil in horror from the suggestion of it, that it looks as if he had no intention of portraying her as a hardened sinner. Her behavior to the other surviving children of her first marriage, and even to this troublesome daughter, for whom she has made secret provision, is certainly not that of an unnatural mother. On the other hand Roxana takes no steps to *prevent* Amy from carrying out her murderous threat, and to that extent she is culpable. Roxana's attitude is fairly summed up in the lines,

> Thou shalt not kill; but needst not strive
> Officiously to keep alive.

At all events Defoe's handling of this dreadful episode is oddly muted: he may already have realized the terrible impact the girl's murder must have on his story, and have felt that by leaving it indefinite he was doing something to lessen the disastrous effect it would have on the reader's attitude to Roxana. The nearest we come to being actually told that Amy has carried out her threat is in a letter from the Quaker lady to Roxana, in which she relates what Amy had reported to her. After giving the Quaker an account of how troublesome the girl had been to her mistress by hunting after her and following her from place to place, Amy had added (as Roxana tells it) that

there was an absolute necessity of securing her and removing her out-of-the-way; and that, in short, without asking my leave, or anybody's leave, she wou'd take care she shou'd trouble her mistress (meaning me) no more; and that after Amy had said so, she had indeed never heard any more of the girl; so that she suppos'd Amy had manag'd it so well as to put an end to it.

The innocent Quaker merely assumed that Amy "had found some way to perswade her to be quiet and easie," but Roxana had no illusions about what that way must have been.

I was struck as with a blast from Heaven at the reading of her letter; I fell into a fit of trembling from head to foot; and I ran raving about the room like a mad-woman. . . . I threw myself on the bed, and cry'd out, *Lord be merciful to me, she has murther'd my child;* and with that a flood of tears burst out, and I cry'd vehemently for above an hour.

Anticipating this ghastly event in her rather rambling narrative, Roxana had already told us that Amy was forming "a more fatal and wicked design in her head against her; which, indeed, I never knew till after it was executed, nor durst Amy ever communicate it to me." The word "fatal" seems to put the issue out of doubt; but what Amy actually did we are never told.[29]

At what stage Defoe decided that his story was going to include cold-blooded murder we cannot know. But once he had allowed it to be committed, all prospects of his usual happy ending became impossible. In the natural process of events Amy would be suspected, apprehended, tried, and almost certainly condemned and hanged at Tyburn. Besides becoming more important as a fictional character than her mistress while all this was going on, she would almost inevitably involve Roxana in her fate; for either Roxana would have to give evidence against her maid, or she would have to stand by her, conceal her knowledge of Amy's intentions, and protest her belief in her innocence. In either case Roxana would inevitably sink lower in our estimation; and whichever course she adopted, the fact that the dead girl was her own daughter was bound to come out, with all the attendant exposure of her past. It looks as if Defoe had involved himself in a train of events that he was unwilling to follow to their natural conclusion. He had been careful, as we have seen, to absolve Roxana from any complicity in the death of her daughter; but in developing the powerful situation in which the persistent girl strove to establish that Roxana was her mother he perhaps failed to weigh the consequences of having her murdered. In any event it is hard to resist the conviction that the novel comes to an abrupt end because

Defoe's hand was being forced, and the ending he had originally planned was no longer possible.

In saying this I am at variance with Professor Starr, who has a special right to be heard on this matter. He sees an essential difference between Roxana and Moll Flanders: whereas Moll underwent a genuine conversion before she left Newgate, Roxana (he suggests) hardened into a final impenitency, and was therefore irretrievably damned. Starr believes that "there are fairly early indications that Defoe meant to consign Roxana to the devil," and that he conceived her as a female counterpart to Bunyan's Mr. Badman. Although Starr admits that there is a considerable similarity between Roxana's spiritual development and Moll's, and considers the hypothesis that "Defoe set out to portray a process of hardening, as in *Moll Flanders,* with every intention of bringing Roxana to eventual repentance, but at some point decided to let her spiritual development complete its natural course, and end with the distinct prospect of damnation," he prefers the alternative supposition that Roxana was doomed to destruction from the first, and that Defoe was therefore consciously writing a different kind of story.

A serious objection to the first hypothesis is that as Roxana relates the story of her life she punctuates it with far more penitent observations than are to be found in Moll's account of her fortunes and misfortunes. She talks at one point of setting herself apart "to the great work which I have since seen so much necessity and occasion for, I mean that of repentance." When she finally leaves off whoring, she explains that she had never loved it "for the sake of the vice," and had not "delighted in being a whore as such." ("I was never able in justice and with truth to say I was so wicked as that.") Like Moll, she had first been tempted by necessity; and as "poverty made me a whore at the beginning, so excess of avarice for getting money, and excess of vanity, continued me in the crime, not being able to resist the flatteries of great persons; being called the finest woman in France; being caressed by a prince. . . ." The point at issue, however, is not whether Roxana was a sinner, but whether in the eyes of Defoe she was so hardened a sinner that she was damned beyond all possibility of redemption. Such confessions as those just quoted

hardly give this impression. When at length she marries the Dutch
merchant whom she might have married nearly ten years earlier,
her whole way of life changes into one of rigid respectability; but
either because Defoe feels she has not yet been sufficiently punished, or because her old way of life has involved her in so much
deception that retribution is bound to follow, she achieves no
settled happiness. The past is continually casting its ugly shadow
on the present. She sleeps little and eats little; she has terrible
dreams "of devils and monsters; falling into gulphs, and off from
steep and high precipices," so that she is "hag-ridden with
frights." It is perhaps worth recalling that Captain Singleton's
mind was similarly troubled when he left off being a pirate, and
he was seriously tempted to put an end to his life by blowing out
his brains until William the Quaker talked him out of it. There
is no casuistical William at hand to console Roxana, and if there
had been she would not have been taken in by his specious arguments. Sometimes, she tells us, she would be transported with joy
at having come "so smoothly out of the arms of Hell" and not
being "ingulph'd in ruin"; but she realised that she had not undergone any real conversion yet:

I was not come to that repentance that is rais'd from a sense of
Heaven's goodness; I repented of the crime, but it was of another and
lower kind of repentance, and rather mov'd by my fears of vengeance
than from a sense of being spar'd from being punish'd, and landed
safe after a storm.

If this was as far as her repentance ever went, we must agree that
in Defoe's reckoning Roxana's soul was in mortal danger; but was
it really Defoe's intention to leave her in that half-way house on
the road to true penitence?[30]
  If he thought of Roxana as a damned soul, why did he allow
her to reproach herself as frequently as she does? Why does she
still seem to have an active conscience? And why, if she is not a
genuine penitent, does she talk so much about repentance? Professor Starr has an answer to those questions: so far as Roxana
herself is concerned, the talk of repentance is no more than talk,
and it is out of character; but Defoe, he suggests, having unfortunately chosen to tell the story of a female Mr. Badman in
the first person, has no other means of bringing home to his

readers the depth of her depravity. He would have done better to tell his story, as Bunyan told his, in the third person, and to leave the commentary to a Mr. Wiseman. If we accept Starr's view of Roxana's ultimate hardening and damnation, all that he says about her frequent moral reflections is sound and unanswerable. But there still remains the distinct possibility that Defoe meant Roxana to be a true penitent (although repentance in her case would entail a prolonged penance), and that the process is never seen to be completed because her story breaks off abruptly before the period of retribution is finished. For what it is worth, it should be noted that the reader's attention is drawn in the Preface to the lesson he can learn from Roxana's repentance: if Defoe himself thought she was not a true penitent he would hardly have made this point. The Preface, however, is so clumsily written, and so muddled in its references to "the relator" and "the writer," who are also apparently the editor of Roxana's narrative, that one wonders whether the Preface was written by Defoe at all. It is at least a possible hypothesis that ill health forced Defoe to abandon *Roxana* before he had completed it, and that the puzzling last paragraph, together with the Preface, were the work of another hand.[31]

Much as she may differ from Moll Flanders, Roxana has all of Moll's intelligence; indeed, she probably strikes most readers as having the superior intellect. Whereas Moll gets through life by acting upon impulse and by bold improvisation, Roxana almost never acts hastily, but weighs up each new situation and draws up her plans to deal with it. This cool and calculating approach, and the very frankness with which she describes her motives, make her for most readers a less attractive character than Moll. We first become aware of her formidable mind when she expresses her disgust with her stupid brewer husband. ("Never, ladies, marry a fool; any husband rather than a fool. . . . What is more shocking than for a woman to bring a handsome, comely fellow of a husband into company, and then be oblig'd to blush for him every time she hears him speak? To hear other gentlemen talk sense, and he be able to say nothing? . . . I had now five children by him; the only work (perhaps) that fools are good for.") Equally impressive is the absence of any illusions in Roxana's mind about the sort of life she has been living, and her calm and clear-headed

assessment of her own motives. This may be all part of Defoe's
determination that the reader shall have no illusions about fornication and adultery; but even if that was his reason for making
Roxana examine herself so frequently and find herself wanting,
the effect of such passages on the reader is to make him more than
ever aware of her intelligence and intellectual honesty. Most
striking of all, perhaps, is Roxana's long debate with her Dutch
lover, who, having been to bed with her, is anxious to make her
an "honest woman," but fails completely in his attempt to marry
her. Roxana has now acquired economic independence: why, she
asks, should she exchange it for the state of matrimony, in which
she and all she possesses would become the property of her husband? This goes far beyond the cry of Congreve's Millamant,
"My dear liberty, shall I leave thee?", when she is about to give
her hand to Mirabel; and it is characteristic of Roxana (and of
Defoe) that it is the economic argument that prevails. Defoe
cannot possibly have approved of Roxana "living in sin," and
Professor Starr believes that the reader is intended to view her as
a woman who is guilty "not merely of fornication but of preaching and promoting it." He points out, too, that Roxana later
acknowledges the foolishness and wickedness of the position she
has defended on this occasion, and he accordingly disagrees with
those who see in her determination to remain free "an extreme
statement of Defoe's characteristic feminism." This would be
more convincing if Roxana were not so eloquent, and if the
Dutchman had anything really substantial to offer in reply. Of
course Roxana's is an extreme statement; but it is hard to believe
that it was not meant by Defoe to shock his readers into recon-
sidering the status of women and the inequality to which they
were traditionally subjected. "I told him," says Roxana,

I had, perhaps, differing notions of matrimony from what the receiv'd
custom had given us of it; that I thought a woman was a free agent
as well as a man, and was born free, and cou'd she manage herself
suitably, might enjoy that liberty to as much purpose as the men do;
that the laws of matrimony were indeed otherwise, and mankind at
this time acted upon quite other principles; and those such that a
woman gave herself entirely away from herself in marriage, and
capitulated only to be at best but an upper-servant. . . . That the very
nature of the marriage-contract was, in short, nothing but giving up

liberty, estate, authority, and every-thing to the man, and the woman was indeed a meer woman ever after, that is to say, a slave.

To this Roxana adds that in her opinion "a woman was as fit to govern and enjoy her own estate, without a man, as a man without a woman; and that, if she had a mind to gratifie herself as to sexes, she might entertain a man, as a man does a mistress." In such passages we are surely listening to the Shavian Defoe, the Defoe who liked to *épater les bourgeois*, who delighted in argument and paradox. But again, so far as Roxana is concerned, the effect of such statements is to impress us with the vigor and independence of her mind, whether we agree with her arguments or reject them.[32]

However we interpret Roxana's determination to keep her liberty, her refusal of the Dutch merchant's offer of marriage was clearly intended by Defoe to be a turning point in her career. It is here that she receives a solemn warning which has been virtually ignored by critics of this novel. When the Dutchman is finally compelled to accept the fact that Roxana will not marry him, he leaves her a letter in which he warns her that her decision will be her ruin, and that she will seriously repent it:

He foretold some fatal things, which, he said, he was well assur'd I shou'd fall into; and that at last I wou'd be ruin'd by a bad husband. . . . This letter stunn'd me: I cou'd not think it possible for anyone that had not dealt with the Devil to write such a letter; for he spoke of some particular things which afterwards were to befal me, with such an assurance that it frighted me before-hand; and when those things did come to pass, I was perswaded he had some more than human knowledge. . . .[33]

In another writer this might not mean very much; but in Defoe, with his frequently expressed belief in predictions, omens, and other occult manifestations, it is clearly meant to be taken seriously. What, then, are we to make of the Dutchman's prediction that Roxana would be "ruined by a bad husband"? Unless this is another reference to the wretched brewer (who was by this time dead, but who had begotten the daughter who was eventually to prove so fatal to Roxana's peace of mind), it looks as if at this point in the composition of his story Defoe had envisaged a different sort of fate for his heroine. Once again we seem to

have come upon one of those loose ends that are so common in
Defoe's fiction, and to which there seems to be no better answer
than Whitman's

> Do I contradict myself?
> Very well then I contradict myself,
> (I am large, I contain multitudes.)

iv

Defoe's views on prose fiction were never very clearly stated,
and such pronouncements as he did make are not always easy to
reconcile, and must to some extent be interpreted in the particular
context in which they were made. It seems clear, however, that
he was prepared to defend "romances" provided they had moral
implications, expressed either overtly or by inference. It was on
those grounds that he recommended the first part of *Robinson
Crusoe*, a story which was "told with modesty, with seriousness,
and with a religious application of events to the uses to which
wise men always apply them, *viz.* to the instruction of others by
this example, and to justify and honour the wisdom of Providence
in all the variety of our circumstances, let them happen how they
will." In the Preface to the *Farther Adventures* he made similar
claims:

All the endeavours of envious people to reproach it with being a
romance [i.e. to reproach it because it *is* a romance] . . . have proved
abortive, and as impotent as malicious. The just application of every
incident, the religious and useful inferences drawn from every part,
are so many testimonies to the good design of making it publick, and
must legitimate all the part that may be call'd invention or parable
in the story.

He went on to complain indignantly of a piratical abridgment of
his story in which all the moral and religious reflections, "which
are not only the greatest beautys of the work, but are calculated
for the infinite advantage of the reader," had been ruthlessly cut
out. If, he continued, *Robinson Crusoe* is, as those pirates assert, a
work of invention, "they take from it the improvement which
alone recommends that invention to wise and good men." This is
clear enough: a mere story of adventure, told for its own sake
and without any moral or religious application, would be un-

acceptable; but if proper inferences were drawn and suitable reflections made, it could be a valuable medium for instruction. In writing his own fiction Defoe unquestionably had various didactic purposes to serve, and he made use of fiction not merely for the sake of moral instruction, but for the propagation of social and economic ideas. The extent to which the "diverting" part takes over from the didactic varies from one story to another.[34]

Defoe's conception of the novel seems to have been remarkably like that of another didactic writer nearer our own day who was also a master of the diffuse, and who, like Defoe, was brimming over with ideas which he was determined to express by means of fiction. "I was disposed," H. G. Wells tells us, "to regard a novel as about as much an art form as a market place or a boulevard. It had not even necessarily to get anywhere. You went by it on your various occasions." In discussing his novel *Marriage* he admits that it might have been more carefully constructed:

It could have been just as light and much better done. But that would have taken more time than I could afford. . . . The fastidious critic might object, but the general reader to whom I addressed myself cared no more for finish and fundamental veracity about the secondary things of behaviour than I.

Defoe would almost certainly have agreed in general with both of those statements, and with the reasons which Wells gave for making a convenience of the novel form in the way he did. But the general resemblance between the two men does not end here. I cite two further passages from Wells's *Autobiography* to show how similar their views on fiction sometimes were. "Who would read a novel," Wells asked, "if we were permitted to read biography—all out?" Substitute "autobiography" for "biography" and we come very near to what Defoe was trying to do in such frank confessions as those of Moll Flanders, Colonel Jack, and Roxana. And when Wells tells us that what he was insisting upon in his novels was "the importance of individuality and individual adjustment to life," we have the central theme of most of Defoe's best fiction.[35]

Where Defoe and Wells (or, at any rate, the later Wells) diverge is in their conception of what constitutes a story worth telling. Here, for a modern parallel, we may turn to Thomas Hardy, whose views on this matter appear to have been similar to Defoe's, however different his novels may have been. Several statements in Hardy's notebooks make it quite clear that he considered a novel was not just a fictitious transcript of ordinary day-to-day life. "A story," he claimed, "must be exceptional enough to be worth its telling. We tale-tellers are all Ancient Mariners, and none of us is warranted in stopping Wedding Guests (in other words, the hurrying public) unless he has something more than usual to relate than the ordinary experience of every average man and woman." I cite another passage in which Hardy develops more fully his conception of the relationship between the unusual (in the events) and the average or usual (in the person who experiences):

The real, if unavowed, purpose of fiction is to give pleasure by gratifying the love of the uncommon in human experience, mental or corporeal.

This is done all the more perfectly in proportion as the reader is illuded to believe the personages true and real like himself.

Solely to the latter end a work of fiction should be a precise transcript of ordinary life; but,

The uncommon would be absent and the interest lost. Hence,

The writer's problem is how to strike a balance between the uncommon and the ordinary so as on the one hand to give interest, on the other to give reality.

In working out this problem, human nature must never be made abnormal, which is introducing incredibility. The uncommonness must lie in the events, not in the characters; and the writer's art lies in shaping the uncommonness while disguising its unlikelihood, if it be unlikely.[36]

Defoe gratifies this love of the uncommon in his tale of a man shipwrecked on a desert island and living alone there for many years; in the narrative of a London citizen who survived the appalling months of the Great Plague; in the story of a female thief whose successful career ended in Newgate and a death sentence; and in that of the deserted wife of a London brewer who became the mistress of a prince and later of Charles II. All of those situations are exceptional enough to satisfy Hardy's requirements. But Crusoe and H. F. of the *Journal* are average men

whose very ordinariness makes their experiences credible; and
Moll and Roxana are women whose careers may be abnormal, but
whose characters make us ready to accept what they do. When
Defoe's main concern is with moral and religious instruction, as
in *The Family Instructor* and *Religious Courtship*, he gives us
"the ordinary experience of . . . average man and woman," and
stays almost painfully close to middle-class manners and conversation; but when he feels free to write fiction less immediately
addressed to improvement, his natural tendency is to tell a tale of
exceptional circumstances that the reader "cannot choose but
hear." Indeed, he said as much himself in his *Serious Reflections
. . . of Robinson Crusoe:*

> Had the common way of writing a man's private history been taken,
> and I had given you the conduct or life of a man you knew, and
> whose misfortunes and infirmities perhaps you had sometimes un-
> justly triumphed over, all I could have said would have yielded
> no diversion, and perhaps scarce have obtained a reading, or at best
> no attention. . . . Even the miracles of the blessed Saviour of the
> world suffered scorn and contempt, when it was reflected that they
> were done by the carpenter's son; one whose family and original
> they had a mean opinion of, and whose brothers and sisters were
> ordinary people like themselves.[37]

In his fiction Defoe was motivated by considerations similar to
those that prevailed with him in his journalistic writing: he had to
catch the ear of an inattentive public. One of his few pronouncements about this public occurs in a passage in *The History and
Reality of Apparitions*, where, after suggesting that premonitions
may be due to the agency of good spirits "that Heaven in its
infinite wisdom and goodness may have appointed," he suddenly
checks himself:

> But hold! whither am I going? This looks like religion, and we must
> not talk a word of that, if we expect to be agreeable. Unhappy times!
> where to be serious is to be dull and grave, and consequently to write
> without spirit. . . .
> Well, we must comply however; the humour of the day must pre-
> vail; and as there is no instructing you without pleasing you, and no
> pleasing you but in your own way, we must go on in that way; the
> understanding must be refined by allegory and enigma; you must

see the sun through the cloud, and relish light by the help of dark-ness.

We would do well not to overestimate Defoe's reluctance to write in allegory (here practically equivalent to fiction); and he obvi-ously enjoyed the freedom to invent and to follow his characters into those dark places that the taste of the public forced upon him. Indeed, when we remember his puritan background and his genuine moral seriousness, we may well wonder at the apparent ease with which he escapes from the sort of world he pictures in *The Family Instructor*.[38]

The autobiographical form in which he chose to tell his stories may sometimes have involved him in narrating events and circum-stances of which he could not possibly approve, and of which, through the comments of a Moll or a Roxana, he sometimes suc-ceeds in expressing strong disapproval. But if he had shown Moll and Roxana repenting *all the time* he would have alienated those readers who could only be instructed if they were pleased, and who would not be pleased if they were given nothing but instruction. He would also have been offering his readers a false view of the life he was seeking to depict, and he would have blurred their impression of a man or a woman living by natural law in a hard and competitive world.

This, then, was Defoe's dilemma. But if he was driven by his own moral principles to make Moll and Roxana express a repen-tance which is not always convincing, the very expression of that repentance has the effect of humanizing what would otherwise be a mere criminal record, and has the further effect of making the reader realize the gap between right and wrong, and the isola-tion of Moll and Roxana from normal human society. And if he was compelled in the interest of decency to make some sacrifice of realism, and in telling Moll's story to "put it into a dress fit to be seen, and to make it speak language fit to be read," he allows himself in *Roxana*, in a passage which must have shocked most contemporary readers and might even attract attention in a twentieth-century novel, to show his heroine putting her maid to bed with the goldsmith while she stands by and looks on.[39] The artist and the moralist are often at loggerheads in Defoe. All things considered, it is remarkable how often it is the artist who has the last word.

6

The Last Years

ELDERLY SCHOLARS, when asked what they are doing now that they have retired, have a way of answering that they have never been so busy. No one could have made that claim with more justification than Defoe. If we date his retirement from the time that he stopped contributing regularly to Mist's and Applebee's journals, we are still left with at least half a dozen years during which he was writing as actively as ever. Some of the books he published in the last years of his life were based on his own personal experience extending over more than sixty years; others were probably compiled in large part from the books in his library, and from the notes he had made from time to time when something caught his attention. Almost all of them were influenced to some degree by his recently acquired habit of writing fiction.

Of the various substantial books he wrote in his old age, the two that will probably survive longest are, improbably enough, guidebooks; and both are characteristic of his later leisurely, rambling, and reminiscent style. The necessary information is imparted to the reader, but it is given with a constant attention to his entertainment. Almost everything that Defoe wrote in those later years is marked by an increased willingness to amuse as he instructs; the style is relaxed and familiar, and the illustrative anecdotes and digressions are frequent and often humorous. Defoe now touches nothing that he does not make human.

The first of those guides, written in the form of familiar letters, is *A Tour thro' the Whole Island of Great Britain*, which ap-

peared in three volumes from 1724 to 1726. Old guide-books
have usually no more than an antiquarian interest, and with the
passage of time become little more than melancholy sources of
misinformation. From obsolete Baedekers the modern tourist can
learn that his father or grandfather could get a good dinner in
Paris for two francs, and that the Campo Santo at Pisa should be
visited on account of its famous frescoes; but the march of
progress has raised the cost of eating, and the frescoes were
bombed out of existence in the Second World War. It is true that
the England and Scotland described by Defoe in the *Tour* have
undergone great changes; but for the economic and social his-
torian his facts retain great interest, and are indeed a prime source
of information. When he was making his numerous circuits
through the country some ancient towns were decaying, and
others, such as Birmingham, Leeds, Manchester, and Liverpool,
were developing rapidly. Defoe is very conscious of change; he is
well aware that the facts he is setting down are becoming out of
date as he writes, and that with every decade the face of England
is altering as new industries are started in one area and old crafts
become moribund in another. "As no cloaths can be made to fit a
growing child," he remarks, ". . . so no account of a Kingdom thus
daily altering its countenance can be perfect."[1] But for Defoe this
is all matter for congratulation; he delights in change, for change
means life, growth, increase of population and of the national
wealth. He is not writing his book for posterity, but for the men
of his own day; if it goes out of date in a few years, so much the
better for England. That posterity is still interested in the *Tour*
is a tribute to his ability as a journalist, with an eye for what is
picturesque, significant, and above all of human interest.

Defoe claimed that his material had been collected in the course
of "seventeen very large circuits, or journeys. . . . and three
general tours over almost the whole English part of the island";
and those travels were obviously the work of many years. He
was mainly concerned with the present state of the country:

The situation of things is given not as they have been, but as they
are; the improvements in the soil, the product of the earth, the labour
of the poor, the improvement in manufactures, merchandizes, in
navigation, all respect the present time, not the time past.

Yet he does not neglect the past. It is true that when he comes in the course of his travels to the ancient walled town of Richmond, which has the ruins of a strong castle, he declines to enter into particulars, and says firmly that "as those things are now all slighted, so really the account of them is of small consequence, and needless; old fortifications being, if fortification was wanted, of very little signification." So, too, after giving a short historical account of Bury St. Edmunds, he abruptly reminds himself that he is not writing history, and that his real business is with "the present state of the place." On the other hand, while he is at York he takes a day off to visit the battlefield of Marston Moor; and this leads him to a digression on the impetuosity of Prince Rupert which led to the defeat of the royal army, and to a further digression on "old General Tilly," who showed much more prudence and military skill at the Battle of Leipzig. Defoe's *Tour* is a ramble in more senses than one. Whatever he may say about not being concerned with past history, he introduces a good deal of it. At Malden in Essex he stops to tell us about Queen Boadicea, and when he comes to Colchester he inserts a long account of the siege of the town in 1648, preserved in a contemporary diary. Quite frequently he quotes from Camden, Dugdale, and other historians and antiquarians. For more recent history he sometimes relies on his own recollections or actual experience, notably when he gives a long and apparently first-hand account of how in 1688 James II's Irish dragoons terrorized a number of towns and villages between Reading and London.[2]

None the less, Defoe's claim that he is mainly concerned with the present state of the country is justified. When he visits towns and cities he inevitably takes some notice of the public buildings, but he seems to prefer them when they are new, and in any case his range of observation goes far beyond that of the normal guidebook. What most interests him is the people, the men and women who are dwelling in the places he visits: how they earn their living, what natural advantages they enjoy, what customs are peculiar to the locality, and so on.

In every country something of the people is said, as well as of the place, of their customs, speech, employments, the product of their labour, and the manner of their living, the circumstances as well as situation of the towns; their trade and government; of the rarities of art, or nature; the rivers, of the inland, and river navigation; also of the lakes and medicinal springs, not forgetting the general dependance of the whole country upon the City of London, as well for the consumption of its produce, as the circulation of its trade.

So we are told a great deal about the various rivers and how far from the sea they are still navigable; about ports and harbors, roads and bridges, markets and fairs, local arts and crafts, the crops grown in various parts of the country, the breeding of horses, cattle and sheep, fishing, sports and pastimes (notably horseracing at such places as Newmarket, Nottingham, and Epsom), the spas (e.g. Bath, Tunbridge Wells, Matlock), and the gentlemen's houses which he frequently goes out of his way to see. These last gave him an especial pleasure. When he described the countryside in the immediate neighborhood of London, with the prosperous seats of noblemen and gentry, he could not contain his delight:

Take them in a remote view, the fine seats shine among the trees as jewels shine in a rich coronet; in a *near sight* they are meer pictures and paintings; *at a distance* they are all nature, *near hand* all art; but both in the extreamest beauty. In a word, nothing can be more beautiful; here is a plain and pleasant country, a rich fertile soil, cultivated and enclosed to the utmost perfection of husbandry, then bespangled with villages; those villages fill'd with these houses, and the houses surrounded with gardens, walks, vistas, avenues, representing all the beauties of building, and all the pleasures of planting. It is impossible to view these countries from any rising ground, and not be ravish'd with the delightful prospect.

Defoe's reaction, we may suspect, is not wholly aesthetic: all this splendor and magnificence is for him a sign of national prosperity. So, too, when he contemplates the Thames near Hampton Court, it is with the eye of the merchant delighting in the commercial greatness of his country. The poets may write their fanciful stuff, but he will stick to the solid and substantial achievements of his countrymen:

I shall sing you no songs here of the River in the first person of a water nymph, a goddess, (and I know not what) according to the humour of the ancient poets. I shall talk nothing of the marriage of old Isis, the male river, with the beautiful Thame, the female river, a whimsy as simple as the subject was empty, but I shall speak of the River as occasion presents, as it really is *made glorious* by the splendour of its shores, gilded with noble palaces, strong fortifications, large hospitals, and publick buildings; with the greatest bridge, and the greatest city in the world, made famous by the opulence of its merchants, the encrease and extensiveness of its commerce; by its invincible navies, and by the innumerable fleets of ships sailing upon it, to and from all parts of the world.

Or again, when he is describing Yorkshire, he notes that "none of the pretended travel-writers and journeyers thro' England" have had much to say about the West Riding, but since he is convinced that the manufactures of England are "as well worth a traveller's notice as the most curious things he can meet with," and since manufacturing is "so prodigious great in this quarter," he makes a point of giving a detailed account of the great wool trade around Halifax. If Wordsworth's heart leapt up when he beheld a rainbow in the sky, Defoe's heartbeat was more likely to be quickened by the sight of the cloth market at Leeds—"a prodigy of its kind, and . . . not to be equalled in the world."[3]

In between those more serious observations Defoe recalls many particular memories and experiences: the swallows gathering for migration on the east coast and covering the whole roof of the parish church at Southwold; a violent snowstorm on the Yorkshire moors in the middle of August, the "ancient lady" in Sussex, of very good quality, being drawn to church in her coach by six oxen, "the way being so stiff and deep that no horses could go in it." Of all the men and women whom Defoe encountered casually in those peregrinations, the most memorable is perhaps the poor woman he met living in a cave in the Peak district of Derbyshire, who to Defoe was a greater wonder than all the so-called Wonders of the Peak. He had been asking her about one of the local tourist attractions, the Giant's Tomb, and in her reply she told him that if her husband had been at home he could have taken him there. At this point Defoe the novelist takes over from Defoe the inquiring traveler:

I snatch'd at the word, *at home!* Says I, Good wife, why, where do you live? *Here, sir,* says she, *and points to the hole in the rock.* Here!

says I; and do all these children live here too? *Yes, sir,* says she, *they were all born here.* Pray how long have you dwelt here then? said I. *My husband was born here,* said she, *and his father before him.* Will you give me leave, says one of our company, as curious as I was, to come in and see your house, dame? *If you please, sir,* says she, *but 'tis not a place fit for such as you are to come into,* calling him *your worship,* forsooth; but that by the by. I mention it to shew that the good woman did not want manners, though she liv'd in a den like a wild body.

However, we alighted and went in. There was a large hollow cave which the poor people, by two curtains hang'd cross, had parted into three rooms. On one side was the chimney, and the man, or perhaps his father, being miners, had found means to work a shaft or funnel through the rock to carry the smoke out at the top, where the Giant's Tombstone was. The habitation was poor, 'tis true, but things within did not look so like misery as I expected. Every thing was clean and neat, tho' mean and ordinary. There were shelves with earthen ware, and some pewter and brass. There was, which I observed in particular, a whole flitch or side of bacon hanging up in the chimney, and by it a good piece of another. There was a sow and pigs running about at the door, and a little lean cow feeding upon a green place just before the door, and the little enclosed piece of ground I mentioned was growing with good barley; it being then near harvest.

As we read on, the image of William Wordsworth begins to blend imperceptibly with that of Daniel Defoe:

I asked the poor woman what trade her husband was? She said he worked in the lead mines. I asked her how much he could earn a day there? She said, if he had good luck he could earn about five pence a day. . . . I then asked what she did? She said, when she was able to work she washed the oar; but looking down on her children, and shaking her head, she intimated that they found her so much business she could do but little, which I easily granted must be true. But what can you get at washing the oar, said I, when you can work? She said, if she work'd hard she could gain three-pence a day. So that, in short, here was but eight-pence a day when they both worked hard, and that not always, and perhaps not often, and all this to maintain a man, his wife, and five small children, and yet they seemed to live very pleasantly, the children look'd plump and fat, ruddy and wholesome; and the woman was tall, well shap'd, clean, and (for the place) a very well looking, comely woman. . . .

This moving sight so affected us all that, upon short conference at the door, we made up a little lump of money, and I had the honour to be almoner for the company; and though the sum was not great, being at most something within a crown, as I told it into the poor woman's hand, I could perceive such a surprize in her face, that, had she not given vent to her joy by a sudden flux of tears, I found she would have fainted away. She was some time before she could do anything but cry; but after that was abated, she expressed herself very handsomely (for a poor body), and told me she had not seen so much money together of her own for many months.

We asked her if she had a good husband; she smiled, and said, Yes, thanked God for it, and that she was very happy in that, for he worked very hard, and they wanted for nothing that he could do for them; and two or three times made mention of how contented they were. In a word, it was a lecture to us all, and that such, I assure you, as made the whole company very grave all the rest of the day. And if it has no effect of that kind upon the reader, the defect must be in my telling the story in a less moving manner than the poor woman told it her self.

Defoe is not a Wordsworth, and he does not make a lyrical ballad out of this emotional experience recollected in tranquillity. Yet, like Wordsworth, he responds to a striking manifestation of resolution and independence and of uncomplaining human dignity, and—like Wordsworth with old Simon Lee—he is emotionally disturbed by the overwhelming gratitude that is sometimes called forth by a small act of kindness.* Perhaps we do not sufficiently take into account the persistent strain of emotionalism in Defoe's character: it is one of the elements in his complex personality that makes him a rather isolated figure in the so-called Augustan age.[4]

Defoe's other guidebook is *The Complete English Tradesman*, published in two volumes, 1726-27, and written, like the *Tour*, in the form of familiar letters. This is ostensibly a manual for young merchants and shopkeepers, telling them how to succeed in business, what pitfalls to avoid, what they should know and how they should conduct themselves. At first sight nothing could seem less likely to attract the general reader; but here again Defoe gives us much more than his title would lead us to expect. If he belonged

* Cf. the gratitude of the poor waterman and his wife in *A Journal of the Plague Year*.

to a nation of shopkeepers, it was a nation that had also produced some of the world's greatest poets; and when he wrote upon trade the merchant and the artist in him came together—one might almost say "sung together."

Looking back with the wisdom of old age on his own career as a London merchant, he passes on his hard-won experience to a younger generation. He preaches a gospel of work, of steady application to business, of regular hours and prudent conduct; everything that he has to say to the young tradesman is informed with the old puritan ethic. "The purposes for which time is given, and life bestow'd," he observes with all the solemnity at his command, "are very momentous; no time is given useless and for nothing; time is no more to be unemploy'd than it is to be ill employ'd." There are three main concerns on which time is properly spent: necessaries of nature (eating, drinking, sleeping, etc.); duties of religion; and duties of the present life (a man's business or profession). But those duties or necessities must not be allowed to "jostle one another" or "be prejudicial to one another." We must eat and we must sleep, and it is the duty of every Christian to worship God. But the proper times for worship are the early morning and the evening: the greater part of the day must be reserved for business. It is utterly wrong for a merchant or trades-man to think of going to worship during business hours; he must resist this temptation—a temptation which Defoe is even willing to believe may have come from the Devil himself. He draws a vivid picture of a man of business in his shop or warehouse with

a vast throng of business upon his hands, and the world in his head, when it is highly his duty to attend it, and shall be to his prejudice to absent himself; then the same Deceiver presses him earnestly to go to his closet, or to the church to prayers, during which time his customer goes to another place, the neighbours miss him in his shop, his business is lost, his reputation suffers. . . .

Defoe follows up his warning about what he calls "this ill-tim'd devotion" with a succession of illustrative anecdotes, including one about a tradesman who was wakened one morning by the cries of his wife calling for a midwife. On his way to fetch one, he passed a church where there was a very early morning service, and finding the door open and the minister just climbing into the pulpit he went in, listened to the sermon, and forgot all about his wretched wife in the pangs of labor. The man (Defoe assures us) was a personal friend of his: perhaps he was, or perhaps Defoe, wishing to drive home his point that there is a time for all things, made the whole story up. Elsewhere in *The Complete English Tradesman* he gives ample attention to the evil effects of luxury and idleness and loose living, as he had already done in *The Family Instructor* and *Religious Courtship*. But by also stressing the danger of unseasonable godliness he is the better able to emphasize his contention that trade "must be work'd at, not play'd with," and that "it is a business *for* life, and ought to be follow'd as one of the great businesses *of* life." Without actually saying that constant application to business is more important than godliness, he can stress its importance by relegating religious exercises to their appointed hours, and by suggesting that it is possible to be righteous overmuch. For the godlier among the readers to whom he was addressing himself such a suggestion must have been startling and even paradoxical, and no doubt Defoe intended it to seem so.[5]

From his earliest writings he had expressed himself with apparent ease and confidence, writing habitually in the first person, and carrying on a kind of conversation with his reader. Now in his old age he had become more relaxed and confidential than ever. *The Complete English Tradesman* (like his last work of all, *The Complete English Gentleman*) abounds in anecdotes and reminiscences and personal confessions; what might have been merely technical and admonitory and pedagogical is made highly readable by its human interest and the constant appeal to experience. Through his pages flit London citizens attending at the counter and displaying their cloths and laces and ribbons, or neglecting their business and heading towards bankruptcy; and here too are their wives, cheapening a piece of linen or gossiping at the tea-table. By the 1720s Defoe had become so accustomed to thinking in terms of fiction that even when he was writing A Young Man's Guide to Success in Trade and Commerce it seemed natural to him to do so by introducing men and women acting, talking, making bargains, working or idling, cheating or being cheated. The same is true of his long, rambling book on the servant problem, *The Great Law of Subordination Considered* (1724), which

is full of real or fictitious anecdotes; or again of that odd expression of his later puritanism, *Conjugal Lewdness, or Matrimonial Whoredom,* a book in which he was so careful to wrap up
his subject in decent language that it is sometimes difficult to
know what he was complaining about.

As a writer Defoe had always tried to make his argument easily
intelligible by means of analogies and allusions that fell within the
experience and comprehension of the ordinary reader. In his old
age his facility for expounding ideas in this way seems, if anything, to have increased rather than diminished. Sometimes, it may
be felt, there was no need for any illustration; but Defoe cannot
resist giving one. In *The Complete English Tradesman,* Letter V
is entitled "Of Diligence and Application in Business," and Defoe
keeps emphasizing how essential it is for the tradesman to attend
personally to his affairs. The point is obvious enough, but Defoe
is not taking any chances:

Trade is like a hand-mill, it must always be turned about by the
diligent hand of the master; or, if you will, like the pump-house at ,
Amsterdam, where they put offenders in for petty matters, especially
beggars; if they will work and keep pumping, they sit well and dry
and safe; and if they work very hard one hour or two, they may rest,
perhaps, a quarter of an hour afterwards, but if they oversleep themselves, or grow lazy, the water comes in upon them and wets them,
and they have no dry place to stand in, much less to sit down in; and
in short, if they continue obstinately idle, they must sink, so that it is
nothing but *pump* or *drown,* and they may chuse which they like best.

Any tradesman who could forget *that* could forget anything.
Again, anxious to make his point that the young tradesman should
never lose a chance of conversing with his fellow tradesmen, since
there is something to be learned from everybody, Defoe dives into
his memories of the past, and comes up with something that is
almost certainly a reminiscence of his old schoolmaster at the
Newington Green academy:

I knew a philosopher that was excellently skill'd in the noble science
or study of astronomy, who told me he had some years studied for
some simily, or proper allusion to explain to his scholars the phenomena of the sun's motion round its own axis, and could never
happen upon one to his mind, 'till by accident he saw his maid Betty

trundling her mop: surpris'd with the exactness of the motion to describe the thing he wanted, he goes into his study, calls his pupils about him, and tells them that Betty, who herself knew nothing of the matter, could shew them the sun revolving about itself in a more lively manner than ever he could. Accordingly Betty was call'd, and bad bring out her mop, when, placing his scholars in a due position, opposite not to the face of the maid, but to her left side, so that they could see the end of the mop when it whirl'd round upon her arm, they took it immediately; there was the broad-headed nail in the center, which was as the body of the sun, and the thrums whisking round, flinging the water about every way by innumerable little streams, describing exactly the rays of the sun darting light from the center to the whole system.

If ignorant Betty, by the natural consequence of her operation, instructed the astronomer, why may not the meanest shoemaker or pedlar, by the ordinary sagacity of his trading wit, tho' it may be indeed very ordinary, coarse and unlook'd for, communicate something, give some useful hint, dart some sudden thought into the mind of the observing tradesman, which he shall make his use of, and apply to his own advantage in trade, when at the same time he that gives such hint shall himself, like Betty and her mop, know nothing of the matter?

Popular education can go no further.[6]

From the time that he had written about the ghost of Mrs. Veal (and no doubt earlier than that) Defoe had been interested in those phenomena which are usually classified in booksellers' catalogues as "the occult." Voices, premonitions, dreams, omens enter frequently into *Robinson Crusoe* and his other works of fiction, and such suprasensory phenomena are discussed in his *Serious Reflections . . . of Robinson Crusoe* and elsewhere. In 1720 there appeared *The History of . . . Duncan Campbell*, a long biographical account of an actual Highlander then living in London who claimed to have second sight, and who was successfully exploiting his gift with those who could afford to pay him for his predictions, and with some who couldn't. This work, traditionally attributed to Defoe, has recently been shown by Professor Rodney M. Baine not to be his at all,[7] and by removing it from the canon Baine has done Defoe a considerable service.

Unfortunately there seems to be no good reason for denying to Defoe the authorship of three other works on the supernatural:

The Political History of the Devil (1726), *A System of Magic* (1727), and *The History and Reality of Apparitions* (1727). Those three catchpenny books are among the most verbose and long-winded that Defoe ever wrote. *The Political History of the Devil* was popular in the eighteenth century, and it has some admirers today; but—what is unusual for Defoe—it seems to be the work of a writer who is scratching about for something to say, and to be indeed the sort of popular compilation that Dr. Johnson would have relegated to the category of "jobs for the booksellers." What is worse, Defoe's attitude throughout is ambivalent. The Devil was no doubt a reality to Defoe in his childhood, as he was still a reality to Moll Flanders when she heard his voice prompting her to steal the bundle, or tempting her to kill the child in the dark alley. But what, or how much the Devil meant to Defoe in the 1720s it would be hard to say. If he had been asked by, say, Robert Harley whether he believed in the old fire-and-brimstone Devil with cloven hoofs he would almost certainly have smiled and said no. But he seems to have been unwilling to give up the Devil entirely, and there was of course no reason whatever why Moll should. At all events, in making the Devil the subject of a long and ambiguous discourse he appears to be either unprepared to commit himself one way or the other, or willing to exploit the superstitious beliefs of the ignorant. Those who like to see Defoe as essentially the journalist turning out popular literature for a half-educated public can point with some justification to his three long books on the supernatural.

ii

It is often, indeed, difficult to disentangle Defoe's motives, and perhaps the greatest mistake we can make about him is to assume that these were invariably direct and simple. Nor is it any easier to define his position as an author, or to decide what made him one in the first place.

> Why did I write? what sin to me unknown
> Dipp'd me in ink . . . ?

Was Defoe a business man who took to writing, and "who pen'd a stanza when he should engross," or was he essentially a writer who became irrelevantly involved in business? He certainly could not have said with Pope that he "left no calling for this idle trade." On the other hand it seems unlikely that anything could have stopped him from writing, although what and how he wrote were largely determined by the circumstances of his life.

Up to the year 1703 there was still a chance that he might have remained first and foremost a man of business who occasionally took time off to produce a pamphlet on contemporary affairs, or on some social problem that interested him. But after the disastrous outcome of *The Shortest Way* he had no choice left but to earn his living by his pen, and to earn it mainly by political journalism, supplemented by what he got from Harley and Godolphin for his work as a political agent. Not that political journalism came hard to Defoe: it is quite unlikely that he had any feeling when he was writing the *Review* that what he should really have been writing was *Robinson Crusoe*. In the pages of the *Review*, and in the pamphlets which he wrote all through the reign of Queen Anne, he was carrying on what he had already begun to do in the 1690s, and did supremely well—addressing his fellow countrymen with unbounded confidence, persuading them, admonishing them, appealing to them, amusing them with his drollery or startling them with his paradoxes, laying down firm lines for their public and private conduct, *preaching* at them from his journalistic pulpit. When a man has caught the attention of his own generation as successfully as Defoe had, nothing is going to stop him from continuing to write. Controversy, argument, the exposure of intellectual folly or moral turpitude were all part of the air that Defoe normally breathed; and so too was his consciousness of himself as a man of moderation, a prophet without honor in his own country, a kind of unreluctant Hamlet born to set things right. On the one side, Daniel Defoe who *knew;* on the other, the public who had to be instructed. "It has been the disaster of all parties in this nation," he wrote in *An Appeal to Honour and Justice* "to be very *hot* in their turn, and as often as they have been *so,* I have differed with them all, and ever must and shall do so. . . . In such turns of tempers and times a man . . . must one time or other be out with every body."[8] For one who was so widely read by his contemporaries he was a strangely isolated figure, both as a man and as a writer.

On the other hand, he was certainly no recluse: the man who wrote with such awareness of the life of his own day must have moved freely in the society of his fellow men and women. Yet the circumstances of his life after 1703 were such that he must frequently have been thrown among strangers. His relationship with Harley was not so much close as secretive, and in his work as a political agent in the English counties and shires and in remote Edinburgh he was sometimes in danger, often in difficulty, and almost always alone. It is this intellectual and physical isolation in the years up to 1719 that makes *Robinson Crusoe* an especially significant document in his literary biography. No one was better able than Defoe to create a character who "lived eight and twenty years all alone" and emerged at the end morally and intellectually undamaged, and with his resolution and will to live as constant as ever.

All the same, the transition from writing mainly on political, religious, and economic affairs to the private world of men and women (even if we remember the domestic setting of the Veal-Bargrave story, the handling of family problems in the miscellaneous sections of the *Review*, or the detailed presentation of parents and children in *The Family Instructor*) is one that Defoe's absorption in public affairs would hardly have led us to expect. Those of his readers who would willingly give up all his political tracts for another *Moll Flanders*, or who are apt to speculate about what we might have had if he had "begun writing fiction at the age of forty or forty-five instead of when he was almost sixty,"[9] are probably asking for something that there was never any likelihood of their getting. Defoe's literary life seems to fall into a natural curve, and at each stage in his career he wrote what it was natural for him to write. With the fall from power of Robert Harley and the death of Queen Anne, his intense involvement in contemporary politics began to diminish; and although for some years he continued to write in the Whig interest, and to conduct his under-cover censorship of several Tory periodicals, he was gradually detaching himself from front-line political action. However much he may or may not have done to tone down the news paragraphs and comment in *Mist's Weekly Journal*, his chief contribution to the effectiveness of that highly successful newspaper was in the form of essays written on non-controversial topics, or on potentially inflammatory topics which he dealt with in a non-controversial way. For the less politically-slanted *Applebee's Journal* he wrote on matters of contemporary interest that had usually little reference to party divisions. It was in this period of retirement, or semi-retirement, from political strife that Defoe turned to writing about men and women, and if he had not become gradually less committed to contemporary politics it is unlikely that he would have given us *Robinson Crusoe* and the other stories that followed it. Yet even here accidental circumstances played some part in determining what sort of fiction Defoe would write: it has often been noted, for instance, that John Applebee specialized in publishing the lives of criminals, and that from writing for Applebee on the lives of actual criminals (and no doubt interviewing some of them in Newgate) it was a natural step for Defoe to create his own Moll or Jacques, and to pass from merely recording their adventures to a realization of their motives and their inner consciousness.

In his last years, as we have seen, he returned to a more general and discursive kind of writing. This was a period, perhaps, of lowered pressure, but one in which the humanizing influence of his years as a writer of fiction frequently makes itself felt. He was still writing when death came to him, on 24 April 1731, in a lodging in Ropemakers Alley. He died, we are told, "of a lethargy." Whatever that may have been, it would be hard to think of a more inappropriate word to associate with Daniel Defoe.

Notes and Sources

The following abbreviations have been used:

Aitken   *Later Stuart Tracts*, ed. G. A. Aitken (1903)

Bohn   *The Novels and Miscellaneous Works of Daniel Defoe*, 7 vols. (1854–67)

Healey   *The Letters of Daniel Defoe*, ed. George Harris Healey (Oxford, 1955)

Lee   William Lee, *Daniel Defoe: His Life, and Recently Discovered Writings*, 3 vols. (1869)

Moore (1)   John Robert Moore, *Defoe in the Pillory and Other Studies* (Bloomington, Indiana, 1939)

Moore (2)   John Robert Moore, *Daniel Defoe, Citizen of the Modern World* (Chicago, 1958)

Moore, *Checklist*   John Robert Moore, *A Checklist of the Writings of Daniel Defoe* (Bloomington, Indiana, 1960)

Secord   *Defoe's Review*, ed. A. W. Secord, 22 vols. (Facsimile Text Society, Columbia University Press, New York, 1938). Reference is made to the number of the facsimile book, and not to that of the original volume; lefthand and righthand columns are indicated by the letters a and b respectively.

Secord (1)   A. W. Secord, *Studies in the Narrative Method of Defoe* (Urbana, Illinois, 1924)

Secord (2)   A. W. Secord, *Robert Drury's Journal and Other Studies* (Urbana, Illinois, 1961)

Starr   G. A. Starr, *Defoe and Spiritual Autobiography* (Princeton, 1965)

Watt   Ian Watt, *The Rise of the Novel* (1957)

Works, 1705   1. *A True Collection of the Writings of the Author of The True Born Englishman* (2nd ed., 1705)

                            2. *A Second Volume of the Writings of the Author of The True-Born Englishman* (1705)

Works, 1840   *The Novels and Miscellaneous Works of Daniel Defoe*, 20 vols. (Oxford, 1840–41)

References to the following works are made to the Shakespeare Head edition, 14 vols. (Oxford, 1927–8): *Robinson Crusoe, The Farther Adventures of Robinson Crusoe, Captain Singleton, Moll Flanders, A Journal of the Plague Year, Roxana.* Quotations for which references are given to *Works, 1840,* Bohn, and other modern collections or editions have been taken from the first editions of the various works cited. In all quotations the original spelling has been retained (except for some expansion of Defoe's contractions in his correspondence); but capital letters and italics have been brought into line with modern usage, and punctuation that seemed likely to impede or confuse the reader has been modernized.

1. *A Biographical Prologue*

1. *Review,* 22 October 1709 (Secord, xv. 341a).
2. *Review,* 11 June 1713 (Secord, xxii. 213b, 214b).
3. *The Complete English Tradesman* (*Works, 1840,* xviii. 88).
4. Public Record Office, S.P. 44/337/1833. See C. D. Curtis, "Daniel Defoe and the Monmouth Rebellion," *Notes and Queries for Somerset and Dorset* (Taunton, 1 March 1966), xxviii. 268f.
5. *An Appeal to Honour and Justice* (Aitken, p. 672).
6. *Report on the Manuscripts of His Grace the Duke of Portland* (Historical Manuscripts Commission), iv. 68.
7. *The Complete Works of George Savile First Marquess of Halifax* ("The Character of a Trimmer"), ed. Walter Raleigh (Oxford, 1912), p. 48.
8. Secord, xviii. 377a.
9. Secord, xxii. 59a.
10. Secord, xxii. 80b.
11. *Review,* 6 June 1712 (Secord, xxii. 209b, 210a).
12. Letter to Charles Delafaye, 26 April 1718; Public Record Office, S.P. 35/11/124 (Lee, i. xff.; Healey, pp. 451ff.)
13. Letters to Harley, 26 November 1706 and 27 January 1707 (Healey, pp. 158f., 196f.).
14. *Robinson Crusoe,* ii. 62, 70f.; *Moll Flanders,* i. 60f., *New Voyage* (Bohn, pp. 261f.); *Colonel Jack,* i. 162f.
15. Letters to Charles Delafaye, 26 April, 23 May, and 4 June 1718 (Lee, i. xiii, xiv, xvf.; Healey, pp. 454, 456, 457f.).
16. Aitken, p. 94.
17. Samuel Johnson, *Lives of the English Poets,* ed. George Birkbeck Hill (Oxford, 1905), iii. 207.
18. *Review,* 5 March 1706 (Secord, vi. 109b).

2. The Journalist

1. Alexander Pope *et al., Three Hours after Marriage* (1717), ed. John Harrington Smith (Augustan Reprint Society, Los Angeles, 1961), p. 153 (Act II).
2. Act IV, Sc. i (Mermaid ed., p. 460).
3. Letter of Pope to Bishop Atterbury; *The Correspondence of Alexander Pope,* ed. George Sherburn (Oxford, 1956), i. 453f.
4. Matthew Arnold, *Essays in Criticism* (First Series: "The Function of Criticism at the Present Time," 1889 ed.), p. 14.
5. *Works, 1705,* i. 203f., 205f., 207.
6. *Ibid.,* i. 207, 208f., 211, 212.
7. *Ibid.,* i. 220f.; Secord, v. 498f.; *Works, 1705,* i. 213.
8. *Works, 1705,* i. 356, 361, 364.
9. *Ibid.,* i. 383.
10. *Ibid.,* i. 246, 224, 253.
11. Letter to Harley, 7 August 1707 (Healey, p. 234).
12. *The History of the Kentish Petition,* 1701 (Aitken, pp. 161, 169); *Legion's Memorial* (Aitken, pp. 180f., 186).
13. G. N. Clark, *The Later Stuarts* (Oxford, 1940), p. 188; *Works, 1705,* i. 239; Aitken, p. 179; G. K. Chesterton, "The Secret People," *Collected Poems* (1927), p. 157.
14. Aitken, p. 184.
15. *Works, 1705,* i. 289.
16. *Ibid.,* i. 300, 293, 301.
17. *Ibid.,* i. 312, 315, 312f.
18. *Ibid.,* i. 316, 304.
19. *Ibid.,* i. 400, 393, 384, 385, 394.
20. *Ibid.,* i. 436; Secord, v. 376a; *Works, 1705,* i. 461, 462; *The Present State of the Parties in Great Britain* (1712), p. 24.
21. Maximillian E. Novak, "Defoe's *Shortest Way with the Dissenters:* Hoax, Parody, Paradox, Fiction, Irony, and Satire," *Modern Language Quarterly,* xxvii (1966), 404; *Works, 1705,* i. 442; *ibid.,* ii. 273; *ibid.,* i. 426; *A Compleat Collection of State-Tryals* (1719), iv. 798, 800. The best discussion of *The Shortest Way with the Dissenters* will be found in Professor Novak's article cited above.
22. Moore (1), pp. 21ff.
23. George Bernard Shaw, *Man and Superman* ("Maxims for Revolutionists," 1939 ed.), p. 230.
24. *Works, 1705,* ii. 436, 437, 438, 439.
25. *Ibid.,* ii. 446, 444, 448, 430, 445, 443.
26. *Ibid.,* ii. 424, 441.
27. *Ibid.,* ii. 419, 420, 422, 449.
28. *Ibid.,* ii. 432, 427.
29. *Reasons Why This Nation . . .* (1711), pp. 3, 5.

30. *Ibid.*, p. 6; *Review*, 24 September 1709 (Secord, xv. 294a); *Review*, 1 October 1709 (Secord, xv. 307a); *Reasons Why This Nation* . . . , p. 6.
31. *Reasons Why This Nation* . . . , pp. 16f., 17f., 22, 39; Secord, xxii. 279a.
32. *Reasons Why This Nation* . . . , pp. 29ff., 39ff.
33. *Appeal to Honour and Justice* (Aitken, p. 87).
34. Bohn, vi. 506, 507, 508.
35. *Ibid.*, pp. 508f., 510.
36. *Ibid.*, pp. 511, 513.
37. *Ibid.*, pp. 514, 515f., 517f.
38. *Ibid.*, pp. 534, 537, 536.
39. *Ibid.*, pp. 537f., 540f.
40. *Ibid.*, pp. 543ff., 546, 547, 548f.
41. Aitken, pp. 87f.
42. Moore, *Checklist*, p. 186; Bohn, ii. 506f.
43. Bohn, ii. 508f.; Samuel Richardson, *Pamela* (Everyman ed.), i. 350.
44. *Daniel Defoe*, ed. James T. Boulton (1965), p. 17.
45. Secord, iv. 138a; *ibid.*, v. 381a; *ibid.*, xxi. 607a; *ibid.*, i, Preface, pp. [3]-[4].
46. *Review*, 13 March 1712 (Secord, xxi. 611a).
47. Secord, xii. 124a-b; *Review*, 12 April 1712 (Secord, xxi. 663 a-b).
48. Secord, xxi. 574b.
49. *Review*, 3 May 1712 (Secord, xxi. 700b); *ibid.*, 8 June 1708 (Secord, xii. 123b); *ibid.*, 19 February 1712 (Secord, xxi. 571b).
50. Secord, xv. 421b–422b, 422b–423a; *ibid.*, xxii. 30a-b.
51. Secord, xxi. 589a–590b, 591b.
52. Secord, xxi. 642a.
53. *Works, 1840*, xvii. 19; *The Works of Daniel Defoe*, ed. G. H. Maynadier (New York, 1903-4), iii. 26 f.
54. Secord, xxi. 582a; Lee, i. v; *ibid.*, iii. 333, 336.
55. Lee, iii. 322f. The letter cited earlier in this paragraph to *The St. James's Journal* is signed "*A. Phyllyps*," who may conceivably be Ambrose Philips.
56. Lee, ii. 396, 22, 48ff., 63; *ibid.*, iii. 263ff.
57. *Ibid.*, iii. 19ff., 27ff. I have given a full account of Marlborough's funeral in *Background for Queen Anne* (1939), pp. 204-24.

3. *The Poet*

1. George Bernard Shaw, *The Admirable Bashville* (Preface), *Prefaces by Bernard Shaw* (1934), p. 739.
2. *The Meditations of Daniel Defoe*, ed. George Harris Healey (Cummington, Mass., 1946), p. 5.
3. *Works, 1705*, ii. 14; *ibid.*, i. 72.
4. Defoe's poem appeared with several others in Charles Gildon, *The History of the Athenian Society* (1692).
5. *Works, 1705*, i. 113, 115.

6. *Ibid.*, ii. 154, 155ff.; *Essay upon Projects*, in Henry Morley, *The Earlier Life and the Chief Earlier Works of Daniel Defoe* (1889), p. 145.
7. *Works, 1705*, ii. 156ff., 162.
8. *Ibid.*, ii. 164, 165ff., 167.
9. *An Appeal to Honour and Justice* (Aitken, p. 72); *Works, 1705*, i. sig. B3ᵛ; *ibid.*, ii. sig. A3ʳ.
10. *Ibid.*, i. 1, 2f., 4, 6f., 7, 8f., 12.
11. *Ibid.*, i. 19, 15f., 17, 17f., 21.
12. *Ibid.*, i. 22ff., 28, 29ff., 33, 34, 34ff.
13. Preface to *The Battle of the Books*, in *A Tale of a Tub* . . . , ed. A. C. Guthkelch and D. Nichol Smith (Oxford, 1920), p. 215.
14. *Review*, 17 May 1712 (Secord, xxi. 724b); *Works, 1705*, i. sig. B4ᵛ; *ibid.*, sig. B2ᵛ; *Review*, 15 February 1709 (Secord, xiii. 554a–555b).
15. *Works, 1705*, i. 27, 11.
16. *Ibid.*, i. 1, 2, 39.
17. *Ibid.*, i. 21, 26, 27, 20, 40; *Conjugal Lewdness: Or, Matrimonial Whoredom* (1727), pp. 400f.
18. *Works, 1705*, i. 62, 49, 60, 59.
19. *Ibid.*, i. 102, 104f.
20. *Review*, 20 January 1708 (Secord, xi. 587a); *Review*, 21 February 1706 (Secord, vi. 91a); *Review*, 12 June 1711 (Secord, xix. 138b); *Conjugal Lewdness*, p. 382.
21. *Works, 1705*, ii. 103; Letter to William Paterson, April 1702 (Healey, p. 6); *Works, 1705*, ii. 116f., 28f.; *ibid.*, Preface, p. [7].
22. *Works, 1705*, ii. 87, 85f., 79.
23. *Ibid.*, ii. 91, 94, 97f.
24. *Review*, 5 September 1704 (Secord, ii. 228a).
25. *Works, 1705*, ii. 178, 180, 181f., 174; *The Consolidator* (Henry Morley, *The Earlier Life and the Chief Earlier Works of Daniel Defoe*, 1889, p. 277).
26. Secord, iv. 214a.
27. *Caledonia, A Poem in Honour of Scotland, and the Scots Nation* (1706), pp. 17, 59.
28. Secord, ii. 251b; iii. 412a; vi. 11b–12b; vii. 372a-b.
29. *Jure Divino. A Satyr. In Twelve Books* (1706), ii. 2 (note a); iii. 6 (note b); iii. 10.
30. Secord, xii. 212a; Samuel Johnson, *Lives of the English Poets*, ed. cit., iii. 7.

4. *The Writer of Fiction (I)*

1. *Accounts of the Apparition of Mrs. Veal by Daniel Defoe and Others*, ed. Manuel Schonhorn (Augustan Reprint Society, Los Angeles, 1965): "Letter from E. B. at Canterbury . . . 13 September 1705," p. 1; "Letter from L. Lukyn at Canterbury . . . 9 October 1705," p. 1; "Letter from Stephen Gray at Canterbury . . . 15 November 1705," p. 1; Defoe, *A True Relation of the Apparition of One Mrs. Veal* . . . , p. 3.

2. *The Family Instructor* (*Works, 1840*, xv. 81f.; xvi. 1ff.).
3. *Ibid.*, xv. 166, 216ff., 236f., 237.
4. *Ibid.*, xvi. 252, 237.
5. Woodes Rogers, *A Cruising Voyage round the World* (1712); Edward Cooke, *A Voyage to the South Sea, and round the World*, 2 vols. (1712). Professor J. Paul Hunter has argued strongly against "the received opinion" that Selkirk's experiences on Juan Fernandez gave Defoe the situation on which he based *Robinson Crusoe*, and that the novel must be considered as a fictitious narrative of travel. "This account of Defoe's design and procedure is, I think, inadequate and inaccurate; and it seriously misleads us as to the rich and complex traditions which nourish *Robinson Crusoe*" (*The Reluctant Pilgrim* . . . , Baltimore, 1966, pp. 2 *et seq.*). While I can readily agree that *Robinson Crusoe* has the religious significance that Professor Hunter demonstrates so ably in his study of Defoe's "emblematic method and quest for form," I do not think that he has shaken the traditional view that Selkirk was what Henry James liked to call the *donnée* of Defoe's story.
6. Richard Steele, *The Englishman*, ed. Rae Blanchard (Oxford, 1955), pp. 107, 109, 107.
7. Secord (1), p. 109 and *passim*.
8. Charles Gildon, *The Life and Strange Surprizing Adventures of Mr. D—— DeF—— of London, Hosier* (1719), p. x (quoted in Lee, i. 298); *Boswell's Life of Johnson*, ed. George Birkbeck Hill, rev. L. F. Powell (Oxford, 1934), ii. 319.
9. *Robinson Crusoe*, i. 73.
10. *Ibid.*, ii. 36f.
11. *Ibid.*, i. 209; *Augusta Triumphans*, 1728 (*Works, 1840*, xvii. 27).
12. *Robinson Crusoe*, ii. 107.
13. *Ibid.*, i. 155, 172, 83, 136, 133, 133f., 74, 137ff.; *The Literary Remains of Samuel Taylor Coleridge*, ed. H. N. Coleridge (1836), i. 197 (quoted in Moore (2), p. 227).
14. *Robinson Crusoe*, i. 58, 63f., 171; *ibid.*, iii. 12.
15. *Ibid.*, i. 145ff.; Wordsworth, Preface to *Lyrical Ballads*, 1800 (*Wordsworth's Literary Criticism*, ed. Nowell C. Smith, 1905, p. 14).
16. *Robinson Crusoe*, i. 77; Watt, p. 72.
17. Wordsworth, Preface to *Lyrical Ballads*, 1800 (ed. cit., pp. 29f.); *Robinson Crusoe*, i. 130; *Serious Reflections . . . of Robinson Crusoe* (1720), Preface.
18. Watt, p. 69.
19. *Robinson Crusoe*, i. 65.
20. *Ibid.*, i. 225; Watt, pp. 67, 70, 65; *Robinson Crusoe*, i. 16, 42.
21. Maximillian E. Novak, *Economics and the Fiction of Daniel Defoe* (Berkeley and Los Angeles, 1962), p. 32; *Robinson Crusoe*, i. 1f., 2, 5, 42, 104; *ibid.*, ii. 111, 112, 111, 117.
22. *Ibid.*, iii. 111, 110; Moore (2), pp. 276ff.; *A Tour thro' . . . Great Britain* (Everyman ed., n.d.), p. 3.

23. Novak, *op. cit.*, pp. 40ff.; Starr, *passim;* J. Paul Hunter, *op. cit.*, *passim;* Watt, p. 81.
24. *Robinson Crusoe*, ii. 91ff., 88; Moore (2), pp. 225f.; *Mist's Weekly Journal*, 4 January 1718.
25. *Robinson Crusoe*, ii. 107; *ibid.*, ii. 149.
26. *Ibid.*, ii. 193; *ibid.*, iii. 81; *ibid.*, ii. 221.
27. *Ibid.*, iii. 13; *ibid.*, ii. 2, 7.
28. Secord (1), *passim.* Defoe's library was sold, along with that of Phillips Farewell, D.D., on 15 November 1731. The sale catalogue is in the British Museum, but it is of course impossible to say which of the items listed were in Defoe's library. See G. A. Aitken, "Defoe's Library," *Athenaeum*, 1 June 1895. The catalogue has been reprinted in *The Libraries of Daniel Defoe and Phillips Farewell*, ed. Helmut Heidenreich (Berlin, 1970).
29. *The Works of Daniel Defoe*, ed. G. H. Maynadier, XVI. xv, xvii.
30. Secord (1), pp. 116ff.; *Captain Singleton*, pp. 137, 130, 124, 137, 128; *ibid.*, pp. 131, 94, 57, 144, 148.
31. *Ibid.*, p. 168. *Pecuniae obediunt omnes* is the title of a long and interesting poem published anonymously in 1698. If it were not rather too early, it might be taken for a work of Bernard Mandeville. It is not unlike the vigorous verse of Defoe.
32. *Captain Singleton*, pp. 175f.
33. *Ibid.*, p. 310; *Colonel Jack*, i. 71; *Captain Singleton*, pp. 69, 322, 333.
34. *Ibid.*, p. 330.
35. Moore (1), pp. 169ff., 171 (*The Four Years Voyages of Capt. George Roberts*, 1726, p. 458).
36. Moore (1), pp. 104ff.; *Madagascar; or, Robert Drury's Journal*, ed. Capt. Passfield Oliver (1890), p. 313.
37. Secord (2), pp. 1–71.
38. Moore (1), pp. 126–88; *Gentleman's Magazine* (1808), lxxviii. 143 (quoted in Secord (2), p. 4); *Read's Weekly Journal*, 1 November 1718.
39. Jane H. Jack, *Huntington Library Bulletin*, xxiv (No. 4, 1961); *New Voyage* (Bohn, vi. 197, 196).
40. *Ibid.*, vi. 197, 194.
41. *Ibid.*, vi. 263ff.; Moore (2), p. 297.
42. Letter to Harley, 23 July 1711 (Healey, pp. 345ff.)
43. *New Voyage* (Bohn, vi. 352).
44. Jane H. Jack, *op. cit.*, p. 323.
45. *Memoirs of a Cavalier*, pp. viii, 313f., 318.
46. Secord (2), pp. 77ff.; *Memoirs of a Cavalier*, pp. 95, 274, 259.
47. Moore (2), p. 260; *Colonel Jack*, i. 10; *The Two Great Questions Further Considered* (*Works, 1705*, i. 371); Secord (2), pp. 130ff., 103f.; *Memoirs of a Cavalier*, pp. 96, vii, ix.
48. *Ibid.*, pp. 236ff., 141, 138, 184f.
49. Moore (2), p. 326; F. Bastian, "Defoe's Journal of the Plague Year Reconsidered," *Review of English Studies*, New Series, xvi (1965), pp. 151ff.; *Applebee's Weekly Journal*, 29 July 1721 (Lee, ii. 408).

50. J. Sutherland, *Defoe* (1938), pp. 8f., 284; Bastian, *op. cit.*, pp. 158, 164f.; *Journal of the Plague Year*, p. 94.
51. Bastian, *op. cit.*, pp. 164f., 160ff.
52. *Ibid.*, p. 172; *Journal of the Plague Year*, pp. 73ff., 68f., 128f.
53. *The Commentator*, 15 August 1720 (Moore (2), p. 22); *Journal of the Plague Year*, pp. 128f.
54. Wordsworth, Preface to *Lyrical Ballads*, 1800, *ed. cit.*, p. 36.
55. *Journal of the Plague Year*, pp. 68f.
56. *Ibid.*, pp. 49ff.; Bastian, *op. cit.*, p. 170; Watt, p. 134.
57. *Journal of the Plague Year*, pp. 298, 301, 302.
58. *Boswell's Life of Johnson*, *ed. cit.*, iv. 334; Secord (1), p. 203.
59. *The Memoirs of an English Officer* (Bohn, ii. 311, 313, 311); Moore, *Checklist*, p. 214.
60. *Ibid.*, p. 215.

5. *The Writer of Fiction (II)*

1. *An Essay upon Projects* (1697), pp. 292f., 294f., 302f.; *Moll Flanders*, i. 13.
2. *Ibid.*, i. 62, 78, 85, 67, 75.
3. *Ibid.*, i. 135, 124; Watt, pp. 63, 114, etc.; *Moll Flanders*, i. 7, 9; *Review*, 15 September 1711 (Secord, xx. 303a); Michael Shinagel, *Daniel Defoe and Middle-Class Gentility* (Cambridge, Mass., 1968), p. 155; *Moll Flanders*, ii. 3; *ibid.*, i. 202; *ibid.*, ii. 4.
4. Virginia Woolf, *The Common Reader* (1933 ed.), p. 122; E. M. Forster, *Aspects of the Novel* (1927), p. 85; *Moll Flanders*, i. 61, 109.
5. *Ibid.*, i. 159, 110, 165, 201; *ibid.*, ii. 1, 2.
6. *Ibid.*, ii. 42, 43f.
7. Arthur Murphy, *An Essay on the Life and Genius of Samuel Johnson, LL.D* (1792), p. 43 (quoted in *Boswell's Life of Johnson*, *ed. cit.*, i. 504); *Moll Flanders*, ii. 110ff., 116; *ibid.*, i. xi.
8. Horace, *Ars Poetica*, ll. 158ff.
9. *Moll Flanders*, i. 167.
10. Watt, p. 126.
11. *Moll Flanders*, i. 57, 131, 185, 187, 188, 190.
12. *Ibid.*, ii. 152; Watt, pp. 110, 111; *Moll Flanders*, ii. 152.
13. *Ibid.*, i. 24.
14. *Ibid.*, ii. 2; *Roxana*, ii. 66; *Moll Flanders*, ii. 4, 6, 8; *ibid.*, i. x.
15. Watt, pp. 98, 116; *Moll Flanders*, i. viii.
16. Robert Bridges, "The Influence of the Audience on Shakespeare's Drama," *Collected Essays* (1927), pp. 13f., 17f.
17. *Mist's Weekly Journal*, 22 September 1722 (Lee, iii. 52).
18. *Colonel Jack*, i. 189; Moore, *Checklist*, p. 184.
19. Letter to John Watts (Healey, p. 473).
20. *Colonel Jack*, i. 121, 122, 11.
21. *Ibid.*, i. 20, 70f., vii, 29.
22. Richard Steele, *The Theatre*, ed. John Loftis (1962), pp. 83, xixff.; *The*

Conscious Lovers, Act IV, Sc. 1; Act IV, Sc. ii (Mermaid ed., pp. 337, 331ff.); *Colonel Jack,* ii. 22, 53f.
23. *The History of . . . Col. Jacque,* ed. Samuel Holt Monk (Oxford, 1965), pp. xvf.; *Colonel Jack,* i. 145, 148, 151, 156ff.; *ibid.,* ii. 87f.
24. *Ibid.,* i. 71, 1f.; *The Complete English Gentleman,* ed. Karl D. Bülbring (1895), p. 74.
25. *Colonel Jack,* i. 6; *ibid.,* ii. 20, 23, 30.
26. *Roxana,* ii. 160. The additional matter to *Roxana* will be found in the Bohn reprint (iv. 292–350).
27. *Roxana,* ii. 174.
28. *Ibid.,* ii. 88, 90, 91, 122, 139.
29. *Ibid.,* ii. 152, 137.
30. Starr, pp. 165, 164; *Roxana,* i. 185; ii. 5, 80f., 76
31. Starr, p. 164; *Roxana* (Preface), i. viiif.
32. *Roxana,* 4f., 7; Congreve, *The Way of the World,* Act IV, Sc. i (Mermaid ed., p. 378); Starr, p. 176; *Roxana,* i. 171f.
33. *Ibid.,* i. 186.
34. *Robinson Crusoe,* ii. viif., viii.
35. H. G. Wells, *Experiment in Autobiography* (1934), ii. 489, 497, 503, 488.
36. F. E. Hardy, *The Later Years of Thomas Hardy, 1892–1928* (1930), pp. 15f.; F. E. Hardy, *The Early Life of Thomas Hardy, 1840–1891* (1928), pp. 193f.
37. *The Works of Daniel Defoe,* ed. G. H. Maynadier, iii. xiii.
38. *An Essay on the History and Reality of Apparitions,* 1727 (*Works, 1840,* xiii. 43).
39. *Moll Flanders,* i. 7; *Roxana,* i. 50f.

6. The Last Years

1. *A Tour thro' the Whole Island of Great Britain,* ed. G. D. H. Cole (1968), i. 4.
2. *Ibid.,* i. 3; ii. 630; i. 50; ii. 640f.; i. 14, 18ff., 293ff.
3. *Ibid.,* i. 3, 168, 173f.; ii. 594f., 611ff.
4. *Ibid.,* i. 56f.; ii. 596ff.; i. 129; ii. 568ff.
5. *The Complete English Tradesman* (1726). i. 61, 61f., 63, 65, 66, 57.
6. *Ibid.,* i. 57, 52f.
7. Rodney M. Baine, *Daniel Defoe and the Supernatural* (Athens, Georgia, 1968), pp. 137ff.
8. *An Appeal to Honour and Justice* (Aitken, pp. 104, 105).
9. W. P. Trent, *Daniel Defoe: How to Know Him* (Indianapolis, 1916), p. 215.

Selected Bibliography

Unless otherwise stated, the place of publication is London.

BIBLIOGRAPHY

John Robert Moore, *A Checklist of the Writings of Daniel Defoe* (Bloomington, Indiana, 1960).

Henry Clinton Hutchins, *Robinson Crusoe and Its Printing, 1719–1731* (New York, 1925).

COLLECTED WORKS

Novels and Miscellaneous Works, 7 vols. (Bohn, 1854–67).

Romances and Narratives, ed. G. A. Aitken, 16 vols. (1895).

Works, ed. G. H. Maynadier, 16 vols. (New York, 1903–4).

Novels and Selected Writings, 14 vols. (Oxford, 1927–8).

A complete facsimile of Defoe's *Review* (1704–13) was edited by A. W. Secord in 22 vols. (Columbia University Press, 1938). There is an index to this (*Index to Defoe's Review*) compiled by William L. Payne (Columbia University Press, 1948).

The Letters of Daniel Defoe have been collected and edited by George Harris Healey (Oxford, 1955).

A more extensive collection of Defoe's writings than any before attempted is now under way, and will be published by the Southern Illinois University Press.

SHORTER COLLECTIONS

Defoe published two volumes of his early pamphlets and poems:

A True Collection of the Writings of the Author of the True Born Englishman (1703), and *A Second Volume of the Writings . . .* (1705).

Modern selections include the following:

The Earlier Life and the Chief Earlier Works, ed. Henry Morley (1889). Contains, *inter alia, An Essay upon Projects* and *The Consolidator.*

A Journal of the Plague Year and Other Pieces, ed. A. W. Secord (New York, 1935).

The Best of Defoe's Review, ed. William L. Payne (New York, 1951).

Daniel Defoe, ed. James T. Boulton (1965).

Selected Poetry and Prose of Daniel Defoe, ed. Michael F. Shugrue (New York, 1968).

Robinson Crusoe and Other Writings, ed. James Sutherland (Boston, 1968).

MODERN EDITIONS OF SEPARATE WORKS

The Meditations of Daniel Defoe, ed. George Harris Healey (1946, Cummington, Massachusetts); Defoe's earliest known verse.

The True-Born Englishman, ed. A. C. Guthkelch (English Association, *Essays and Studies,* IV, 1913).

Accounts of the Apparition of Mrs. Veal by Daniel Defoe and Others, ed. Manuel Schonhorn (Augustan Reprint Society, Los Angeles, 1965).

A Tour thro' the Whole Island of Great Britain, ed. G. D. H. Cole, 2 vols. (1927; also available in Everyman ed., 2 vols.).

Memoirs of Captain Carleton, ed. Cyril Hughes Hartman (1929).

Conjugal Lewdness; or, Matrimonial Whoredom, ed. Maximillian E. Novak (Gainesville, Florida, 1967; facsimile reproduction with Introduction).

A number of Defoe's pamphlets have been edited for the Augustan Reprint Society and the Luttrell Society.

Most of Defoe's fiction is available in modern editions and reprints, more especially *Robinson Crusoe* and *Moll Flanders.* The Oxford English Novels series now has editions of *Roxana* (Jane H. Jack), *Colonel Jack* (Samuel H. Monk), *A Journal of the Plague Year* (Louis A. Landa), and *Captain Singleton* (S. Kumar).

STUDIES—MAINLY BIOGRAPHICAL

William Lee, *Daniel Defoe: His Life and Recently Discovered Writings,* 3 vols. (1869). Vols. II and III reprint contributions to *Mist's Journal* and other periodicals which Lee attributed to Defoe.

W. P. Trent, *Daniel Defoe: How to Know Him* (Indianapolis, 1916). Includes numerous brief excerpts from Defoe's writings.

Paul Dottin, *Daniel Defoe et ses romans,* 3 vols. (Paris, 1924). Vol. I is biographical.

James Sutherland, *Defoe* (1937; 2nd ed., 1950).

John Robert Moore, *Daniel Defoe: Citizen of the Modern World* (Chicago, 1958).

STUDIES—MAINLY CRITICAL

BOOKS

A. W. Secord, *Studies in the Narrative Method of Defoe* (Urbana, Illinois, 1924); *Robert Drury's Journal and Other Studies* (Urbana, Illinois, 1961).

John Robert Moore, *Daniel Defoe and Modern Economic Theory* (Bloomington, Indiana, 1934); *Defoe in the Pillory, and Other Studies* (Bloomington, Indiana, 1939; includes Moore's reasoned attribution to Defoe of "Captain Johnson's" *History of . . . the Pyrates); Defoe's Sources for Robert Drury's Journal* (Bloomington, Indiana, 1943).

Rudolf G. Stamm, *Der Aufgeklärte Puritanismus Daniel Defoes* (Zurich, 1936).

William L. Payne, *Mr. Review. Daniel Defoe as Author of the Review* (New York, 1947).

Francis Watson, *Daniel Defoe* (1952).

Maximillian E. Novak, *Economics and the Fiction of Daniel Defoe* (Berkeley and Los Angeles, 1962); *Defoe and the Nature of Man* (Oxford, 1963).

G. A. Starr, *Defoe and Spiritual Autobiography* (Princeton, 1965).

J. Paul Hunter, *The Reluctant Pilgrim: Defoe's Emblematic Method and Quest for Form* (Baltimore, 1966).

Michael Shinagel, *Daniel Defoe and Middle-Class Gentility* (Cambridge, Mass., 1968).

Rodney M. Baine, *Daniel Defoe and the Supernatural* (Athens, Georgia, 1968).

Defoe's fiction is discussed in the following general works on the novel: E. M. Forster, *Aspects of the Novel* (1927); Dorothy van Ghent, *The English Novel, Form and Function* (New York, 1953); A. D. McKillop, *The Early Masters of English Fiction* (Lawrence, Kansas, 1956); Ian Watt, *The Rise of the Novel* (1957); John J. Richetti, *Popular Fiction before Richardson* (1969).

ARTICLES

In listing the various articles given below, the following abbreviations have been used: *HLQ: Huntington Library Quarterly; MP: Modern Philology; PQ: Philological Quarterly; RES: Review of English Studies; SEL: Studies in English Literature; SP: Studies in Philology.*

Miscellaneous and General Articles

C. E. Burch, "British Criticism of Defoe as a Novelist, 1719–1860" (*Englische Studien*, lxvii, 1932); "Defoe's British Reputation, 1869–1894" (*ibid.*, lxviii, 1934).

Rudolf G. Stamm, "Daniel Defoe: An Artist in the Puritan Tradition" (*PQ*, xv, 1936).

Herbert G. Wright, "Defoe's Writings on Sweden" (*RES*, xvi, 1940).

Hans H. Andersen, "The Paradox of Trade and Morality in Defoe" (*MP*, xxxix, 1941).

Bonamy Dobrée, "Some Aspects of Defoe's Prose" (*Pope and His Contemporaries*, ed. James L. Clifford and Louis A. Landa, Oxford, 1949).

Benjamin Boyce, "The Question of Emotion in Defoe" (*SP*, i, 1953).

Fritz Wölken, "Major Ramkins' *Memoirs*" (*Anglia*, lxxv, 1957).

Albert Rosenberg, "Defoe's *Pacificator* Reconsidered" (*PQ*, xxxvii, 1958).

Maximillian E. Novak, "The Problem of Necessity in Defoe's Fiction" (*PQ*, xl, 1961); "Defoe's Theory of Fiction" (*SP*, lxi, 1964); "Defoe's *Shortest Way with the Dissenters* . . ." (*Modern Language Quarterly*, xxvii, 1966); "Defoe's Use of Irony" (*The Uses of Irony: Papers on Defoe and Swift Read at a Clark Library Seminar, April 2, 1966*).

Laurence Poston, "Defoe and the Peace Campaign, 1710–1713: A Reconsideration" (*HLQ*, xxvii, 1963).

Richard I. Cook, " 'Mr. Examiner' and 'Mr. Review': The Tory Apologetics of Swift and Defoe" (*HLQ*, xxix, 1966).

Rodney M. Baine, "Defoe and the Angels" (*Texas Studies in Literature and Language*, ix, 1967).

James Sutherland, "The Relation of Defoe's Fiction to His Non-Fictional Writings" (*Imagined Worlds: Essays . . . in Honour of John Butt*, ed. Maynard Mack and Ian Gregor, 1968).

G. A. Starr, "From Casuistry to Fiction: The Importance of the *Athenian Mercury*" (*Journal of the History of Ideas*, xxviii, 1967).

Articles on Defoe's chief works of fiction

Robinson Crusoe: H. W. Hausermann (*RES*, xi, 1935); William H. Halewood (*Essays in Criticism*, xiv, 1964); Martin J. Grief (*SEL*, vi, 1966); Robert W. Ayers (*PMLA*, lxxxii, 1967).

Captain Singleton: Gary J. Scrimgeour (*HLQ*, xxvii, 1963).

Moll Flanders: Pierre Legouis (*Revue . . . des langues vivantes*, xlviii, 1931); Robert C. Columbus (*SEL*, iii, 1963); Dennis Donoghue (*Sewanee Review*, lxxi, 1963); Howard L. Koonce (*English Literary History*, xxx, 1963); Maxmillian E. Novak (*College English*, xxvi, 1964); Arnold Kettle (*Of Books and Humankind . . .*, ed. John Butt, 1964); Ian Watt (*Eighteenth-Century Studies*, i, 1967).

A Journal of the Plague Year: F. Bastian (RES, New Series, xvi, 1965); Manuel Schonhorn (*ibid.*, xix, 1968).

Colonel Jack: William H. McBurney (*SEL*, ii, 1962).

Roxana: Spiro Peterson (*PMLA*, lxx, 1955); Maximillian E. Novak (*Journal of English and Germanic Philology*, lxv, 1966); Robert D. Hume (*Eighteenth-Century Studies*, iii, 1969); G. A. Starr (*The Augustan Milieu. Essays Presented to Louis A. Landa*, ed. Henry Knight Miller *et al.*, Oxford, 1970).

A New Voyage round the World: Jane H. Jack (*HLQ*, xxiv, 1961).

Index

Main entries are in bold figures.